Soviet Interview Project Series

Restructuring the Soviet economic bureaucracy

T0312091

Soviet Interview Project Series

James R. Millar, editor

Also published in the series:

James R. Millar, editor, *Politics, Work, and Daily Life in the USSR: A Survey of Former Soviet Citizens*

Data for this study were produced by the Soviet Interview Project. The project was supported by Contract No. 701 from the National Council for Soviet and East European Research to the University of Illinois at Urbana-Champaign, James R. Millar, principal investigator. The analysis and interpretations in this study are those of the author, not necessarily of the sponsors.

Restructuring the
Soviet economic bureaucracy

PAUL R. GREGORY
University of Houston

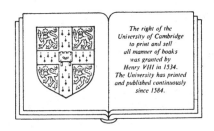

CAMBRIDGE UNIVERSITY PRESS
Cambridge
New York   Port Chester   Melbourne   Sydney

CAMBRIDGE UNIVERSITY PRESS
Cambridge, New York, Melbourne, Madrid, Cape Town, Singapore, São Paulo

Cambridge University Press
The Edinburgh Building, Cambridge CB2 2RU, UK

Published in the United States of America by Cambridge University Press, New York

www.cambridge.org
Information on this title: www.cambridge.org/9780521363860

First published 1990
This digitally printed first paperback version 2006

A catalogue record for this publication is available from the British Library

Library of Congress Cataloguing in Publication data
Gregory, Paul R.
  Restructuring the Soviet economic bureaucracy / Paul R. Gregory.
    p. cm.
  ISBN 0-521-36386-1
  1. Government economists – Soviet Union. 2. Bureaucracy – Soviet
Union. 3. Perestroĭka. 4. Central planning – Soviet Union. 5. Soviet
Union – Economic policy – 1986– I. Title.
HC336.26.G76 1990
338.947′009048 – dc20   89-27260
                              CIP

ISBN-13 978-0-521-36386-0 hardback
ISBN-10 0-521-36386-1 hardback

ISBN-13 978-0-521-03268-1 paperback
ISBN-10 0-521-03268-7 paperback

Contents

Foreword

Although our knowledge of Soviet affairs and institutions has grown by leaps and bounds over the past four decades, much remains unknown and undescribed in both the Soviet and the Western literature. Relatively speaking, the management of the industrial enterprise and its dealings with the higher economic bureaucracy have been well described and extensively analyzed in the West. The economic bureaucracy itself, however, has for the most part remained a "black box." We know something of how it interacts with enterprise managers, but we do not know what happens within the black box, among the ministries or between the ministries and the state committees, for example. Paul Gregory's contribution in this volume is to throw beams of light into the black box and to illuminate facets of the interrelations within the economic bureaucracy above the enterprise level.

The study presented in these pages is based on two main sources. One is unique. Gregory was able to interview former members of the Soviet economic bureaucracy about its inner workings. Most of these individuals were located for him by the Soviet Interview Project, which conducted a census of adult emigrants from the USSR to the United States between the beginning of 1979 and the end of 1984 and was able, therefore, to identify individuals who had job experience in the economic bureaucracy. With only a handful of exceptions, the migration did not include persons from the top elite of the bureaucracy; the study focuses, therefore, on the middle elite. The second source is the literature on planning both in the USSR and in the West.

Because the number of former members of the Soviet economic bureaucracy available in the West is severely limited, Gregory was not able to draw a proper sample for purposes of statistical analysis. Technically, he was obliged to work with a group of "informants," rather than with a sample of respondents. His informants represent, however, persons with expert knowledge of certain aspects of the Soviet economic bureaucracy. The method is analogous to that of the ethnographer, who interviews knowledgeable members of a society in order to develop an understanding of how certain institutions, such as marriage, religion, or money, function within it.

The use of a limited number of individuals as expert informants has limitations, of course. Because the investigator does not have a proper sample, he cannot treat his interview results as though they describe a referent population of economic bureaucrats. He cannot, therefore, say anything about variations in the way the bureaucrats work among, for example, geographical regions or among different industries. Variation of this sort would require a relatively large, randomly selected sample. But this is not to say that there is not much to learn from expert informants, and especially when the unit of observation and analysis is not the individual bureaucrat but the institution within which he was employed. Suppose, for example, that you wanted to learn something about the job of vice-chancellor for academic affairs in an American university, something about the way it really works, as opposed to the official job description. You would not have to interview very many former vice-chancellors to learn that they are preoccupied by budget allocations among divisions of the university, promotions, and hiring and retaining faculty. These patterns and the problems they entail would emerge clearly even if you were totally innocent about the job before the interviews. Differences between private and public institutions, between large and small institutions, between highly visible and less known institutions would require a larger sample, and an even larger sample would be required to control for denominational or regional differences.

Evaluating results of expert testimony can be a frustrating experience, because it is frequently difficult or impossible to interpret variation among informants. A formal sample represents the statistical limit one would reach if random sampling from the referent population could be continued without restriction. That is, one could draw respondents until variation ceased to be discovered and patterns were well established. When the number of respondents is limited, one finds some clear patterns, some suggested patterns, and many unique observations that defy interpretation. Gregory has restricted his "conclusions" to the first of these categories, and he describes as "hypotheses" the second category. The third category is ignored unless it is confirmed by some other (e.g., literary) source.

Gregory's method is, therefore, both careful and modest, but he still comes up with significant, interesting results. Let me mention only two that strike me as important. First, the newspapers and the literature are replete today with stories of bureaucratic resistance to the Gorbachev reforms. It is clear from Gregory's interviews, however, that the bureaucracy is not a homogeneous entity. There are those who are obliged to make decisions and to reap the consequences, good or bad. Gregory calls these the economic managers (*khoziaistvenniks*). There are others whose work is not uniquely associated with any particular outcome. These are the rule setters and the measurers, whom Gregory labels the *apparatchiks*. Because their functional roles are radically different and because their work is evaluated differently, one can expect these two components of the economic bureaucracy to react differently to reform proposals. Gregory's interviews reveal, therefore, a new realm of complexity confounding any attempt to determine where the economic bureaucracy taken as a whole stands with respect to *perestroika,* and especially with respect to any particular reform proposal.

Second, the Soviet economic bureaucracy is a very complex piece of machinery, one that has developed not only to deal with the allocation of resources in Soviet society, but specifically to deal with a fundamental characteristic that is peculiar to Soviet-style planning: supply insecurity. The people who manage and oversee resource allocation in the Soviet economy operate in a world of perpetual deficit supply. This is not the hypothetical scarcity of a world in which unlimited wants confront finite resources. It is actual deficit supply, which means that some potential buyers must do without or with inferior substitutes year in, year out. Merely reducing the degree of shortage is not likely to be productive. Moving to a position of surplus in most markets would seem to require unthinkable changes in supply and demand conditions in the USSR, but only this would be likely to make the bureaucracy as it now operates unnecessary. Only this would create a situation in which enterprise inventories of final products would be positive or zero at any given time. The more one thinks about Gregory's findings, the less confidence one has in the prospects for the success of such extensive reforms.

Gregory's study raises a major research issue as well. Although he has found a number of bureaucratic practices that may very well be unique to the Soviet economic system, many are quite familiar to anyone who has experience with bureaucracy in other systems. Like their counterparts elsewhere, Soviet bureaucrats, for example, seek "insurance" against uncertain outcomes, are sedulous about creating paper trails to protect themselves against criticism, and are constantly trying to shift responsibility by having others "sign off" on decisions. The research question is: What is peculiarly Soviet and what is general bureaucratic behavior?

Mikhail Gorbachev is, perhaps, running against the bureaucracy much as former President Reagan used to do. It is an unpopular institution, one that is viewed as inefficient, overstaffed, and indifferent to the public's needs. Running against the economic bureaucracy is likely to be popular, therefore, even if the leader fails to curtail its actual power. The implication is, however, that the bureaucracy may survive and continue to function *normal'no* for the indefinite future. Given Gregory's findings, the alternative would appear to be the conversion of the Soviet economy into a buyer's market generally, one in which the monopoly power of sellers was broken and one, therefore, in which central planning as practiced by the economic bureaucracy would be abolished. The economic bureaucracy would disappear along with the "dictatorship of supply."

James R. Millar

Preface

Conventional wisdom both inside and outside the Soviet Union is that the bureaucracy represents the greatest threat to Gorbachev's *perestroika* (restructuring). This fear has aroused Soviet interest in how the economic bureaucracy works. In fact, the cumbersome and bloated bureaucracy has been singled out as a chief source of economic stagnation. The bureaucracy's press has been uniformly bad, and the bureaucracy's malpractices have been gleefully exposed by an unleashed Soviet press.

This book examines the way the Soviet economic bureaucracy has worked over the years. As of mid-1989, the bureaucracy continued to operate in much the same way that it had since the 1930s. Numerous complaints from enterprise officials and ministry personnel in the Soviet press confirm this point. In effect, this book is about the bureaucratic practices that *perestroika* seeks to change. Understanding how the bureaucratic system works sheds light on why the system has been so difficult to change and on the bureaucratic resistance that *perestroika* will face. In fact, the risk that the findings of this book will be outmoded by the successes of restructuring is small. Previous efforts to change bureaucratic practices have failed; at best, significant changes will be achieved slowly.

The research reported in this book is based on Soviet and Western published accounts and on interviews with former members of the Soviet economic bureaucracy who emigrated to the West. The published and interview sources complement each other. A study of this sort could not have been done with only one source.

I am grateful for the financial support of the National Council for Soviet and East European Research, Contract No. 701 to the Soviet Interview Project, James R. Millar, University of Illinois, Urbana-Champaign, principal investigator. I am also grateful to the Volkswagen Foundation for its support of an International Fellowship for Advanced Soviet and East European Studies at the Bundesinstitut fuer ostwissenschaftliche und internationale Studien, Cologne, Germany.

Numerous colleagues have provided valuable advice and assistance. I wish to thank James R. Millar, Peter Rutland, and Thomas Mayor for their advice on earlier drafts. I benefited from discussions with Joseph Berliner at the early stages of this research and want to single him out for special thanks. I also want to thank Susan Linz, Philip Hanson, Heinrich Vogel, Marvin Jackson, and Hans-Hermann Hohmann for their advice. The errors and faults in this study are, of course, my sole responsibility.

CHAPTER 1

Perestroika and bureaucracy

This book describes how the Soviet economic bureaucracy works – how bureaucrats big and small make the routine and extraordinary decisions that determine Soviet resource allocation. The Soviet economic bureaucracy operates according to rules and practices that have proved resistant to change. Soviet bureaucratic practices represent a "spontaneous order." That the working arrangements of the Soviet economic bureaucracy have much in common with bureaucracies everywhere shows that they were not created randomly. In fact, one of the most difficult problems of studying Soviet bureaucracy is to distinguish peculiarly "Soviet" features from those that are common to any large bureaucratic organization.

Soviet bureaucratic arrangements have been remarkably stable. The practices described in this book represent responses to an inherently complex resource-allocation problem that defies easy solution. The bureaucracy must manage hundreds of thousands of enterprises of various sizes and shapes, producing millions of distinct goods and services. The bureaucracy must implement the general directives of the political leadership, operating at a level of aggregation well above that at which production enterprises work. In many cases, it must impose tasks on its subordinates that are inconsistent and sometimes irrational.

The Soviet economic bureaucracy must manage an economy that lacks private property rights, the natural equilibrating forces of markets, and the discipline imposed by the need to seek out profit opportunities. It has had to establish a system of rewards and punishments that motivates participants to act in the interests of their superiors in an environment in which information is distributed unequally. It is often difficult to judge outcomes and to assign responsibility for success or failure. Moreover, the bureaucracy, in imposing accountability, must limit the opportunistic (or dysfunctional) behavior that subordinates engage in to avoid failure.

The Soviet economic bureaucracy currently has many critics and few admirers. The criticized irrationalities of the Soviet bureaucracy, however, have their own internal logic and consistency. Simple palliatives – like changes in personalities or decrees against specific practices – have not worked in the past. Soviet reformers of bureaucracy will continue to find that the entrenched system is difficult to change for good reason.

Who are the Soviet economic bureaucrats?

The Soviet economic bureaucracy (as of 1987) consisted of 38 state committees, 33 union ministries, 28 union-republican ministries, and more than 300 regional ministries and authorities.[1] Each of these nearly 400 organizations has its own bureaucracy – departments, main administrations, offices – as well as associated units. It employs millions of persons and manages 1.3 million production units (43,000 state enterprises, 26,000 construction enterprises, 47,000 farming units, 260,000 service establishments, and more than 1 million retail trade establishments.[2]

Soviet bureaucrats are located in a hierarchy, ranging from the top elite to those who occupy responsible professional (but not managerial) positions. The political and executive elite, to use Gerd Meyer's term, is composed of the political elite (from the Central Committee down to first secretaries of provinces, regions, and cities) and the executive elite (from members of the Supreme Soviet and Council of Ministers, to minister presidents of the republics and chairmen of regional and city executive committees, down to the directors of the hundred or so largest enterprises). Fewer than a thousand individuals belong to this top elite.[3]

The middle elite can be delineated in different ways. According to recent estimates, more than 17 million persons work in the sphere of administration (*upravlenie*), which amounts to 15 percent of the labor force.[4] This figure includes the administrative staff of enterprises, which account for some 90 percent of the total. The remaining 2 million work above the enterprise level in state and party organizations. The share of administrative personnel of labor force appears to have remained relatively stable, accounting for 14 percent in 1966.[5]

[1] "Ubytochyne, no svoi," *Trud*, June 2, 1987.
[2] These figures are from A. G. Aganbegian, *Upravlenie sotsialisticheskimi predpriatiiami* (Moscow: Ekonomika, 1979), p. 20.
[3] Gerd Meyer, *Buerokratischer Sozialismus: Eine Analyse des sowjetischen Herrschaftssystem* (Stuttgart-Bad Cannstatt: Frommann, 1977), pp. 143–9.
[4] *Argumenty i fakty*, September 30, 1988, p. 7.
[5] This estimate is from D. M Gvishiani, "Problemy upravleniia sotsialisticheskoi promyshlennosti," *Voprosy filosofii*, No. 11 (1966), p. 7.

Although we are interested primarily in bureaucrats operating above the enterprise level, Soviet statistics commonly include the management of enterprises in the economic bureaucracy (*upravlenie*).[6] Soviet enterprises employ almost 16 million persons in administrative positions. The top management of enterprises (the manager, his deputies, and chief engineers, accountants, and so on) would number more than 3 million.

This book focuses on the middle elite, defined as leadership positions below the *nomenklatura* (people occupying positions requiring formal approval by the party cadres departments of the union central committee or of the central committees of the republics). Examples of middle elite positions are main (*glavny*) engineers, constructors, accountants, and economists of large enterprises, institutes, or trusts, main (*glavny*) bookkeepers or accountants of state bank branches, department heads, main engineers, main accountants, main economists in state committees such as Gosplan (State Planning Commission), Gossnab (State Committee for Material Technical Supply), or the Ministry of Finance, and deputies of main administration heads in republican and union ministries. Most belong to the half-million "leaders of party, state, union, and komsomol organizations," and all belong to the 4 to 5 million "leading cadres" category of Soviet statistics.[7] Virtually all would be included in the 2.2 million members of "higher" (*verkhnye*) organs of administration cited in a prominent Soviet source on the economic bureaucracy.[8]

Soviet bureaucrats perform different tasks in the management of the economy. They operate under different reward structures and with different levels of responsibility. A useful distinction (developed in Chapter 4) is between those who bear responsibility for final results and those who do not. Trust or enterprise managers and industrial ministers and ministry officials in charge of particular production branches are responsible for final results. If their production units fail to fulfill their economic plans, they suffer the consequences. Selected party officials are also responsible for final results. Chapter 7 shows that local party officials are held broadly responsible for the economic results of their region. The top political leadership bears responsibility for macroeconomic performance. Nikita Khrushchev's ouster in 1964 has been attributed to economic shortcomings along

---

[6] See, e.g., Iu. M. Kozlov, *Upravlenie narodnym khoziaistvom SSSR* (Moscow: Izdatel'stvo Moskovskogo Universiteta, 1971), Part 1, Chap. 1.

[7] These figures are cited in Meyer, *Buerokratischer Sozialismus,* p. 149.

[8] D. B. Averianov, *Funktsii i organizatsionnaia struktura organov gosudarstvennogo upravleniia* (Kiev: Akademiia Nauk, 1979), pp. 132–3.

with other factors, and Mikhail Gorbachev's regime will ultimately be judged on the basis of economic performance. The posthumous discreditation of Leonid Brezhnev has focused on the economic stagnation of the Brezhnev years.

The majority of Soviet economic bureaucrats are not held responsible for final results. They occupy largely "functional" positions. They make rules and norms, draw up technical and accounting balances, set prices and wages, prepare documentation requirements. They issue instructions to operating units; yet they are not responsible for the fulfillment of these instructions. Their actions affect different production units; they may report to different bosses.[9] Although they establish the rules, norms, and directives under which industrial ministries and enterprises operate, they are not (and often cannot) be held accountable for the effects of their actions on production outcomes.

Perestroika's attack on the bureaucracy

General Secretary Mikhail Gorbachev has announced a radical restructuring of the Soviet economy – perestroika.[10] One of perestroika's aims is to change the way the Soviet economic bureaucracy works. The restructuring program calls for more decisions to be made by the production units themselves and fewer by higher bureaucratic bodies. Administrative organs are to turn their attention to long-run issues and cease intervening in routine operations. The economy is to be directed more by laws and norms than by binding decrees. Economic units are to have more freedom in their dealings with one another and with higher authorities. If implemented as designed, perestroika would radically alter the way the Soviet bureaucracy does business.

Why does the Soviet reform leadership wish to change the bureaucratic system described in this book? What features of the Soviet bureaucratic system have caused it to fall into disrepute? This book shows that Soviet economic bureaucrats have behaved rationally in the sense that their actions are consistent with the prevailing reward

---

9 The Soviet literature distinguishes between two types of functional unit: The first, the *shtatnoe* unit, reports to one boss; the second is specialized according to function and reports to different bosses. V. G. Vyshniakov, *Struktura i shtaty organov sovetskogo gosudarstva i upravleniia* (Moscow: Nauka, 1972), Chap. 3.

10 Abel Aganbegyan and Timor Timofeyev, *The New Stages of Perestroika* (New York: Institute For East–West Security Studies, 1988).

structure. Soviet bureaucratic behavior is a predictable response by rational agents to a well-understood incentive system. Soviet bureaucratic practices did not appear out of thin air. They have their own logic, and similar practices are found in other large bureaucracies.

Successful restructuring requires an understanding of how and why the bureaucracy acts as it does. *Perestroika's* designers must devise an incentive system that motivates bureaucrats to change their behavior. Over the years, Soviet authorities have relied on decrees, organizational shuffling, and personnel changes to change the way things work, rather than focusing on changes in underlying rewards and incentives.

Perestroika is the most recent effort to change bureaucratic behavior. The failures of previous reforms and experiments show that bureaucratic behavior patterns are deeply entrenched. Previous reforms have had little lasting effect on bureaucratic practices. In fact, bureaucratic inertia is cited as a prime source of the Soviet leadership's chronic inability to change the economic system.

The Soviet leadership's radical restructuring program has been sparked by deteriorating economic performance. Economic performance is the outcome of millions of decisions made on the shop floor, by enterprise management, by bureaucratic organizations above the enterprise, and by external shocks. Above all, economic outcomes are dictated by the institutional structure of the economic system. *Perestroika's* designers believe that the Soviet bureaucracy has contributed to declining economic performance. *Perestroika* raises specific questions: Exactly how has the Soviet economic bureaucracy contributed to deteriorating economic performance? How can bureaucratic working arrangements be improved? What bureaucratic practices work well and deserve to be preserved? Is the Soviet economic bureaucracy, as currently constituted, capable of performing the more limited interventions envisioned by *perestroika?*

The Soviet bureaucracy affects economic performance by devising reward structures, setting rules and norms, and intervening directly into enterprise affairs. If the bureaucracy devises bad rules, norms, and reward systems and intervenes counterproductively, it harms economic performance. The literature provides numerous examples of bureaucratic inefficiencies at the enterprise level: Soviet managers work under a reward and promotion system that encourages dysfunctional behavior. Managers reduce quality when plan targets are based on physical outputs, they conceal capacity from superiors when current plan targets are based on past performance, and they resist technological change.[11] Enterprise managers are subject to bureaucratic rules or norms that reduce efficiency. Capital-allocation rules allow differential rates of return, and pricing rules encourage managers to use expensive inputs. Direct bureaucratic interventions, such as the diversion of enterprise resources to local projects by the local party or the petty tutelage by remote ministry officials, can reduce the efficiency of enterprise operations.[12]

Soviet reform economists criticize bureaucratic performance. In fact, some reform economists identify the bureaucracy as the major source of economic inefficiency.[13] They view the bureaucracy as too conservative and too ready to meddle in the routine affairs of Soviet enterprises. Antibureaucratic reformers propose simple and perhaps naive solutions. Limiting the size of the bureaucracy will reduce petty tutelage. Redirecting the tasks of the bureaucracy away from routine enterprise matters will give enterprises more autonomy. Merging the bureaucracy into larger units will refocus bureaucratic attention on broader matters.

Although Soviet reformers disparage the "administrative-command economy" associated with the name of Stalin, they do not propose to do away with the economic bureaucracy. Rather, *perestroika* proposes to restrict and redirect bureaucratic actions. Even with the successful implementation of *perestroika*, the rationality of bureaucratic behavior will remain a key issue.

Soviet reformers fail, by and large, to address the more fundamental issue – why have bureaucrats systematically devised inefficient

---

[11] The major works on this subject are Joseph S. Berliner, *Factory and Manager in the USSR* (Cambridge, Mass.: Harvard University Press, 1957) and David Granick, *Management of Industrial Firms in the USSR* (New York: Columbia University Press, 1954). The work of Barry M. Richman, *Soviet Industrial Management* (Englewood Cliffs, N.J.: Prentice-Hall, 1965), should also be noted.

[12] The works by Berliner and Granick identify inefficient working arrangements between ministry and enterprise. Abram Bergson, *The Economics of Soviet Planning* (New Haven, Conn.: Yale University Press, 1964), has studied material-balance planning, labor allocation, and capital-allocation procedures from an efficiency standpoint. Judith Thornton, "Differential Capital Charges and Resource Allocation in Soviet Industry," *Journal of Political Economy, 79*, No. 3 (1971), pp. 545–61, has attempted to measure the efficiency losses caused by Soviet capital investment rules.

[13] The most well known Soviet proponent of the antibureaucratic view is the Soviet sociologist T. Zaslavskaia. For a statement of her views, see T. Zaslavskaia and V. Efimov, "Slomat' mekhanizm tormozhenia," *Sovetskaia Rossiia*, March 24, 1987. In 1987, it was difficult to read a Soviet newspaper without finding an article deploring the inefficient workings of the bloated Soviet bureaucracy.

rules, intervened counterproductively, or used reward structures that promote dysfunctional behavior? Why have these practices persisted over time? *Perestroika* reformers are following a long Soviet tradition of believing that behavior patterns can be changed by the rewriting of formal rules, organizational reshuffling, or the replacement of certain members of the bureaucracy. True to form, *perestroika* calls for high-level organizational changes but pays little attention to matters of bureaucratic incentives.

By neglecting deeper, underlying forces, Soviet reformers under-estimate the complexity of bureaucratic reform. It is unlikely that the economic performance of the bureaucracy can be improved in a sig-nificant way by simple palliatives.[14]

The actual working arrangements of the Soviet economic bureau-cracy must be better understood before an "optimal" bureaucratic structure can be found. We have learned a great deal about the work-ing relationships of Soviet enterprises. We know relatively little about the internal workings of Soviet bureaucratic units, and we know even less about interrelationships among bureaucratic organizations. We know more about how and why quality and technology are under-produced by Soviet enterprises than about why ministries redistribute profits among enterprises or devote a substantial portion of their efforts to producing goods and services outside the ministry's main "profile."

Political scientists have attempted to pierce the veil of the bureau-cracy, but they have focused more on party–state relationships than on internal working arrangements within the state bureaucracy.[15] Economists have studied bureaucratic behavior, both by theorizing

14 Fyodor Kushnirsky, *Soviet Economic Planning, 1965–1980* (Boulder, Colo.: Westview Press, 1982), points out that past Soviet reforms have been based on the naive belief that an ideal planning indicator can be found that eliminates the natural friction between planner and enterprise. When the latest ideal indicator is found to have faults, reformers move on to a new indicator in a never-ending quest.

15 Merle Fainsod, *Smolensk Under Soviet Rule* (Cambridge, Mass.: Harvard University Press, 1958), has come the closest to penetrating the party bureaucracy, using actual regional party archives from the Smolensk province to study the role of the party in economic affairs. Unfortunately, Fainsod's study focuses more on party–agriculture relations because of Smolensk's rural nature. Jerry Hough, *The Soviet Prefects: The Local Party Organ in Industrial Decision Making* (Cambridge Mass.: Harvard University Press, 1969), uses Soviet sources and interviews with Soviet officials to investigate the economic role of the party. Peter Rutland, "The Role of the Communist Party in Economic Decision Making," Ph.D. dissertation (University of York, 1987), uses Soviet literature and press accounts to describe the economic role of the party.

about rational bureaucratic strategies and by testing theories of bureaucratic behavior using data on economic outcomes.[16] Some hints
about the internal workings of Soviet bureaucratic organizations can
be gleaned from historical studies and from autobiographical works
of Soviet bureaucratic administrators.[17]

The Soviet planning literature describes primarily how the bureaucracy is supposed to work, not how it actually works, but Soviet writings provide some glimpses into actual working arrangements.[18] Soviet interest in decision-making processes has led to statistical studies of
decision-making processes of bureaucratic units.[19] Soviet journalistic
writings of the late 1980s have provided behind-the-scenes glimpses
of actual bureaucratic working arrangements, especially since the reform leadership has singled out the bureaucracy for blame for Soviet
economic problems.[20] These press accounts are designed to express a
negative view of the bureaucracy, but they illuminate bureaucratic
practices in the process.

Published sources and interviews

The choice of bureaucratic institutions to be studied is dictated by the
availability of information. A variety of sources are used. They in-

16 On this, see Alice C. Gorlin, "The Power of Soviet Industrial Ministries,"
    Soviet Studies, 37, No. 3 (1985), pp. 353–70; Gregory Grossman, "The
    Party as Manager and Entrepreneur," in Gregory Guroff and Fred Car-
    stensen (eds.), *Entrepreneurship in Imperial Russia and the Soviet Union*
    (Princeton, N.J.: Princeton University Press, 1983), pp. 284–305.
17 For an example of an historical study of the Soviet planning bureaucracy,
    see Tatjana Kirstein, *Die Rolle der KPdSU in der Wirtschaftsplannung, 1933–
    1953/54* (Wiesbaden: Harrassowitz, 1985). Examples of rare autobiog-
    raphies of Soviet economic administrators are I. V. Paramanov, *Uchitsiia
    upravliat'* (Moscow: Ekonomika, 1970); A. G. Zverev, *Zapiski Ministra*
    (Moscow: Izdatel'stvo politicheskoi literatury, 1973); and A. I. Iakovlev,
    Tsel' zhizni (Zapiski aviokonstruktora) (Moscow: Izdatel'stvo politicheskoi lit-
    eratury, 1972).
18 For example, Soviet monographs from the 1970s discuss conflicts between
    line and functional units and the tendency of bureaucratic units held
    responsible for "final results" to paint an overly optimistic picture of eco-
    nomic results.
19 V. A. Lisichkin and E. I. Golynker, *Priniatie reshenii na osnove prog-
    nozirovaniia v usvloviiakh ASU* (Moscow: Finansy i statistika, 1981).
20 For an example of the greater use of Western-style investigative reporting
    in the Soviet press, see "Prospekt Kalinina, 19. Pis'ma iz ministerstva,"
    Izvestiia, December 16–20, 1986. Also see "Prosim skorrektirovat' plan!"
    Izvestiia, September 2, 1986.

clude Soviet academic writings on bureaucracy, official Soviet handbooks, articles from the technical journals of various state institutions,
and materials from the Soviet press. The Soviet press offers a variety
of views of bureaucratic working arrangements in letters to editors,
accounts of legal proceedings, and investigative reports. The most
valuable Soviet sources are those that give insights into how things
actually work as opposed to how they are supposed to work. Biogra-
phies or autobiographies of persons who served in the economic bureaucracy represent a promising source of information, but there are
unfortunately few valuable writings of this genre.

With liberalized emigration from the Soviet Union since the early
1970s, former members of the Soviet economic bureaucracy offer a
relatively new source of information. The 1970s witnessed a substantial emigration of former Soviet citizens to Israel, the United States,
and Western Europe. These emigrants represent an important living
archive on life in the Soviet Union. Emigré writings on the economic
bureaucracy are an important channel for information.[21] Interviews
with former members of the Soviet economic bureaucracy offer another way to gain new insights.[22]

The author's interviews with fifty former members of the Soviet
economic bureaucracy serve as a key source of information. Interviews cannot support a full-scale study of Soviet bureaucracy alone.
There are too few highly placed respondents; too few institutions are
represented. However, general outlines of Soviet bureaucratic behavior can be perceived from the interviews when used in combination
with published sources.

The lack of highly placed respondents dictates that this be a study
of middle bureaucracy. No respondents were industrial ministers or

[21] Three of the most influential works of this genre are Kushnirsky, *Soviet
Economic Planning, 1965–1980;* Aron Katsenelinboigen, *Studies in Soviet
Economic Planning* (White Plains, N.J.: Sharpe, 1978); and Igor Birman,
"From the Achieved Level," *Soviet Studies, 31,* No. 2 (1978), pp. 153–72.
Sergei Friedzon's account of high-level decision making is controversial
because it relies heavily on personal recollections, but it gives the most
comprehensive account of the high-level state and party bureaucracy. Ser-
gei Friedzon, "Top-Level Administration of the Soviet Economy: A Partial
View," *Rand Memorandum,* January 1986.
[22] See, e.g., Susan J. Linz, "Managerial Autonomy in Soviet Firms," *Soviet
Studies, 40,* No. 2 (1988), pp. 175–95; Linz, "Emigrants as Expert Informants on Soviet Management Decision-Making," *Comparative Economic
Studies,* 28, No. 3 (1986), pp. 65–89; Philip Hanson and Stephen Shenfield, "State Statistical Work in the USSR: Findings from Interviews with
Former Soviet Statistical Personnel," *SIP Working Paper,* March 1986.

their deputies, or heads of state committees or their deputies. None were from the less than 100,000 political/executive elite. A number of them, however, did belong to the numerically prominent middle elite. The Soviet emigration of the 1970s included a reasonable number of individuals who worked in a professional or managerial capacity in state committees, ministries, institutes associated with state committees or ministries, local and regional executive committees, in trusts, and in the management of large enterprises. The most highly placed respondents occupied responsible positions in ministry main administrations (*glavki*), in state committee departments, in departments subordinated to executive organs of Soviet government at republican or city levels, or in institutes attached to state committees, ministries, or large enterprises.

Studies of middle Soviet elites have provided valuable insights into Soviet institutions.[23] Studying Soviet middle elites has its advantages. First, more Soviet material is published on middle-level than on top-level decision making. Published Soviet sources can therefore be used to confirm or deny the personal testimony of respondents because both sources refer to the middle bureaucracy. Second, middle elites interact as subordinates with top elites; top elites can be studied indirectly through the observations of subordinates. Third, and perhaps most important, the top elites spent their formative years in the middle bureaucracy. One would expect them to continue the practices they learned on their way up. Decision-making procedures of the middle bureaucracy should carry over to higher levels.

The goal of this book

This book describes how the Soviet economic bureaucracy works above the level of the enterprise. It does so by seeking to answer a number of questions: How do people in the bureaucracy make decisions? What are their goals; what are they trying to accomplish? Who moves up the administrative ladder and why? How are they judged by their superiors? Who trusts whom? Why do subordinates sometimes act contrary to the interests of their superiors? Do bureaucrats who are judged on the basis of production results behave differently than those who are not? What are the interactions among the levels of the bureaucracy? How do superiors keep tabs on their subordinates? Is

---

[23] Two of the most notable studies in Soviet politics were studies of middle elites. See Fainsod, *Smolensk Under Soviet Rule* and Hough, *The Soviet Prefects*.

there an independent auditing authority within the bureaucracy? What are the relationships between state and party organizations?

Answers to these questions must be drawn from the limited published sources and interview information just described. Trying to describe how the Soviet economic bureaucracy works is like the blindfolded men of the familiar story trying to describe an elephant. Just as each man's description of the elephant depends on the anatomical feature he happens to touch, so does the availability of material determine the conclusions of this study.

This book is a highly personal account of the Soviet economic bureaucracy. It covers only selected institutions. It relies heavily on the actual work experiences of former bureaucrats and published anecdotes of bureaucratic practices. Just as the blindfolded men must rely on the incomplete information acquired by touch, so must we rely on incomplete information gleaned from Soviet writings and the life experiences of a small group of émigré respondents. The information is qualitative and not suitable for conventional statistical analysis. The Appendix discusses the methodology of interviewing former Soviet economic bureaucrats and interpreting the results.

Just because information is incomplete and qualitative does not mean that we cannot draw meaningful conclusions. The blindfolded men can use their incomplete data to answer important questions. They can conclude, for example, that the elephant is a living being, that it seems to be large and mobile, that it makes noises, and that it has a peculiar smell. On the observations about which they are less certain, such as the use of the tusk or the exact size of the elephant, they can formulate hypotheses, which subsequent observers unimpeded by blindfolds can test.

The principal–agent problem that confronts all hierarchical organizations provides the logical framework for studying the Soviet economic bureaucracy. The principal–agent framework elaborates the information and motivation problems with which any bureaucratic organization must deal. It suggests what to look for in written accounts and in respondent testimony. In particular, it requires focusing on how information is gathered, the checks and balances used, who trusts whom, how people are motivated, and the techniques used to ensure the successful completion of tasks. The principal–agent framework also raises the question of how bureaucratic agents who are not responsible for final results operate and how they interact with those who are held responsible.

Findings are presented as *conclusions* when certain conditions are met. Both the written records and interview testimony appear to be in agreement. There are clear repetitions in interviews that simply jump out at the researcher. Respondents consider the bureaucratic practices described to be matters of general knowledge. Moreover, the bureaucratic practices make logical sense in the context of the Soviet economic bureaucracy. Examples of conclusions are the importance of "not spoiling relations" within the bureaucracy, the practice of "overinsuring," and the job security provided by technical experience. Other bureaucratic practices are presented as *hypotheses*. Whether they constitute an integral part of Soviet bureaucratic working arrangements cannot be established conclusively with the information at hand. The interpretation of practices that cannot be corroborated by repetitions or published sources depends on the researcher's "feel" for how things fit together.

CHAPTER 2

Design

Theory of socialist bureaucracy

Organization theory provides a general framework for studying the way bureaucratic organizations work.[1] The nature of organizations is defined by the individuals that staff them, by their formal and informal structures, by interactions among constituent parts, and by procedures for determining status and roles within the organization. Communications systems link the components of the organization and determine how information flows within the organization. Members of the organization make decisions, which depend on jobs, individual expectations, motivations, and the organization's structure. Organizations are composed of people and institutions. The classical organization theory of Frederick W. Taylor, James Rooney, and Alan Reiley focused on the anatomy of formal organization. Modern organization theory combines formal hierarchies with informal organization, human motivations, and information.[2]

Organization theory, although general in focus, has been applied primarily to business organization, seldom to bureaucracy.[3] Bureaucracy theory, like organization theory in general, has evolved in the direction of greater emphasis on human motivation and information flows. Max Weber, the most prominent student of bureaucracy, portrayed the bureaucrat as a professional dispassionately following well-defined orders.[4] Weber saw no reason for the interests of bureaucrats

[1] For discussions of modern organization theory, see James March and Herbert Simon, *Organizations* (New York: Wiley, 1958), and Mason Haire (ed.), *Modern Organization Theory* (New York: Wiley, 1959).

[2] For a survey of classical, neoclassical, and modern organization theories, see William G. Scott, "Organization Theory: An Overview and an Appraisal," *Academy of Management Journal*, April 1961, pp. 7–26.

[3] For example, the indexes of modern texts on organization theory contain no reference to bureaucracy. See, e.g., John Ivancevich and Michael Matteson, *Organizational Behavior and Management* (Plano, Tex.: Business Publications, 1987). Such texts also rarely mention Max Weber, the most prominent student of bureaucracy.

[4] Max Weber, *Wirtschaft und Gesellshaft*, 4th ed. (Tuebingen: Mohr, 1956).

13

to diverge from those of their superiors. The Weberian bureaucrat had no room for discretionary action; any two competent Weberian bureaucrats would carry out a given set of orders in exactly the same fashion. Accurate information would be volunteered at all levels of the bureaucracy. Weberian bureaucrats did not have to make choices based on costs and benefits. Lacking the discretion to make choices, the Weberian bureaucrat did not appear an interesting object of study.

Critics of socialist resource allocation focused on bureaucratic problems. Ludwig von Mises, Friederich von Hayek, and Abram Bergson argued that the socialist bureaucracy's computational and information burden would be unmanageable and that, without private ownership and market allocation, socialist managers would make poor decisions and be improperly motivated.[5] Even public-spirited bureaucrats would not know how to operate in the public interest.[6]

The writers who formulated the theoretical foundations of planned socialism – Enrico Barone, Oskar Lange, Karl Marx, and V. I. Lenin – failed to lay out the formal design of its bureaucracy.[7] They paid little

---

[5] The most prominent skeptics are Ludwig von Mises and Friederich von Hayek. On this see Abram Bergson, "Socialist Economics," in *Essays in Normative Economics* (Cambridge, Mass.: Harvard University Press, 1966), pp. 193–236.

[6] For an analysis of this issue, see Abram Bergson, "Managerial Risks and Rewards in Public Enterprises," *Journal of Comparative Economics*, 2, No. 3 (1978), pp. 211–25.

[7] Enrico Barone, the nineteenth-century Italian economist who laid the theoretical framework for socialist resource allocation, gave little thought to its bureaucratic requirements. Barone demonstrated that, in a world of perfect information and perfect computation, planners could allocate resources efficiently. Barone's solution required conditions that could scarcely be met, and he despaired of a real-world socialist economy ever creating a planning bureaucracy that could produce his efficient solution.

Oskar Lange's well-known model of market socialism was conceived as an answer to the informational and computational problems of planned socialism. In Lange's model, most resource-allocation decisions (except investment) are made by the market, and the market assists planners in setting relative prices by trial and error. Lange devoted little attention to the bureaucratic arrangements required to implement his planning scheme. Lange wrote of a central planning board that would carry out the trial-and-error pricing, make investment decisions, and correct externalities. He also wrote of intermediate bodies (resembling ministries) that would be a part of the socialist bureaucracy.

Marxist-Leninist writings also fail to spell out the institutional details of the bureaucracy of planned socialism. Lenin did note that state planners would control only heavy industry, transport, and banking during the early

attention to bureaucratic matters, information and computational burdens, or motivation. These writers felt that the elimination of class struggle would allow socialist bureaucrats and managers to work in harmony. All would direct their efforts toward achieving broad social goals, and none would be deflected from these goals by narrow self-interest.

In effect, the socialist writers had in mind a Weberian bureaucrat schooled in socialist principles – a professional official crisply carrying out well-defined orders from superiors and passing down clearly defined orders to subordinates. There would be no need to worry about bureaucratic motivation, because self-interest would not be involved, and tasks would be so well defined that no discretionary choices would have to be made. Information would flow smoothly without distortion among the various levels of the socialist bureaucracy.[8]

Modern organization theory postulates a different view of the neutrality of bureaucrats. If bureaucrats, like other economic agents, are interested in maximizing their utility, they can be motivated to act contrary to the interests of their superiors.[9] The utility-maximizing view of bureaucratic behavior is less narrow than it appears: Bureaucratic utility can be defined broadly to encompass both private and social goals. Private goals could include rapid advancement or higher income, while social goals could include improving social welfare. Because utility can be broadly defined, bureaucratic utility maximization is consistent with different views of bureaucratic behavior.[10]

Principal–agent problems

Socialist bureaucrats operate in a hierarchy of superior and subordinate organizations. At each level, bureaucratic agents take actions that

years of the socialist state and that this would limit their administrative burden. Contemporary Marxist-Leninist writers use vague notions such as "scientific planning," "proportional development," and "harmonious interests" to demonstrate the manageability of the bureaucratic problem.

[8] Weber, *Wirtschaft und Gesellschaft*.
[9] The pioneers in the economic study of bureaucracy are Kenneth Arrow, *The Limits of Organization* (New York: Norton, 1974); Gordon Tullock, *The Politics of Bureaucracy* (Washington, D.C.: Public Affairs Press, 1965); and Herbert Simon, *The Science of the Artificial* (Cambridge, Mass.: MIT Press, 1969).
[10] For a discussion of Marxist theories of bureaucracy, see the discussion in Gerd Meyer, *Sozialistische Systeme* (Opladen: Leske, 1979).

serve their own goals. Different organizations in the bureaucracy possess different amounts of information, and they can have divergent interests. Subordinate organizations typically have more "local" information than their superiors. If the interests of the subordinate organization differ from those of the superior, the subordinate organization can take advantage of its greater information.[11]

A principal–agent relationship exists between bureaucrats at different levels. The subordinate bureaucrat acts as an *agent* for the superior bureaucrat, or the *principal*.[12] The agent carries out the orders of the principal, and the principal wishes the agent to act in his, the principal's, interest. At the highest levels, bureaucrats have broad social goals, but they must issue specific orders to their agents, who then issue orders to their agents. Career-minded agents want to fulfill their tasks in a manner judged satisfactory by the principal.

As tasks are handed down from principals to agents through a hierarchy, they become more narrow and specific. The high-level principal translates broad social goals into specific, measurable tasks for intermediate-level agents. Intermediate-level agents seek to be in formal compliance with these specific tasks, and they must in turn translate their tasks into even more narrow measurable tasks for their agents. As principals hand down more and more specific and narrow tasks to their agents, agents may be motivated to act contrary to the interests of their principals.

The principal can state well-defined objectives for only certain spheres of the agent's activity. In other areas, the agent has the discretion to act contrary to the interests of the principal. A *principal–agent problem* exists when the agent is motivated to act in areas of discretionary behavior contrary to the interests of the principal.

If a principal possessed perfect information, he could issue detailed and mutually consistent instructions to his agent that would require the agent to act in the principal's interest in all activities. With perfect information, the principal could monitor all of the agent's actions. However, the principal's information is not perfect, and the more complex the hierarchy, the less perfect it is. Principals and agents have

---

[11] Pioneers in the economics of information are F. A. Hayek, "The Use of Knowledge in Society," *American Economic Review, 35* (1945), pp. 510–30; Michael Spence, "Job Market Signalling," *Quarterly Journal of Economics, 87,* No. 3 (1973), pp. 355–74; and G. J. Stigler, "The Economics of Information," *Journal of Political Economy, 69* (1961), pp. 213–25.

[12] For discussions of the principal–agent literature, see Roy J. Ruffin, *Modern Price Theory* (Glenview, Ill.: Scott, Foresman, 1988).

asymmetric information. The agent has more detailed knowledge of local circumstances. With asymmetric information, the principal cannot monitor the agent perfectly, thus allowing the agent to engage in *opportunistic behavior* – to pursue goals not consistent with those of the principal.

Confronted with opportunistic behavior, a principal can try to devise a reward system that motivates the agent voluntarily to act in the principal's interest. However, the principal can reward (or penalize) selected, measurable tasks. The agent's other activities are not subject to rewards or sanctions, and in these areas the agent is free to engage in opportunistic behavior. The agent is entirely rational in behaving opportunistically as long as the chances of meeting the principal's specific reward targets are improved.[13]

The documented opportunistic behavior of Soviet enterprise managers illustrates the principal–agent problem in the Soviet context.[14] The principals of Soviet enterprises (the ministries) want enterprise managers to produce assigned current outputs with maximum efficiency, while also providing for future output assignments by installing new technologies. The principals of Soviet enterprises cannot convert these broad objectives into a consistent set of measurable targets for their enterprises. They lack the local information and monitoring capability, so they select a limited number of concrete tasks on which to judge enterprise performance. The superiors of an enterprise have no way of knowing to what extent the enterprise is achieving their broad objectives.

Soviet managers must be in formal compliance with the concrete tasks given them by their superiors (such as meeting physical output targets). In other areas of enterprise operations, they are left with a considerable amount of discretion. "Rational" Soviet managers en-

---

13 Fyodor Kushnirsky, *Soviet Economic Planning 1965–1980* (Boulder, Colo.: Westview, 1982), clearly describes the frustration of Soviet planners in seeking appropriate success indicators for subordinate organizations. If gross output targets are the criterion, quality is sacrificed and expensive materials are used to build up the gross value of the output. If net output is the indicator, subordinate units use too much labor. If product quality is used, enterprises limit physical outputs. Kushnirsky pictures the stream of reforms of planning indicators as a futile search for a nonexistent ideal incentive system.

14 Joseph Berliner, *Factory and Manager in the USSR* (Cambridge, Mass.: Harvard University Press, 1957); Berliner, *The Innovation Decision in Soviet Industry* (Cambridge, Mass.: MIT Press, 1976); David Granick, *Management of the Industrial Firm in the USSR* (New York: Columbia University Press, 1954).

gage in dysfunctional activities, like concealing enterprise capacity, overordering inputs, or avoiding new technologies, because these opportunistic actions improve their chances of fulfilling their formal assignments. Although these dysfunctional activities are contrary to the interest of the principal, the reward system motivates the manager to engage in opportunistic behavior.

The design of the Soviet economic bureaucracy

The Soviet economic bureaucracy has been shaped by the problems of bureaucratic burden, divergent bureaucratic goals, and asymmetric information. Since the early days of Soviet rule, the political leadership has insisted upon an economic system in which major priorities are set by the party, the most important resources allocated by administrative means, and the means of production owned by the state.

The intent of the system

The Soviet political leadership wants a bureaucracy that faithfully interprets and implements its instructions. It wants a bureaucracy that does not behave opportunistically. The leadership wants its economic goals carried out at the least cost of society's resources. Resource misallocations or waste that cause the economy to fall short of the maximum output consistent with the leadership's preferences should be avoided.

Opportunistic behavior occurs when agents have divergent goals and possess more information than their principals. Opportunistic behavior can be reduced by a reduction in the principal's information disadvantage. We would therefore expect the design of the Soviet bureaucratic system to emphasize "honest" third-party information. There are resource costs of gathering honest information in the form of a larger bureaucracy. To elicit "honest" information, the principal must relieve the information agent of responsibility for final outcomes. If information agents were held responsible, they would be tempted to distort information to their advantage. However, it is dangerous to have responsibility-free agents who are in a position to affect economic outcomes.

The Soviet economic system is said to use "scientific" planning to replace the "anarchy" of the market. Resources are allocated by administrative decree, and in such a system, the work of subordinates is judged by formal compliance with instructions and orders. The more agents who are free of responsibility for final results, the weaker "scientific" planning becomes. The Soviet bureaucratic system requires agents who are held responsible for economic outcomes in order for the planning system to work.

If principals and agents throughout the bureaucracy had the same goals, principal–agent problems would not exist. In a complex, multilayered bureaucracy, it is difficult to devise a foolproof reward structure. The political leadership desires good macroeconomic performance, but it can give assignments to its agents that cover only a portion of their activities. In their other activities, agents have discretion and are in a position to act contrary to the interests of the principals. Bureaucrats who are freed from responsibility for economic performance present a difficult incentive problem. Their principals wish them to perform well but have no way to measure their performance.

The major actors

Soviet writings on state bureaucracy lay out its logical structure.[15] This literature subdivides the multilayered bureaucracy into three general categories:

1. High-level decision makers
2. Those who assist high-level decision makers in the making of their decisions
3. Those who implement and are held responsible for the instructions of high-level decision makers

Soviet planning handbooks specify in great detail who is authorized to make decisions and, accordingly, who is responsible for these decisions.[16] Although it gives mechanical rules to be applied by decision

[15] The most detailed official discussion of the Soviet planning system is Gosplan SSSR, *Metodicheskie ukazaniia k razrabotke gosudarstvennykh planov ekonomicheskogo i sotsial'nogo razvitiia SSSR* (Moscow: Ekonomika, 1980).

[16] *Metodicheskie ukazaniia* gives literally thousands of exact instructions concerning what organization is to approve what decisions. For example, it states that investment and construction projects are "to be approved according to the following order: For ministries and authorities (*vedomstva*) of the USSR carrying out construction-installation work – by the Council of Ministers in the plan of economic and social development of the USSR according to the nomenclatures of projects developed by the Council of Ministers. For union-republican ministries and authorities, republican

makers,[17] the major decisions are to be made by people, not by rules.[18]

It is easy to lose sight of the Soviet bureaucratic forest for all the trees. We begin by presenting the Soviet economic bureaucracy in an idealized form that illustrates the main functions of the three bureaucratic layers just listed.

The board of directors. The Soviet system uses a board of directors (the Council of Ministers of the USSR) to oversee the economic bureaucracy. The board serves as the political leadership's executive arm. The board exercises general supervision and coordination, and it handles disputes among bureaucratic units. It is not supposed to carry out the details of resource allocation but to set broad strategy, such as investment planning, and to supervise key appointments.

The planning commission. The board sets broad policy without working out the actual details. A planning commission (the State Planning

ministries and authorities, all-union construction trusts, main administrations of ministries of the USSR, provincial authorities for construction not directly subordinated to a construction ministry of the USSR – by the ministries and authorities of the USSR and by the Councils of Ministers of the republics" (p. 472).

Or on the matter of material input norms, it states: "Individual norms of expenditures on production are confirmed by the directors of ministries and authorities of the USSR and union republics according to the orders approved by them or by directors of enterprises if they can guarantee the fulfillment of the plan of average reductions of material expenditures" (p. 154).

17 *Metodicheskie ukazanie:* "The confirmed norms of expenditures in the planning year on one unit of production must be, as a rule, lower than the norm of the current year and of the actually expended expenditures for the accounting year. An increase of individual norms for the planning year over current norms or actual expenditures is possible only in the case of documented major changes in the construction of parts or procedures of production for the goal of raising their quality, durability, or reliability or also in the case of a deterioration in the quality of materials used in their production" (p. 154).

18 Soviet writings recognize that decisions cannot be based entirely on norms and rules of conduct. In fact, the looser the rules of organization, the more local discretion the decision maker has. The Soviets use a pejorative term, "local norm creation" (*lokal'noe normotvorchestvo*), to describe a situation in which a decision maker operates too independently of rules and norms set from above. On this, see D. B. Averianov, *Funktsii i organizatsionnaia struktura organov gosudarstvennogo upravleniia* (Kiev: Akademiia nauk Ukrainskoi SSSR, 1979), Chap. 1.

Commission, or Gosplan) acts as the board's executive agent. The planning commission translates the board's directives into operational input and output plans and monitors their fulfillment. The planning commission draws up balances of supplies and demands of key inputs on which to base its input and output plans. *The planning commission does not manage enterprises directly.* If the planning commission were responsible for enterprise plan fulfillment, it might act contrary to the interests of the political leadership.

Industrial ministries. Industrial ministries deal directly with enterprises and are responsible for implementing the planning commission's plan at the operational level. With industrial ministries responsible for enterprises, the planning commission is free to concentrate on operationalizing the board's general directives in the form of ministry input and output plans. Industrial ministries do the operational input and output planning for enterprises based on the ministry plans of the planning commission. Ministries allocate inputs to enterprises administratively subject to limits set by the planning commission.

The system's directors want the ministry to produce the outputs ordered by the planning commission and to allocate materials efficiently. *The ministry is held responsible for the results of the ministry's enterprises.* The ministry is monitored and rewarded on the basis of fulfillment of ministry output plans, because it is too difficult to judge how well the ministry has used inputs.

Functional committees. The planning commission uses a multitude of functional committees (e.g., a price committee, an investment committee, a technology committee) for advice. Functional committees study engineering and financial relationships to advise the planning commission on ministry input requests and the feasibility of planned outputs. The planning commission uses functional committees to establish norms and rules of conduct for ministries and enterprises. The functional committees have no direct authority over enterprises (only the ministries have such power), but they can indirectly affect resource allocation through their rules and norms. *Functional committees are not held responsible for enterprise results.* Functional committees should serve as honest brokers of information for the planning commission.[19]

[19] The Soviet literature is emphatic on the point that functional organizations are the honest information brokers in the economy because they are

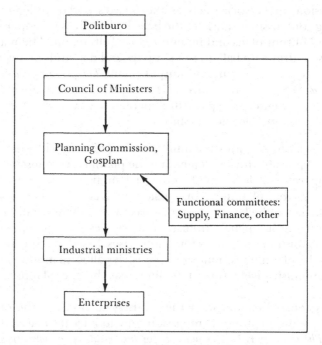

Figure 1. A schematic presentation of the Soviet economic bureaucracy.

The local party. The ministries are organized on branch lines; functional committees specialize in engineering relationships and financial activities. Yet production takes place on a regional basis, and some production and supply are local. The local branches of the party are suitable for coordinating territorial output. In addition, local party units can monitor local enterprises, which are managed by the industrial ministries. Local party units also deal with matters that transcend ministry boundaries yet require regional coordination. Local party units, like the industrial ministries, deal directly with enterprises. *The local party is held responsible for the results of its enterprises.*

Figure 1 gives a schematic rendering of the organization of the

not held responsible for final results. In contrast, industrial ministries, which are held responsible for final results, are suspected of providing biased information to superiors in order to make their performance appear better than it was in reality. For a clear statement of this, see V. G. Vyshniakov, *Struktura in shtaty organov sovetskogo gosudarstva i upravleniia* (Moscow: Nauka, 1972), Chap. 3.

Soviet economic bureaucracy. At the apex of the chart is the political leadership (the Politburo of the Communist Party), which is placed above the bureaucracy. The chart divides the bureaucracy into a "board of directors" level (an upper level dominated by the planning commission but including its functional assistants), an intermediate level composed of the industrial ministries, and a lower level composed of the producing enterprises.

We began with a three-way classification of the Soviet economic bureaucracy. The board of directors (the Council of Ministers) and the planning commission (Gosplan) belong in the high-level decision-maker category. The functional committees belong in the second category. They assist high-level decision makers by their information-gathering and rule-making activities. The ministries, enterprises, and local party are responsible for implementing the instructions of high-level decision makers.

Summary

The board of directors (the Council of Ministers) is supposed to set broad policy, including investment strategy and key appointments; it should not handle the routine details of resource allocation. As the executive arm of the political leadership, it should have interests that coincide with those of the political leadership. Like the latter, the board is held accountable for economic results – for macroeconomic performance.

The planning commission translates the policy directives of the board into ministry plans. It should use the functional committees as honest brokers of information. The functional committees are not to be held responsible for production results, but should influence economic outcomes through their advice and rules.

The industrial ministries are in charge of the actual operation of the economy and are to be held responsible for production results. They formulate the actual operational plans of the economy (in conjunction with the planning commission) and allocate materials among enterprises.

The local party deals directly with enterprises as well, and local party officials, like ministries, are held responsible for production results. Party officials are judged on the basis of regional economic outcomes, whereas ministries are judged on sectoral economic outcomes.

Potential principal–agent conflicts are located in the system. Both the industrial ministries and the local party are held responsible for production results and hence are prepared to act opportunistically. Both possess "local information" on production circumstances that is superior to that held by their principals.

CHAPTER 3

Organization

Implementation of the bureaucratic design

The preceding chapter elaborated the logical design of the Soviet economic bureaucracy. We turn in this chapter to the implementation of this design in Soviet practice. We discuss the roles of the Council of Ministers, Gosplan, the functional committees, and the industrial ministries. Using the literature and interviews with middle-level bureaucrats as a basis, we study the functions, staff, and hierarchical conflicts of the Soviet economic bureaucracy.

The oversight level: the Council of Ministers

The USSR Council of Ministers (Sovet Ministrov SSSR) is the highest oversight and executive committee of the Soviet economic bureaucracy. It is responsible for the enactment of the economic policies of the Communist Party by the state bureaucracy.

Functions. The Council of Ministers is the highest executive organ of state power. Its duties and authority are spelled out in the Soviet constitution, which empowers the Council of Ministers to issue decrees and to monitor their execution.[1] The Council of Ministers is the main source of economic legislation, orders, and decrees. Its edicts (called *postanovlenie*) vary from important statements of enterprises or ministry law to routine guidelines for individual ministries or organizations.[2]

The Council of Ministers coordinates and directs the activities of

---

[1] *Konstitutsiia (Osnovnoi zakon) SSSR* (Moscow 1975), articles 64–77.

[2] *Postanovlenie* are issued either by the Council of Ministers alone (an example would be a *postanovlenie* about "raising the effectiveness of scientific work in the . . . industry") or jointly with the Central Committee of the Communist Party (examples would be a *postanovlenie* about "raising the effectiveness of the organization of work in the industry" or on regulations governing the operation of socialist enterprises).

the state committees and the ministries and the organizations subordinate to them. It supervises national economic planning, the state budget, and credit and currency systems. It forms state committees and has the right to countermand orders of ministers and heads of state committees. The Council of Ministers' authority to reverse the decisions of ministers and heads of state committees makes it the most powerful executive body in the Soviet economic bureaucracy. It is authorized to make and execute the key resource-allocation decisions of the Soviet economy.[3]

Does the Council of Ministers limit itself to a board-of-directors role? High Soviet party and state officials have intervened regularly in routine economic matters over the course of Soviet history. Stalin and Molotov, for example, were personally involved in routine resource allocations, often operating outside the established planning system.[4] The Council of Ministers' continued involvement in routine affairs can be gleaned from the intrusive and detailed nature of its decrees.[5]

It therefore comes as no surprise that even middle-level bureaucrats have regular dealings with the Council of Ministers, often on routine matters. Respondents reported active involvement of high Council of Ministers officials in routine operations, especially in supply matters. Middle-level respondents who worked in ministries and state committees received detailed instructions from the Council of Ministers, a number signed by either the chairman or his personal representative. There were so many routine Council of Ministers orders in circulation that relevant parties were not impressed and frequently failed to respond.[6] Ministers were reported as taking routine

[3] See David Lane, *State and Politics in the USSR* (New York: New York University Press, 1985), pp. 191–5, for a discussion of the Council of Ministers' role as the acting executive responsible for the economy.

[4] The historical literature gives ample evidence of hands-on management of operational economic affairs. On this see Tatjana Kirstein, *Die Rolle der KPdSU in der Wirtschaftsplannung, 1933–1953/54* (Wiesbaden: Harrassowitz, 1985). To judge by the autobiographies of Soviet economic officials, the highest level of the Communist Party participates actively in operational decisions. On this see A. G. Zverev, *Zapiski ministra* (Moscow: Izdatel'stvo politicheskoi literatury, 1973), and A. I. Iakovlev, *Tsel' zhizni (Zapiski aviokonstruktor)* (Moscow: Izdatel'stvo politicheskoi literatury, 1972).

[5] As these examples show, Council of Ministers *postanovlenie* can vary from relatively minor matters to matters of great importance such as the definition of the rights and powers of socialist institutions such as socialist enterprises or ministries.

[6] One respondent who worked for a supply agency reported taking a Council of Ministers order (signed by a high-level official) to a supply enterprise and being shown disdainfully a drawer full of such orders.

ministry matters to the top leadership of the Council of Ministers, and high Council of Ministers officials were said to work on operational matters such as pipe allocations or the engineering details of ministry investment projects.

The involvement in detail of high-level officials is a recurring theme in this study. It appears to occur because administrators find it difficult to distinguish the important from the routine. If the allocation of pipe is done poorly, it is felt, this can reverberate throughout the economy. At the ministry level, it is thought that if a key factory fails to meet its supply plan, the entire ministry plan could fail.

Many of the dealings of former middle-level bureaucrats with the Council of Ministers entailed the broad policy matters consistent with its board-of-directors function. The involvement of the Council of Ministers in investment decisions is covered in Chapter 6. The Council of Ministers is without question deeply involved in high-level state appointments. Ministerial employees reported that either the ministry or the Council of Ministers could nominate persons for high-level positions and that personnel matters were a cooperative effort. Not a single respondent reported outright conflicts between the Council of Ministers and other state organs on matters of high-level appointments. Although frictions of this type probably exist, if they were commonplace, they would be picked up by interviews such as these. Respondents did report that their organization had to take on unqualified persons nominated by higher authorities who had been removed from party positions or who had connections to high officials.[7] Such appointments were accepted grudgingly as a natural part of doing business in the bureaucracy. Virtually every respondent had some tale about the imposed appointment of incompetent relatives, friends, or deposed party officials.

Middle-level bureaucrats typically knew what positions in their organization were on the appointment list (*nomenklatura*) of the Council of Ministers and which could be decided by the organization's directors. They distinguished the appointments on the *nomenklatura* of Director X, Minister Y, or Manager V from those of the Council of Ministers. Ministry positions from the head of a main administration (*glavk*) on up were said to be Council of Ministers appointments. Generalizations, however, are difficult to make. Even the position of

---

[7] Jerry F. Hough, *The Soviet Prefects: The Local Party Organs in Industrial Decision Making* (Cambridge, Mass.: Harvard University Press, 1969). Chapter 7 shows that a ministry will often appoint someone dismissed at the behest of party to a higher position.

chief engineer of a giant enterprise falls under the appointments list of the Council of Ministers.

The fact that middle-level economic bureaucrats had relatively common dealings with the highest executive arm of the Soviet economic bureaucracy confirms that it is not just a policy-setting oversight body as called for by the theoretical system design. Rather, it is involved in routine economic affairs in addition to broader policy matters. The Council of Ministers is called upon to make thousands of decisions concerning resource allocation. These decisions range from mundane matters such as who gets steel pipe to more important issues, such as the location of major new industrial complexes.

Staff. The size and structure of the Council of Ministers are largely hidden from public view.[8] The council consists of more than 130 members. Its regular activities are handled by a standing body, its presidium. It is organized into functional departments and branch departments.[9] Its permanent branch commissions are formed by the Politburo. The branch commissions manage the industrial ministries that report to them. The Council of Ministers' permanent commissions are staffed by Council of Ministers personnel as well as by high officials from Gosplan, Gossnab, and other state committees. The Council of Ministers has a technical staff that does the documentation work and technical studies on which Council of Ministers decisions are based. The Department of the Assistant for Economic Questions, according to one account, plays the most prominent role in documenting and analyzing Council of Ministers economic decisions.[10]

Since the council is the highest executive arm of the Soviet political leadership, the technical competence of its staff is an important issue. To what extent are the council's decisions based on information supplied by a staff that is well versed in practical economic matters?

Respondents who had contact with the Council of Ministers' branch departments report that branch technocrats (called curators, or *kuratory*) oversee (*kuriruet*) specific state committees and ministries. The technical staff of the Council of Ministers is considered highly

---

[8] See William J. Conyngham, *The Modernization of Soviet Industrial Management* (Cambridge University Press, 1982), Chap. 1, for a discussion of what is known about the operations of the council. Also see David Lane, *State and Politics in the USSR* (New York: New York University Press, 1985), pp. 199–5.

[9] This information is based on Sergei Friedzon, "Top-Level Administration of the Soviet Economy," *Rand Memorandum*, January 1986, pp. 145–73.

[10] Ibid., pp. 140–4.

competent, most members having had branch experience. One former ministry official had frequent meetings with Council of Ministers branch department officials; he described them as well-versed, young technocrats who prepared most of the decision papers for the Council of Ministers. The respondents, who had working contacts with Council of Ministers staff, spoke highly of their technical qualifications.

Documents were channeled through the overseer, and implicit rules concerning the working relationship between state committee heads and ministers were well understood. A former employee of a state committee described the working relationship with the committee's *kurator:* All documents concerning the committee went through the *kurator.* If the document was signed by the head of the state committee, the *kurator* was not allowed to alter it, even if he had a different opinion. In cases of difference of opinion between the *kurator* and state committee head, the *kurator* was obliged to call the state committee head to seek a resolution. A former member of a republican ministry described a similar set of arrangements between the minister and the Council of Ministers of the republic. From these accounts, it appears that the Council of Ministers technocrat is obliged to work cooperatively with the head of the committee or ministry. The system aims to iron out differences before they reach higher levels.

The most important economic matters are handled in joint sessions of the Politburo and Presidium of the Council of Ministers.[11] Each voting member must sign off on basic economic policy for the action to become fundamental law.

The high technical competence of Council of Ministers staff is explained by the fact that most staff members had previous experience in the branch that they oversee. Chapter 4 discusses bureaucratic career patterns and shows that Soviet bureaucrats tend to remain within their field of technical training. Persons working in the petrochemicals branch of the Council of Ministers will have had a technical education in petrochemicals and will have worked in that area before their appointment to the Council of Ministers staff.

Principal–agent problems. Little is known of the relationship between the Central Committee of the Communist Party and the Council of Ministers, but we see no grounds to suspect a principal–agent problem. The Central Committee and the Council of Ministers appear to have a common interlocking directorship in which the leading members of the Council of Ministers are also members of the Central

[11] Ibid., pp. 101–3.

Committee. Middle-elite respondents can shed little light on the working relationships between the two organizations. Some respondents observed dealings between the central committees of the republics and the council of ministers of the republics. None of them reported conflicts between the two.

A former Soviet official, Sergei Friedzon, provides the most comprehensive account of high-level economic decision making. His account gives some evidence of the absence of principal–agent problems between the Council of Ministers and the Politburo.[12] First, the top-level economic decision makers of the USSR form an interlocking directorate of party and Council of Ministers officials. In fact, the chairman of the Council of Ministers is placed a level above powerful regional party officials to ensure that there is one party line.[13] Regional party leaders compete for limited resources; so the chairman of the Council of Ministers must be in a position to prevent this competition from deflecting the economy from the council's national objectives. Second, although the industrial ministries report to the branch commissions of the Council of Ministers, the branch commissions and the council itself are not held responsible for the final results of the ministries. The chairman of the permanent commission of the Council of Ministers represents the interests of the collective leadership. Ministers are not part of this collective leadership, because they manage individual branches. Ministers are held responsible for production results; the Council of Ministers is not held responsible for ministry results.[14]

The available evidence suggests that the Council of Ministers and the party leadership are one. The Council of Ministers is not held responsible for final results; there is no compelling reason for the council or its branch commissions to behave opportunistically vis-à-vis the party leadership.

The top level: Gosplan

Gosplan SSSR (the State Planning Committee of the USSR) is the core state committee of the Soviet economic bureaucracy. Gosplan is re-

---

12 Ibid., pp. 173–5, 193.
13 Ibid., p. 97–8.
14 This is an important point. Friedzon claims that the interpretation that the Council of Ministers is not held responsible for ministry outcomes is based on his reading of the Standard Regulation on Permanent Branch Commissions of the USSR Council of Ministers Presidium. This regulation concerns the branch commission's obligation to hear ministry reports on plan fulfillment and to take corrective measures in case of plan shortfalls. On this, see ibid., p. 193.

sponsible for executing the directives of the Council of Ministers and for advising the council on a wide range of issues. The range of duties, rights, and responsibilities of Gosplan testify to its importance in the economic affairs of the Soviet Union.

Functions. The task for which Gosplan is best known is the preparation of annual operational plans. Gosplan's job is to translate the general directives handed down by the Council of Ministers into operational plans for the ministries. Gosplan plans for the ministries, not for enterprises. Gosplan's statute charges it with working out current (*tekushchie*) plans for the ministries and authorities (*vedomstva*). Its operational plans are for the intermediate ministry levels and not for specific production enterprises, although some large enterprises are planned directly by Gosplan.[15] Gosplan's organizational statute expressly states that operational plans are to be compiled with the participation of the ministries.[16] Operational planning is indeed a cooperative effort between Gosplan and the ministries, as will be shown in Chapter 5.

Gosplan is also charged with preparing long-term plans (typically on a five-year basis) and longer-term "perspective" plans. Insofar as these are not operational plans, this type of planning activity is of lesser importance than annual planning. Gosplan's long-term planning does, however, have operational significance for investment planning. Permission to begin construction projects is tied to long-term plans. Respondents confirmed that there is room to fit in construction projects desired by the leadership at the last minute, but respondents who worked in construction felt that major construction projects were normally based on long-term plans. The lengthy and detailed process of site selection, feasibility study, and creating groups of contractors and subcontractors appeared to be dictated by five-year and even perspective plans.

Gosplan approves all large-scale construction projects by entering

---

[15] At least two interviews revealed that certain large enterprises and trusts enter into Gosplan's plans as line items (*otdel'naia stroka*) that cannot be altered by the ministries. The existence of line item enterprises means that Gosplan in some instances does directly plan for enterprises. Respondents reported that there were substantial advantages to being a line item enterprise because it meant that other agencies could not touch your allocations.

[16] "Polozhenie o gosudarstvennom planovom komitete Soveta Ministrov SSSR" (Gosplan SSSR); "Resheniia partii i pravitel'stvo po khoziaistvennym voprosam," Moscow 1970; *Spravochnoe posobie-direktoru proizvodstvennogo obedineniia predpriiatiia* (Moscow: Ekonomika, 1977), Part 2, p. 328.

them in "title lists" (*titul'nye spiski*), giving legal authority to proceed on the project. Respondents active in industrial construction reported that their operational "plan" consisted of the title list, which gives technical documentation, much being organized by Gosstroi (the State Committee for Construction Affairs), and of material and financial "limits" (the latter provided by the Ministry of Finance). Gosplan serves as the coordinator of construction projects that transcend ministry boundaries (which is often the case for large projects), and Gosplan (or the Council of Ministers) can set the priority of the project if it so desires. Respondents were able to report which types of projects had to be placed on Gosplan's title list and which could be approved by lower planning bodies. Respondents who worked in construction confirmed that Gosplan exercises rigid control over construction planning, a view that is consistent with the available literature on investment planning.[17]

Soviet law gives Gosplan considerable responsibilities concerning supply planning. Gosplan is specifically charged with preparing and confirming plans for the distribution of production (supplies) among ministries. Basically, it is Gosplan's task to prepare general material "limits" (*limity*) for the ministries, to be broken down into product "profiles" by the State Committee for Material Technical Supply, Gossnab.

Respondents confirmed that Gosplan prepared general supply plans that Gossnab disaggregated, but they were divided over the relative importance of Gosplan and Gossnab. Requests to make major changes in supply allotments had to go to Gosplan, and changes that called for increases of more than 10 percent of the limit had to be approved by the head of Gosplan for key "funded" commodities. Some former ministry employees felt that Gossnab was more important in determining supplies than Gosplan, but it may be that the more detailed the supply work, the more respondents would have felt that Gossnab was the key organization. One former ministry official even claimed that Gossnab was simply a technical arm of Gosplan that made few if any important decisions. Gossnab's true source of authority, however, may be its better knowledge of local circumstances. One respondent noted that Gosplan rarely changed Gossnab decisions because Gossnab was much better informed about the details of supply.

Gosplan also arbitrates disputes among ministries or state committees. One respondent described how Gosplan handled disputes

---

[17] David Dyker, *The Future of the Soviet Economic Planning System* (Beckenham, Kent: Croon Helm, 1985), Chap. 5.

(*raznoglasii*). In disputes over subcontracts, the different ministries went to Gosplan for arbitration. Sometimes the dispute would be submitted first to a lower agency such as Gosstroi. If the matter could not be resolved at the lower level, the chairman of Gosplan would issue a judgment. Soviet press accounts give a number of examples of Gosplan arbitrating disputes involving ministries.[18]

In addition to arbitrating disputes, Gosplan coordinates activities that cross regional or ministerial boundaries or both. More will be said about this later. Gosplan has been involved virtually since its founding with problems of regional coordination.[19] In Chapter 6, Gosplan's role in coordinating large regional projects (such as the BAM railway) will be discussed.

Staff. Former ministry employees generally expressed favorable opinions of the technical qualifications and expertise of their Gosplan counterparts. Gosplan branch officials have typically had considerable practical experience in the branch they oversee.[20] Gosplan required ministry officials to bargain over minute details of enterprise output and input plans, and a number of respondents attended such bargaining sessions. When asked whether it was foolish for Gosplan to be involved in the details of planning, one respondent replied that Gosplan technical experts had as many years of experience in the branch as he did and that he was not put off by Gosplan's close supervision. Another former ministry official reported that Gosplan officials had a good feel for resources and could be useful in sniffing out resources for the ministry if necessary. One respondent who had worked in construction complained about Gosplan's inability to keep informed about his ministry's five hundred or so construction projects. Gosplan did not even know where the tractors were located. Although this is slim evidence, it may suggest that Gosplan can keep better track of industrial production than of construction projects that are spread throughout the country.

People who had had dealings with Gosplan felt that they had dealt with persons who were experts in the branch. Sometimes Gosplan was able to help them in their quest for resources. In most cases, Gosplan

---

18 "Osleplenie firmoi," *Sotsialisticheskaia industriia*, May 7, 1987, e.g., tells of a dispute between two ministries being taken to Gosplan for resolution.

19 V. Kotolov and G. Petrovich, *N. A. Voznesensky (Biograficheski ocherk)* (Moscow: Izdatel'stvo politicheskoi literatury, 1963).

20 Fyodor Kushnirsky, *Soviet Economic Planning, 1965–1980* (Boulder, Colo.: Westview, 1982), Chap. 3, points out that Gosplan branch officials tend to be industry specialists.

was pictured as a tough bargainer, demanding that petitioners make a good technical case if they wish to receive resources.

Gosplan and the Council of Ministers. Does a principal–agent problem exist between Gosplan and its principal, the Council of Ministers? Although middle-level respondents cannot provide direct answers, they can provide indirect evidence. Indirect signs of principal–agent problems would be close Council of Minister monitoring of Gosplan's activities or a lack of autonomy accorded Gosplan in its decision-making authority.

A key question for establishing a principal–agent problem is whether Gosplan employees are held accountable for the outcome of their planning. "Good" planning is defined as the construction of plans whose major objectives are feasible and can be fulfilled if the ministries perform their work well. If Gosplan officials are judged on this basis, there should be evidence that they resist unrealistic growth targets handed down from above.

The Soviet literature is quiet on the matter of the Gosplan reward system, but former Gosplan employees shed light on this issue. They reported that Gosplan translated Council of Ministers directives faithfully into operational plans even if this meant constructing unrealistic plans. They also reported that Gosplan had no choice but to accept the sectoral and economywide growth targets handed down by the political leadership through the Council of Ministers. Even in its capacity as a technical expert on planning, Gosplan was not in a position to resist growth targets that it felt were not achievable. One former Gosplan employee cited the cases of a republican Gosplan official being fired for arguing for lower, more realistic targets and of a "scandal" created by an internal projection of declining growth rates. According to one former Gosplan employee, "It is impossible to construct a plan without growth [*bez rosta*]."

When asked about the desire to produce realistic plans not requiring constant corrections, former Gosplan employees answered that they knew when their plans were unrealizable, but if the party made arbitrary (*volevye*) decisions, these decisions had to be incorporated into the operational plan. One former Gosplan employee complained about the enormous pressure for new construction that Gosplan knew would make the construction plan unrealistic. Insofar as plan fulfillment depended on planned construction capacity coming on stream as scheduled, Gosplan's output plans were automatically unrealistic. Another Gosplan employee complained of the arbitrary decision of a former Soviet party leader to have a sewing machine in each household. Gosplan had no choice but to compile operational plans that would lead to the fulfillment of this political objective even though it meant presenting an unrealistic plan. Virtually all former Gosplan employees identified the obligatory growth targets imposed on their divisions as the source of unrealistic plans, but none indicated that Gosplan seriously attempted to resist or that Gosplan employees were punished for the unrealistic nature of plans.

Friedzon's analysis of relations between the Council of Ministers and Gosplan relations is consistent with these accounts. Friedzon writes that Gosplan, despite its broad-ranging functions, does not have the authority to determine whether its operational and long-run plans correspond to enunciated party policy.[21] This is done by the branch departments of both the Council of Ministers and the Central Committee, working under the supervision of the political leadership. In other words, it is not Gosplan's job to question growth targets handed down from above that are judged by the Council of Ministers to implement party policy.

No former Gosplan official spoke of penalties exacted for the formulation of unrealistic plans. There were few performance-based rewards, and former Gosplan employees shrugged off bonuses as insignificant. Although they did work in a tense atmosphere with a heavy work load, the main performance criterion appeared to be meeting formal deadlines, not the quality of planning work. One former Gosplan official, however, did note that Gosplan employees could be penalized in the case of major planning shortfalls. In anything but a major disaster, the blame could be passed fully on to responsible ministry officials. Major plan shortfalls that disrupted the overall plan, however, could cause "unpleasantness" (*nepriiatnosti*) in Gosplan branch departments. In this case, higher officials might have to look further than the ministries for scapegoats. Under normal circumstances, ministries would be unwilling to "spoil their relations" (*isportit' otnosheniia*) with their Gosplan lifeline and could be counted on to take the blame.

When asked whether it would be feasible to use a reward system to evaluate the work of Gosplan, respondents emphasized the joint nature of Gosplan planning work. Any one person's contribution to the planning process is obscured by the many changes and amendments that are made. Declared one respondent, "After all the changes and amendments that go on, the only one you can actually hold responsible for the operational plan is the chairman of Gosplan."

---

[21] Friedzon, "Top-Level Administration of the Soviet Economy," pp. 143–4.

Eugene Zaleski claims that the Soviet economy is a "managed" rather than a "planned" economy.[22] He argues that plan realism has not been a prime goal of the Soviet economic leadership. The plan is supposed to motivate actors to achieve the unachievable. Plan imbalances can be corrected at the resource-management stage of plan implementation. Middle-level respondents had not occupied positions sufficiently high to witness possible struggles between Gosplan's leadership and the political leadership over realistic growth targets. What they were able to report is that they knowingly engaged in unrealistic planning on the basis of growth targets passed down from above, and they apparently suffered few ill consequences.

Former Gosplan and ministerial employees described administrative procedures that point to a nonadversarial relationship between Gosplan and the Council of Ministers. Former Gosplan employees who worked in branch administration were unexpectedly modest concerning Gosplan's power. They argued that Gosplan had no authority to order anyone to do anything. It was the ministries, in their view, that possessed the power and authority to issue actual operational orders. It was Gosplan's job to suggest, to serve as the technical expert.

In contrast, ministry officials felt that their ministries could not get anything done except through Gosplan. Further questioning, however, revealed the apparent key to Gosplan's authority. Although ultimate decision-making authority rests with the Council of Ministers, Gosplan serves as the council's chief technical consultant and adviser. Ministry officials report that all appeals for significant plan corrections or permission to exceed material input limits have to be addressed to Gosplan. Although ministry officials have the right to appeal Gosplan decisions to the Council of Ministers or even to the Central Committee, the Council of Ministers typically turns such appeals back to Gosplan for its recommendations. This handling of appeals makes it difficult for the ministries to make end runs around Gosplan. Moreover, the Council of Ministers almost automatically accepts the recommendations of Gosplan.[23]

Gosplan and the ministries. Soviet planning texts declare operational

---

22 Eugene Zaleski, *Stalinist Planning For Economic Growth 1933–1952* (Chapel Hill: University of North Carolina Press, 1980).

23 One respondent noted that Alexei Kosygin, a former chairman of the Council of Ministers, did personally overturn the recommendations of Gosplan in the 1960s. Kosygin was an experienced, self-assured bureaucrat who may have been more inclined to substitute his judgment for that of Gosplan.

planning a joint venture between Gosplan and the ministries. Former Gosplan and ministry employees confirm that output and input planning are indeed cooperative efforts, with most operational planning done by the ministry planning departments. Although planning is a cooperative venture, it appears to take place in an adversarial situation with the defense (*zashchita*) of a plan carried out in an atmosphere of intense debate. When asked whether the ministry could blame Gosplan for a plan that went wrong, one respondent noted that the plan was formulated by both the ministry and Gosplan; therefore, the ministry could not very well blame Gosplan for poor planning. This statement appears to corroborate the evidence that Gosplan is not held responsible except in extraordinary circumstances for bad planning.

If ministries possess better information than Gosplan, ministries could use that advantage to engage in opportunistic behavior. One indicator of principal–agent problems between Gosplan and the ministries would be evidence of independent data gathering by Gosplan to correct its information imbalance. It might be noted that the bulk of Soviet economic data is generated by the ministries.[24] This practice raises the question of the extent to which Gosplan has an independent data-gathering network.

Former Gosplan employees provided ample evidence of Gosplan's independent information-gathering activities. Two reported extensive on-site visits to factories to verify the reports of ministry or regional authorities. Although Gosplan does not manage enterprises directly, such reports show that it does gather independent information at the enterprise level. One long-time Gosplan branch official reported on numerous visits to enterprises to gather independent information on their production capacity. Kushnirsky confirms that Gosplan conducts regular audits of representative firms to gather independent information.[25]

Gosplan devotes a great deal of attention to compiling material input norms and other engineering data that allow it to operate independently of local information.[26] Former Gosplan employees reported on the massive amount of technical documentation work done by Gosplan and its associated research institutes. This documentation work focuses on material input norms, which serve as guides to material input planning.

[24] On this see Stephen Shenfield, "The Functioning of the Soviet System of State Statistics, *Soviet Interview Project Working Paper*, No. 23, July 1986.
[25] Kushnirsky, *Soviet Economic Planning, 1965–1980*, pp. 35–42.
[26] Ibid., pp. 67–78.

It seems there is sufficient evidence to conclude that Gosplan is wary of ministry data (which is the dominant source of economic data) and attempts to gather information independently of the ministries.

Gosplan is charged with battling parochial tendencies (*vedomstven-nost'*), such as the unwillingness of ministries to supply other ministries, the ignoring of regional needs, a failure to work cooperatively on interministerial projects, and supply autarky. To combat ministry parochialism, Gosplan has the authority to assign ministries special tasks and to form interdepartmental commissions to manage projects that transcend ministry boundaries. Several respondents served on interdepartmental commissions created by Gosplan. The general impression one gains from their accounts is that Gosplan was able to arrange and enforce interministerial cooperation. One respondent reported on the work of an interministerial commission created by Gosplan to carry out a large high-priority construction project. Gosplan played the role of organizer and observer, leaving the actual detailed work to the participating ministries. Respondents who worked for ministries also told of projects that involved several ministries that were coordinated by Gosplan. These accounts suggest orderly working arrangements, with Gosplan remaining in the background and with a general-contractor ministry in charge of coordinating the work of the different ministries. Respondent accounts of orderly ministerial cooperation supervised by Gosplan jibes with evaluations of published Soviet sources.[27]

The functional state committees

Figure 1 of the preceding chapter placed the other state economic committees under Gosplan and divided them into three groups: the State Committee on Material-Technical Supply, the financial state committees, and other functional state committees.

Functions. It is not possible, given the limited scope of this book, to discuss all the state committees that deal with economic affairs. There are almost forty state committees, and most of them are involved in economic affairs. This section describes the functions of a few key state committees in order to provide a general flavor of their work.

The State Committee for Material Technical Supply, or Gossnab

---

[27] There is evidence of well-coordinated interministerial cooperation, especially in matters of defense. On this see Ronald Amann and Julian Cooper (eds.), *Industrial Innovation in the Soviet Union* (New Haven, Conn.: Yale University Press, 1982), p. 43.

SSSR, assists Gosplan with the allocation of key material inputs, called funded (*fondiruiumye*) goods, to the ministries.[28] Gosplan prepares material allocations by general product groups, and Gossnab works out the operational details for detailed assortments (or "profiles") of funded goods. Gossnab maintains actual warehouses and distribution points from which the ministries draw materials. In this sense, Gossnab acts as an executive arm for Gosplan in matters of supply planning. The respective roles of Gosplan and Gossnab in supply planning were discussed briefly above, and Gossnab's planning activities will be discussed in Chapter 5.

A second group of functional state committees consists of the State Committee on Prices (Goskomtsen), the State Committee on Labor and Wages (Goskomtrud), the State Committee on Science and Technology (Goskomtekhnika), the State Committee on Construction (Gosstroi), and the State Committee on Standards (Goskomstandart). These functional committees work primarily in setting rules and establishing norms that the ministries and their constituent enterprises must observe.

The State Committee on Prices sets prices for goods for which prices are set centrally and establishes rules for price setting for prices that are set by ministries. The State Committee on Labor and Wages establishes staffing norms and spells out the rules of compensation and pay. The State Committee on Science and Technology sets norms for scientific work and works with Gosplan on science policy. The State Committee on Construction sets standards for documenting construction projects and assists Gosplan in site and project selection. The State Committee on Standards establishes rules for judging quality standards.

Two financial state committees, the Ministry of Finance and the State Bank (Gosbank), work directly with enterprises, unlike other functional state committees. Their work is discussed in Chapter 5. The Ministry of Finance sets up the credit plans for the economy's enterprises (working with the ministries), plays a role in limiting managerial staff positions, and is responsible for collections of revenues for the state budget. Gosbank works directly with enterprises to carry through their credit plans, and it monitors the supply of money in the economy.

[28] The key raw materials and producer goods that are allocated centrally by Gosplan SSSR and Gossnab SSSR are called funded goods and are allocated to the ministries in the form of limits (*limity*). Other raw materials and producer goods are called "planned" (*planiruiumye*) and are allocated by the ministries and by local authorities.

Respondents reported an unheralded role of the Ministry of Finance in influencing the structure of the Soviet economic bureaucracy. The Ministry of Finance sets the number of staff positions in state bureaucratic organizations and monitors compliance. Its monitoring of bureaucratic positions is apparently undertaken seriously, and a number of respondents reported that their organizations had trouble with the Ministry of Finance because of overstaffing.[29]

Friedzon's writings suggest that the Ministry of Finance plays a more important role in the state bureaucracy than has been expected.[30] The Ministry of Finance is authorized to give an independent opinion on the correspondence of economic plans to party economic policy – a right that Gosplan does not have. This authority is derived from the ministry's responsibility for the development and execution of the state budget.

The main function of functional state committees appears to be the generation of information useful to the Council of Ministers and Gosplan in making planning decisions. Their information on norms, technology, and quality standards gives Gosplan independent information on which to evaluate ministry requests. Moreover, the Council of Ministers and Gosplan can use the rules developed by the functional state committees to constrain the activities of the industrial ministries in order to limit their opportunistic behavior.

Staff. It is difficult to generalize about the quality of staffing of functional committees. Those who worked in banking and finance tended to have higher education in finance and displayed a great deal of technical expertise. Others who worked on norms, specifications, and standards came from more diverse backgrounds. Although ministry officials (as noted above) tended to be impressed by the technical qualifications of the staffs of Gosplan and the Council of Ministers, they expressed more reservations about the qualifications of those who worked in various functional state committees. A number of respondents worked in technical areas of functional departments in which they had no specialized background. Soviet sources suggest that movement up the administrative ladder is more rapid in functional units.[31] If this pattern is valid, persons from operational units

---

[29] These respondent reports are confirmed by ministry complaints about the Finance Ministry's rigid control of ministry staffing levels. On this, see "Kadry. Pis'ma iz ministervstva," *Izvestiia*, December 19, 1986.

[30] Friedzon, "Top-Level Administration of the Soviet Economy," pp. 144, 152.

[31] V. G. Vyshniakov, *Struktura i shtaty sovetskogo gosudarstva i upravelniia* (Moscow: Nauka, 1972), Chap. 3.

would feel that their functional counterparts were less well qualified. Respondents also spoke of the confusing and poorly worded instructions and rules issued by functional committees, a concern also voiced in the Soviet press.[32]

Respondents who worked in ministry branches and in enterprises voiced frequent complaints about the ill-conceived suggestions of functional authorities who knew little about the real world of production. These complaints echo similar concerns expressed in the Soviet planning literature.[33]

Former employees of functional committees expressed more concern about their job stability than did other members of the Soviet economic bureaucracy. When asked about their prime objective at work, respondents frequently reported that their main goal was to keep their job. Respondents who worked for functional committees reported that everyone "fears for their chair" (*boitsiia za svoi stul*). This fear may be justified insofar as the Soviet literature claims that position cuts take place first in functional units during periods of budget stringency.[34]

Principal–agent issues. To what extent do functional committees serve as the "honest" information brokers called for by the theoretical system design? Interviews with former employees of functional state committees reveal clearly that they worked in an environment of limited risks and limited scrutiny. They did technical work; they were not rewarded for the success or failure of the rules, standards, and norms that they devised. Although their work load was heavy at times, they were rarely judged on the quality of their work. They were judged primarily on the basis of compliance with formal deadlines or completion of page limits.[35] Gossnab employees receive bonuses for fulfilling the supply plan – monitoring the shipment of goods, and receipt of payments – irrespective of whether enterprises receive the goods they need.[36]

Although the norms, rules, and specifications prepared by functional committees affect economic outcomes (when applied by Gos-

---

[32] See, e.g., "Ne bez ogrekhov," *Eko*, No. 3, 1985, pp. 209–12.

[33] Vyshniakov, *Struktura i shtaty*, Chap. 3.

[34] Ibid.

[35] Soviet bureaucrats refer to plans that are expressed in number of pages as *bumazhny val* (paper output). On this see "Pisma iz ministerstva," *Izvestiia*, December 16, 1986.

[36] Andrew Freris, *The Soviet Industrial Enterprise: Theory and Practice* (New York: St. Martin's, 1984), Chap. 1.

plan to actual planning decisions), there appears to be no way to relate this type of work to economic outcomes. Hence, the leadership cannot reward functional committees on the basis of economic outcomes. The Soviet planning literature has long recognized that functional units cannot be held responsible for "final results."[37] Functional units therefore are not given authority over resource allocations but should influence outcomes through the "authority of knowledge."

Former employees of functional units were taken aback by questions like "How did your superiors judge whether you were doing a good job?" or "Was good performance rewarded by bonuses or other means?" Most of them had not received bonuses that they perceived to be performance based, and they were unable to explain what constituted good or bad work.

A number of respondents expressed cynicism concerning their work. Although they spent a great deal of time devising norms, rules, and specifications, they felt that in reality their work was ignored. Instead of using their "scientific" norms, resource managers would use rough rules of thumb. The rules they devised for evaluating investment projects and scientific inventions were so confusing and obscure that they could scarcely be used in practice. The Soviet press is also full of complaints about instructions that cannot be understood or rules that superiors are unaware of.[38]

One respondent related the case of proposing a new scheme for evaluating quality standards to Gosstandart. The scheme (which he felt was a good one anyway) was readily accepted by Gosstandart officials because they incurred zero risks in taking on the project. If the new system proved a failure, no one would know. If it was successful, the agency could use it to demonstrate its progressiveness to higher authorities.

A large-scale Soviet study of bureaucratic decision making confirms the feeling of workers in functional units that their "scientific" work was not seriously applied in the economy.[39] Most decisions concerning the organization of production and material-technical supplies are made intuitively, by rules of thumb (*ottsenka "na glazok"*), or on the basis of past experience. Relatively few decisions are based on methodological instructions, internal or external expert advice, or optimizing calculations – the kind of work done by functional departments.

[37] Vyshniakov, *Struktura i shtaty*, Chap. 3.
[38] On this see "Ne bez ogrekhov," pp. 209–12, and "Kvartira za bumazhnym bar'erom," *Sotsialisticheskaia industriia*, May 21, 1987.
[39] V. A. Lisichkin and E. I. Golynker, *Priniatie reshenii na osnove prognozirovaniia v usloviiakh ASU* (Moscow: Finansy i statistika, 1981), p. 51.

In some cases, the work of functional committees could be directly linked to economic outcomes. Employees of Gossnab could send machinery to the wrong address. Designers in the State Committee for Construction Affairs (Gosstroi) had to make concrete recommendations about factory sites. When functional agencies were involved in specific planning decisions (which could turn out to be wrong), they exercised the caution characteristic of those held responsible for final results. When Gosstroi was involved in site selection for major construction projects, it would work out a series of variants with a list of caveats to which it could later point if there were later problems with the site. In its other areas of work (such as building specifications), Gosstroi exercised less caution because it felt that it could not be held responsible.[40]

We see little reason for the various functional committees to engage in opportunistic behavior. Their principals are unable to link the work of functional committees to concrete economic outcomes; there are few (if any) performance-based rewards or penalties. Functional committees do not stand to gain from relating incorrect or distorted information to their principals (Gosplan or the Council of Ministers). The downside is that there is little incentive for functional committees to devise rules, norms, and specifications that encourage efficient resource allocation by those agencies held responsible for economic outcomes. In fact, employees of functional committees are cynical about the eventual application of their work in the economy, and they are poorly motivated to establish "rules of the game" that promote economic efficiency.

Soviet writings suggest one reason that functional units may not be honest information brokers.[41] They receive few if any benefits from supplying honest information to principals who are unable to evaluate the quality of their work. Yet they affect the economic performance of those units held responsible for final results through their activities. What is to prevent functional units from looking the other way when operational units distort reality to their principals?[42]

---

[40] In the aftermath of the Armenian earthquake of December 1988, it is likely that Gosstroi officials will be blamed for the fact that their building specifications were not appropriate for an earthquake-prone region. In the case of major disasters, there is a tendency for Soviet authorities to compile a long list of scapegoats. People who had not anticipated that they could be held responsible find themselves being held responsible.

[41] Vyshniakov, *Struktura i shtaty*, Chap. 3.

[42] One respondent gave an example of looking the other way. On a factory inspection trip, he found that a republican Gosplan office was trying to cover up falsifications of production reports by a key regional enter-

The industrial ministries

The industrial ministries are intermediate bodies that deal directly with production enterprises. As such, they play a key role in Soviet resource allocation. More has been written about them than about other bureaucratic agencies. Soviet sources provide a great deal of information about the formal duties, responsibilities, and decision-making processes of the industrial ministries.

Functions. Soviet law charges the industrial ministries with the distribution of operational planning tasks to enterprises and with the allotment of state-controlled resources to enterprises. The ministries organize the work of subordinated enterprises to fulfill state plans and bear responsibility for these results. Each ministry is responsible for devising a unified technology policy and for creating an appropriate system of incentives for its enterprises.[43]

Soviet law calls for Gosplan to prepare operational plans in conjunction with the industrial ministries. The ministries negotiate branch output targets and input limits with Gosplan. Once the output and input targets of a ministry are set, it organizes the activities of its enterprises to achieve ministry output targets and stay within input limits. A ministry must petition Gosplan for nonmarginal changes in ministerial output and input targets if plan fulfillment is threatened. The Council of Ministers, as already noted, has the formal authority to decide on these petitions, but in most cases, these decisions are made by Gosplan.

Each ministry breaks its branch output plan into enterprise plans, whose totals must, by law, add up at all times to the current ministry target. The ministry has the legal right to reallocate plan targets among its enterprises during the course of plan fulfillment.

The industrial ministries are the fund holders (*fondoderzhateli*) of the economy. The most important industrial raw materials, equipment, and semifabricates are allocated to the industrial ministries by

prise. The republican Gosplan office was not officially responsible for this factory, but regional authorities had much to lose by revelation of the falsification. The Soviet press is full of similar accounts of regional functional authorities covering for regional line authorities.

43 *Postanovlenie Soveta Ministrov SSSR ot 10 Iulia 1967 g.* "Ob utverzhdenii obshchego polozheniia o ministerstvakh SSSR," SP SSSR, 1967 No. 17; "Polozhenie ob obrazovanii i ispol'zovanii rezervov po fondam ekonomicheskogo stimulirovaniia ministerstva (vedomstva)," *Ekonomicheskaia gazeta*, No. 7, 1972; *Spravochnoe posobie direktoru proizvodstvennogo obedineniia predpriiatiia* (Moscow: Ekonomika, 1977).

Gosplan and Gossnab. The ministries have their own supply departments that work with (and often independently of) central supply organizations. Centrally allocated materials are called "funded" (*fondiruiumye*) commodities, and they can be allocated to the enterprises (through legal channels) only by the ministries. Enterprises are not allowed to exchange funded goods legally, although they do have some limited leeway for interenterprise exchange.

Whereas employees of Gosplan and functional committees find it difficult to explain how their superiors judge their performance, ministerial employees have no such problem. Each ministry receives concrete output targets from Gosplan. These targets are broken down into targets for the ministry main administrations (*glavki*). Main administration officials have to juggle outputs, inputs, wage funds, and profits to make sure that their enterprises produce an aggregate output that equals the unit's plan. Success or failure is easy to judge in a ministry. Each line unit of the ministry must produce its apportioned share of ministry output. The main ministry indicators (as of 1980) were the growth of ministry output in constant prices, production of main indicators in natural form, and the growth of products of high quality.[44]

As this discussion shows, the industrial ministries do a variety of things. They plan production, manage material-technical supplies, arrange transportation, devise scientific policy, and project capital investment. A Soviet study of ministry decision making finds that 30 percent of ministry decisions concern production matters, 20 percent concern scientific policy, 18 percent concern material-technical supply, and 15 percent concern capital investments.[45] The bulk of ministry activity, therefore, is devoted to current production and supply matters. However, long-range issues, such as science policy and capital investments, do occupy a significant portion of ministry activities. On the planning front, the ministries devote most of their planning activities to the operational plan and its fulfillment.[46] Only a small portion of ministry activities are devoted to long-run planning (about 12 percent). The bulk of ministry decision making is devoted to implementing and monitoring the operational plan *after* the annual plan has been approved. This finding supports Eugene Zaleski's description of the Soviet economy as a resource-managed economy insofar as

[44] M. Chistiakov (nachalnik podotdel Gosplana SSSR), "Novye metodicheskie ukazaniia k razrabotke gosudarstvennykh planov," *Planovoe khoziaistvo*, No. 7, July 1980, pp. 73–83.
[45] Lisichkin and Golynker, *Priniatie reshenii*, p. 45.
[46] Ibid., pp. 46–7.

the ministry's key resource-allocation decisions are made *after* the annual plan has been approved.[47]

Staff. The ministry consists of a relatively small central apparatus and a number of main administrations (*glavks*). The central apparatus consists of functional departments (such as the finance department, the planning department, the supply department, the cadres department, and the summary department). Most of the operational work of the ministries is done by the main administrations. Most ministry employees who occupy responsible positions have completed a higher education in economics, engineering, finance, or engineering-economics. Those with engineering training do not stray from their area of engineering specialty. If trained in metallurgy, they work in this specialty. If trained in finance, they work in some banking or finance capacity.[48] Women employees of ministries are more likely to occupy technical than managerial positions. Ministry workers tend to be mature, because it is difficult to attract younger people to the ministries.[49] A good number of them have worked in industry before joining the ministry, but individuals occupying positions in Moscow administrative units may not have had experience in the factory.[50]

Those who have worked in the ministry for a long time are proud of their skill and experience and of the value that superiors place on their work. Most have worked in the same organization for many years, and they have a sense of loyalty to the ministry. They feel that their experience shields them from summary dismissal. They speak with respect of their minister, who is described as hard working and knowledgeable in technical matters.

---

47 Zaleski, *Stalinist Planning For Economic Growth 1933–1952*, Chap. 19.
48 In his autobiography, former finance minister A. G. Zverev, *Zapiski ministra* (Moscow: Izdatel'stvo politicheskoi literatury, 1973) relates that he was unwilling to accept a high position (offered directly by Stalin) because he had graduated in finance. A number of respondents received their positions through colleagues with whom they had studied. This networking would tend to keep individuals in the field in which they had received their degrees.
49 The statistics on age and status of employment come from a series of articles on the ministry of heavy-machine building (mintiazhmash) entitled "Prospekt Kalinina, 19. Pis'ma iz ministerstva," *Izvestiia*, December 16–20 1986.
50 The *Izvestiia* series points out that ministries located in Moscow have trouble getting entry permits for their employees. Accordingly, it is difficult to bring in workers with factory experience, especially since this ministry has few enterprises in Moscow. I do not know whether this experience can be generalized to other ministries.

Principal–agent problems. As noted above, the industrial ministries are held responsible for economic outcomes, primarily for fulfilling their output plans. Although the Council of Ministers branch commissions monitor the ministries, it is the ministries that must bear responsibility for plan failures. Ministerial officials stand to be penalized for their failure to produce the "final results" ordered by their superiors. Sanctions for failure include loss of bonuses, as well as administrative, collective, and party sanctions. Within the ministry, the most prevalent sanction is the "administrative" sanction, which places a black mark in the official's record and could lead to demotion or firing if the offense is repeated. Ministerial officials are deprived of bonuses when production targets are not met.[51]

Former ministerial employees confirm the widespread use of penalties and sanctions within the ministry. They report on a well-defined reprimand system that begins with a simple reprimand (*vygovor*) and is followed by a severe reprimand (*strogy vygovor*), which could lead to dismissal or demotion. Reprimands can be removed from the employee's record if the offense is not repeated. Former employees reported as well on the fear and trembling caused by an invitation to appear before a ministry's collegium. One respondent reported, "You are not called before the ministry collegium to be praised."

Surprisingly, former ministerial officials reported few firings and dismissals, either of high-level or of other ministry officials, for reasons of plan failure. In fact, those with many years of experience in a ministry felt that their experience protected them from job loss. When asked about their fear of dismissal, former ministry employees would say, "Whom would they get to replace me? No one else had as many years as I in my particular job."

Just as ministries possess better information on local circumstances than their superiors, so do ministry enterprises have an information advantage. This information advantage is offset by the experience of the ministry branch staff.

Ministerial officials, held responsible for final results, wish to minimize the risks of failure. The previously referenced Soviet study of ministry decision making finds that high ministry officials cite *risk minimization* as their prime consideration when they make production and supply decisions.[52] A necessary condition for opportunistic behavior is that the agent have an information advantage over the prin-

---

[51] For distributions of penalties according to ministry activities, see Lisichkin and Golynker, *Priniatie reshenii*, p. 61.

[52] Ibid., p. 56.

cipal. Respondents gave ample evidence of the information advantages that ministries have over their principals. No matter how well informed the Gosplan or Gossnab official, there is no way for that official to have as much information as the ministry.

What is noteworthy is the generally high opinion held by former ministry officials of the expertise of their technical counterparts in superior organizations. The interviews suggest that, although information asymmetries are bound to exist, they have been limited by the recruitment and retention of experienced technical people in the planning hierarchy. Ministry officials felt that they could fool their superior organizations only at the margin.[53] A ministerial official reported negotiating with Gosplan over fairly fine engineering details and felt that the Gosplan experts were very well informed about the respondent's business. Important dealings with superior organizations involved meetings with the technical-engineering representatives of the subordinate and superior organization. Gosplan and Gossnab appeared to be interested much more in the technical recommendations of the specialists than in the reports of ministry officials.

Do the objectives of the ministries differ from those of Gosplan or the Council of Minister? The Soviet theoretical literature recognizes that interests among bureaucratic units diverge, citing differences between functional units (in which Gosplan would be included) and line units (primarily the ministries). Soviet sources further suggest that functional units are more likely to consider national interests, while line units (like ministries) are more likely to consider narrow interests.[54] Soviet ministry law declares that each ministry must ensure the general development of its subordinated enterprises as a component part of the national economy. In other words, the ministry should not ignore national interests in managing its enterprises. The wording of Soviet ministry law, therefore, anticipates potential conflicts of interest between ministry objectives and national interests, and the frequent complaints against ministry parochialism in the Soviet press confirm the practice of ministries opportunistically placing their own interests above national interests. Western experts on Soviet

---

53 Former enterprise management officials felt the same about their ability to fool ministry officials. Their ministry counterparts were sufficiently well informed about enterprise matters that they could be fooled only at the margin. On this see Susan Linz, "Managerial Autonomy in Soviet Firms," *Soviet Studies*, 40, No. 2 (1988), pp. 175–95.

54 For this discussion, see Averianov, *Funktsii i organizatsionnaia struktura*, pp. 110–15, and Vyshniakov, *Struktura i shtaty*, Chap. 3.

ministries also conclude that there are strong principal–agent problems between the ministries and their superiors.[55]

Soviet industrial ministries are rewarded primarily for fulfilling output targets. The emphasis of Gosplan and the Council of Ministers on ministry output targets is reflected in the requirement that the ministry plan be "specified" at all times. Former ministry employees emphasized the legal requirement that the ministry not have an "unspecified plan" (*neraspredelenny plan*) at any time in the process of plan implementation. An unspecified plan indicates a situation in which the sum of the enterprise output plans does not add up to the current ministry plan. Avoiding having an unspecified plan is a legal requirement that ministry officials take seriously. Getting caught with an unspecified plan is apparently a serious offense.

Evidence of opportunistic behavior. Faced with the constant pressure to meet their output targets, the industrial ministries would be tempted to engage in three types of opportunistic behavior:

1. To bargain for outputs below the collective capacity of their constituent enterprises
2. To convince Gosplan that inputs in excess of real needs are required
3. To integrate themselves excessively both vertically and horizontally to be independent of outside supplies

How great an incentive do Soviet industrial ministers have to bargain opportunistically for low outputs? Presumably, this would depend on the ambition of the minister, and mostly ambitious persons would strive to become industrial ministers. Ambitious industrial ministers must have successes to show in order to advance. If they bargain for low outputs, they will have little to show. Respondents who knew their ministers well confirmed such pressure. Ministerial reputations could be made and progress up the political ladder accelerated by a minister taking on ambitious output targets and fulfilling the plan successfully. Ministers are under pressure to appear progressive in the eyes of the leadership and are likely to respond favorably to ambitious programs. Other respondents noted that important industrial ministers are part of the "state" (*pravitel'stvo*) and are not entirely free to pursue parochial interests. Moreover, respondents speak of

[55] Alice C. Gorlin, "The Power of Soviet Industrial Ministries," *Soviet Studies*, 37, No. 3 (1985), pp. 353–70.

"branch patriotism," which expresses itself as a general desire of ministry officials to push the branch ahead of competing ministries. Branch patriots are unlikely to bargain for opportunistically low outputs, because choice investment projects and higher material "limits" would go to rival ministries.

The minister stands to benefit from ambitious output plans that can be met but obviously stands to lose from plans that cannot be met. Former ministerial officials reported that negotiations between their ministry and Gosplan over outputs were intense adversarial encounters and that their ministers often had to fight against unrealistic output targets. A minister would appeal all the way to the Central Committee. The fact that ministers fight against unrealistic targets does not prove that they fight for easy targets. They must achieve realistic output targets to reduce the risk of plan failure.

Given the industrial ministries' superior information on enterprise technologies, ministers stand to benefit more from opportunistic behavior on the input side. Ministers can ensure output-plan fulfillment by obtaining liberal material and labor limits from Gosplan or Gossnab. The makeup of the Soviet planning system suggests that ministries direct their opportunistic behavior toward overstating input requirements. Much of the work of Gosplan, Gossnab, and the functional committees is devoted to input norms – which is necessary if a ministry opportunistically overdemands inputs.[56] Respondents reported that it was impossible to obtain any type of "limited" resource, including the use of engineering norms to justify the input request, without complete and careful documentation. A multitude of respondents reported that Gosplan was much more interested in the testimony of technical ministerial personnel with reputations of professional integrity than in the testimony of ministry officials, whose job it was to present the ministry's request in the most favorable light.

Finally, there is ample empirical evidence of the "excessive" integration of industrial ministries. On this matter, Soviet experts have gathered sufficient data to demonstrate the lack of specialization of Soviet ministries, which not only produce manufactured goods, but also provide raw materials, repair services, and plant construction, as well as transport their own goods.[57] Cost comparisons by Soviet au-

---

[56] Kushnirsky, *Soviet Economic Planning 1965–1980*, pp. 67–78.
[57] For Western discussions of this problem, see Gorlin, "The Power of Industrial Ministries," pp. 353–70; Gerhard Fink, *Gossnab SSSR: Planung und Planungsprobleme der Produktionsmittel verteilung in der USSR* (Berlin: Duncker & Humblot, 1972), Chap. 3. For Soviet discussions of ministry autarkic tendencies and regional maldistributions, see I. M. Egorov, "Re-

thors reveal the inefficiencies caused by ministry autarky. Goods outside the main profile of the ministries are produced at high multiples of the cost of producing them in the ministry that has primary responsibility for that branch.

Respondents readily testified about the autarkic tendencies of their ministries. They gave many examples and offered explanations for why these tendencies existed. It was particularly difficult to get outside producers to manufacture anything that was not suitable for mass production. Specialized machinery in particular had to be manufactured in-house. Many respondents worked in enterprises that produced goods and services that had little to do with the ministry's title. Some respondents wondered out loud why their enterprises were called upon to perform tasks for which other enterprises in other ministries were much more qualified.

Numerous respondents reported difficulties in extracting supplies and service work from enterprises in other ministries and the difficulty of crossing ministerial boundaries. One of the most touted managerial skills was the ability to pick up a phone and talk with responsible persons working in other ministries to obtain supplies. Respondents noted autarkic tendencies even within a single ministry, reporting that enterprises often duplicated central ministry facilities (with the tacit support of the ministry) to avoid reliance on outside organizations.

Informal mechanisms. Organization theory emphasizes that informal organizational arrangements can be as important as formal ones. The Soviet administrative literature, as well, emphasizes that, when a formal organization does not work well (or when rules are poorly spelled out), informal working arrangements emerge. The literature of Soviet enterprises has long emphasized the importance of informal arrangements among enterprises, particularly with reference to informal supply networks. Respondents told of an established informal exchange system among ministries based on the barter concept of equivalent exchange. They gave accounts of the exchange of materials between ministries and with local party officials. These informal exchanges appear to have their own structure and rules, such as what types of exchange can be approved by a deputy minister or by a main administration head. Judging from these accounts, ministries may be

mont − na uroven' sovremennykh trebovanii," *Eko,* No. 3 (129), 1985, pp. 23–33; and "Ubytochnye, no svoi," *Trud,* June 2, 1985. Soviet writers refer to thee tendencies as *mestnichestvo* and *vedomstvennost'*.

more willing to cross ministerial boundaries on matters of informal exchange. These matters are discussed in Chapter 5.

Summary

Like any complex hierarchy, the Soviet economic bureaucracy experiences principal–agent problems. The opportunistic behavior of Soviet enterprises (overdemanding inputs, sacrificing quality for physical output targets, avoiding new technology) has been known for a long time.

The Soviet economic bureaucracy is headed by the Council of Ministers of the USSR, which serves as the board of directors of the bureaucracy. Although it is supposed to limit itself to a general policy-making and oversight role, the council is actively involved in the routine operations of the planned economy. The branch commissions of the council oversee the industrial ministries, but they are not held responsible for ministry plan fulfillment.

Gosplan is the executive arm of the Council of Ministers; its main task is to operationalize the directives of the council in the form of input and output plans for the industrial ministries. There is no evidence that Gosplan is held responsible for bad planning. Indirect evidence in the form of a lack of oversight committees, general acceptance of Gosplan's recommendations, channeling of documentation through Gosplan, and lack of a well-defined incentive system for Gosplan employees points to a lack of principal–agent problems between Gosplan and the Council of Ministers.

Functional state committees specializing in engineering, technical, price, and finance matters set rules that govern the conduct of industrial ministries and provide technical information and advice to Gosplan and the Council of Ministers. Their main function is to correct the information imbalance that exists between the ministries and Gosplan, especially in matters of supply and technology. Although they affect economic outcomes through their information gathering and rules, functional committees are not held responsible for economic outcomes.

The industrial ministries do the actual operational planning of the economy in conjunction with Gosplan. They also allocate funded commodities among ministry enterprises. Insofar as ministries are judged on the basis of their fulfillment of output targets, principal–agent problems exist, particularly in matters of supply. The opportunistic behavior of ministries includes excessive vertical integration and overdemanding of inputs. Ministers, who wish to advance, do not necessarily bargain for low outputs, because they make their reputations through output successes, but they fight hard to defend themselves against unrealistic output targets. Soviet ministry law clearly states that ministries are held responsible for the results of their enterprises and that the sum of enterprise output plans must at all times equal the ministry output target. Whereas respondents who worked for Gosplan and the functional committees did not feel they were held responsible for the results of their work, there was a clear understanding among former ministry officials that they were judged on the basis of output results.

CHAPTER 4

Bureaucratic behavior

This chapter focuses on the individuals who staff the Soviet economic bureaucracy. It divides Soviet bureaucrats into three general categories: *khoziaistvenniks* (persons who perform resource allocation and are held responsible for results), *apparatchiks* (persons who issue instructions and rules to the *khoziaistvenniks*), and *technocrats* (individuals who serve the former two groups in a technical rather than decision-making capacity). We show that each bureaucratic type behaves differently and works under different conditions of reward and risk.

Organization of Soviet bureaucratic units

Each Soviet bureaucratic organization is set up according to official instructions concerning its functions and makeup. For high-level organizations, these instructions are issued by the Central Committee and the Council of Ministers. At lower levels, they are issued by ministries or republican authorities. These instructions provide the operating rules and bylaws of the organization.

Each organization is supposed to operate according to a set of instructions, called *dolzhnostnye instrukstsii*, which describe the duties and responsibilities of the organization and its management personnel. In many cases, these operating instructions are vague and general (e.g., "the obligation to organize on a scientific basis the work of subordinates"). Soviet authors complain about vague instructions, which give the management of the organization the opportunity to define responsibilities in its own way.[1] Staffing instructions are typically worked out by the State Committee on Labor and Wages (Goskomtrud), which gives a "unified nomenclature of positions" (*nomen-*

---

[1] D. B. Averianov, *Funktsii i organizatsionnaia struktura organov gosudarstevennogo upravleniia* (Kiev: Akademiia nauk, 1979), pp. 90–4, complains about the imprecision of the various *polozheniia* and legal acts that set up governing institutions. If organizations receive vague instructions, they are able to define their own responsibilities, a practice called local norm creation (*lokal'noe normotvorchestvo*).

klatura dolzhnostei sluzhashchikh). In addition, the Ministry of Finance sets limits on the administrative staff of the organization in the form of a staffing limit *(shtatny kontingent).* This limit appears to serve as an irritation to the organizations that feel themselves understaffed, and complaints about the miserly staffing limits of the Ministry of Finance can be found both in the Soviet press and in interviews.[2] One ministry response to such limits has been to create positions that are technically outside the ministry but that in reality are for ministerial employees. Ministries also evade the limit by creating semiautonomous research institutes, which relieve the ministries of their planning obligations and even carry out some of their production. A couple of respondents worked for institutes that were created to get around staffing limits imposed on various ministries and state committees.

Soviet administrative organizations are divided into main administrations, departments, offices, subdepartments, units, shops, and so on. In some cases, the internal organization of the unit is prescribed by law (as in the case of ministries). In other cases, the director of the organization is largely free to determine its internal structure. According to Soviet law, the Council of Ministers determines the structure of each ministry (how it will be divided into units), names the minister, the minister's deputies, and the composition of the collegium that advises the minister. These positions fall under the appointive powers of the Council of Ministers, and they must be approved by the Central Committee of the Communist Party. The minister determines the staffing of the remaining administrative positions of the ministry and of the ministry's enterprises. The prevailing diversity of structures of different ministries suggests that ministries have leeway in determining their internal organization at least in matters of technology.[3] Enterprise managers can appoint subordinates not subject to appointment by the ministry or higher authorities. There is a great diversity by type of organization, region, and location as to how the structure and staffing of an administrative organ are handled.

New Soviet bureaucratic organizations are created by higher authorities. The Council of Ministers establishes new state committees and new ministries. Ministries can establish new branches or indepen-

[2] For a typical ministry complaint about the strict control exercised by the Ministry of Finance over ministerial staffing, see "Prospekt Kalinina 19. Pis'ma iz ministerstva," *Izvestiia,* December 16–20, 1986.

[3] Stephen Fortescue, *The Technical Administration of Industrial Ministries,* Soviet Industry Science and Technology Work Group, Centre for Soviet and East European Studies, University of Birmingham, February 1986.

dent research institutes with the approval of the Council of Ministers. The structure of the Soviet economic bureaucracy is fluid, with new organizations being created and (a few) older organizations disappearing from sight.

New bureaucratic organizations are typically created by splitting off a branch or department of a standing organization. For example, the State Committee on Prices (Goskomtsen) and the State Committee for Material Technical Supply (Gossnab) were split off from Gosplan.[4] There has been an especially strong tendency to create new ministries from a standing ministry. The combination of factors required for the splitting off of a new ministry are the development of a new technology that clearly distinguishes the branch product, an ability to separate out the enterprises that produce, and an ambitious deputy minister. One respondent told how the ministry in which he worked was created: An important group of technical experts was prompted by the minister and his deputy to write a letter to the Council of Ministers pointing out the need for a new ministry. The minister and potential new minister (a deputy minister), meanwhile, worked behind the scenes to grease the wheels of the process. Because all parties agreed, it was not difficult to obtain the Council of Ministers' approval.

Once a new ministry is spun off, it quickly establishes an independent identity. An older respondent who began work in a ministry in the 1930s remembered the process. Initially, the new ministry and parent ministry would work together in the same quarters. After a while, access from one ministry to the other would be limited, and workers from one ministry would be admitted only with special passes. New ministries erect barriers quickly to shield themselves from the influence of their parent ministry.

More than one respondent reported cases in which organizations were created to establish a suitable position for an important political figure. One respondent told of a republican party official who was removed from his position because of a conflict. Because of his stature, it was necessary to create an all-union institute. The institute soon had branches in Moscow and Leningrad even though its head office was located in the Ukraine.

The principle of *edinonachalie*

Each Soviet bureaucratic organization is supposed to have a single head (*rukovoditel'*), who issues all orders and bears responsibility for the

---

[4] William J. Conyngham, *The Modernization of Soviet Industrial Management* (Cambridge University Press, 1982), Chap. 1.

results of the organization.[5] The head derives power and authority from the principle of one-man management (*edinonachalie*) – the concentration of decision-making authority in the hands of one person, the *edinonachalnik*.[6] The *edinonachalnik* can be an enterprise manager, a minister, the head of a research institute, or the chairman of Gosplan.

To say that all decision-making authority is concentrated in the hands of one person does not literally mean that the *edinonachalnik* personally makes all decisions. The head cannot specialize in all spheres of activity or be everywhere at once. Deputies, who specialize in different aspects of the unit's operations, are responsible for managing various spheres of activity. They are authorized to make executive decisions in the name of the *edinonachalnik* in designated areas. One ministerial official reported that material exchanges among ministries up to a specified level could be handled by the deputy ministers. More important exchange deals had to be approved by the ministers themselves. Another respondent reported that deputy ministers worked out the operational details of coordinating major construction projects involving several ministries. The ministers had little to do with such negotiations and operations. Another respondent explained that managers of large enterprises assigned deputies specific responsibilities, such as overseeing environmental rules or fulfilling scrap metal plans. Once this authority was granted, enterprise managers gave full responsibility to the appointed deputy and did not even wish to know how the deputy fulfilled the task.

The *edinonachalnik* bears ultimate responsibility for the decisions of deputies. When asked whether an *edinonachalnik* can pass the blame for poor decisions to subordinate deputies, one respondent replied that the *edinonachalnik*'s superiors could not care less about why things have gone wrong. What is important is that assignments have not been fulfilled and the *edinonachalnik* is to blame.

The concentration of decision-making authority and responsibility dictates a strict hierarchical order. Each *edinonachalnik* is responsible for a unit, and if subordinates could deal directly with higher authorities, the head would no longer control decision-making processes for which he bears full responsibility. Soviet law dictates a strict obser-

---

[5] See V. G. Vishniakov, *Struktura i shtaty organov sovetskogo gosudarstva i upravleniia* (Moscow: Nauka, 1972).

[6] For a discussion of the history of the principle of *edinonachalie*, see Silvana Malle, *The Economic Organization of War Communism, 1918–1921* (Cambridge University Press, 1985), Chap. 3.

vance of the hierarchical order. Individuals, however, can report a superior who is violating laws and rules to higher authorities.[7]

Interviews show that the Soviet economic bureaucracy does work along designated channels. Within a ministry, for example, construction materials enterprises handle all their business through the head of the main administration of construction materials. The head of the main administration carries out all his business with the deputy minister in charge of that product area. The deputy minister has to handle all his business through the first deputy minister, and so on. If anyone attempts to appeal directly to a higher authority, the appeal is turned back to his immediate superior. If ministers attempt to appeal over Gosplan's head to the Council of Ministers, their appeals are turned back to Gosplan.

Respondents often accompanied their superiors to meetings with higher authorities, and in some cases, they were allowed to go by themselves because "their superior trusted them." They distinguished between contacts with their boss's superior on purely technical matters, which were allowed, and contacts on policy matters, for which permission was required.[8]

Consultative bodies

The *edinonachalnik* is supposed to seek advice from an organized group of colleagues, called a collegium, a council of experts, or some such name. The consultative group is composed of deputies, departments heads, key technical personnel, and worker representatives. Membership in the organization's consultative group appears to de-

---

[7] Merle Fainsod, *Smolensk Under Soviet Rule* (Cambridge, Mass.: Harvard University Press, 1958), describes the manner in which local party organizations received and dealt with such appeals. The Soviet press is full of examples of individuals and organizations that appeal above the heads of their immediate superiors to report wrongdoing. For examples, see "Priniato k . . . neispolneniu," *Sotsialisticheskaia industriia*, May 6, 1987, and "Neumestnye ambitsii," *Sotsialisticheskaia industriia*, May 6, 1987. A number of respondents reported on the problems that could be caused by such appeals, especially when the substance of the report was true. In such cases, the *edinonachalnik* would attempt to take the easiest way out, either admitting guilt and promising he would not make the same mistake again or appealing to important allies in the higher bureaucracy to quash the matter.

[8] I. V. Paramanov, *Uchitsiia upravliat'* (Moscow: Ekonomika, 1970), p. 143, in his memoirs reported that he was so trusted by his superiors that he could go directly to ministers but that he usually had to tell the *glavk* that he was going.

termine status within the organization.[9] The consultative body can be appointed by higher bodies and operate according to highly formal rules, or it can be a more informal body. Each industrial ministry, for example, has a well-organized collegium (*kollegiia*) whose structure is specified by ministry law and whose members are appointed by higher authorities. Soviet law is so specific with regard to the ministry collegium that it even specifies its maximum size. In addition to the collegium or collegium-like consultative body, the *edinonachalnik* can also consult a scientific-technical council, composed of the leading scientific and technical personnel of the bureaucratic unit.

Consultative bodies can make decisions and give advice, but their decisions can be implemented only by the *edinonachalnik*, who is free to ignore their advice. The ministry collegium has the right to inform higher authorities of differences of opinion with the minister, but the decisions are still made by the minister and by no one else.[10] The existence of a consultative body apparently prevents the *edinonachalnik* from shifting blame to the consultative body.

The Soviet press is full of complaints about the boring and useless meetings of ministry collegiums, but respondents assess the meetings differently.[11] In some ministries, collegium meetings were forums for resolving major policy issues, reprimanding ministry officials, and discussing key personnel matters. A number of respondents attended ministry collegium meetings, in either management or technical capacities. They presented different versions of the importance of such meetings. One regular participant referred to them as "gab sessions" in which collegium members sat around and complained about supply problems. Another described them as often heated discussions of basic ministry policy and felt that important matters were resolved. Several respondents noted that an invitation to a nonmember to appear before the collegium evoked foreboding. Collegium meetings were an occasion for publicly reprimanding ministry officials whose work was deemed poor. Personnel matters were also discussed in the collegium. It is therefore understandable that an invitation to appear was not greeted with enthusiasm.

---

9 Kushnirsky, *Soviet Economic Planning, 1965–1980*, (Boulder, Colo.: Westview, 1982) Chap. 3.

10 On the rules governing the relationship between a minister and his collegium, see *Spravochnoe posobie direktoru proizvodstvennogo obedineniia predpriiatiia* (Moscow: Ekonomika, 1977), pp. 42–6.

11 For typical Soviet press complaints about useless, wasteful meetings of a ministry, see "Diktuet vremiia: Zametki s zasedaniia komiteta narodnogo kontrolia SSSR," *Izvestiia*, February 11, 1987.

Soviet economic bureaucracies use the practice of "signing off" (*vizirovanie*) to involve lower-level officials in the decision process.[12]

According to Friedzon, decisions made by joint sessions of the Politburo and the Presidium of the Council of Ministers must go through a process of signing off by all members of the two bodies. Politburo decisions that go through the signing-off process have higher authority than those that do not. Council of Ministers decrees that go through signing off have the force of legal acts of state administration.[13]

Signing off works as follows: A pending decision is circulated to all affected units. These units can then either sign off or express their disagreement with the decision. In this manner, all local disputes are brought to the attention of the *edinonachalnik*, who can then make decisions with the knowledge of local circumstances.[14]

The mechanics of decision making

A valuable Soviet statistical study of decision making sheds considerable light on the mechanics of decision making within ministries.[15] It reveals that the most common type of decision made by ministry officials is the command (*prikazyvaiushchi*) or directive (*rasporiaditel'ny*) action; together they account for 35 percent of all decisions emanating from ministries. Notification-warning (*preduprezhdaiushchi*) actions account for 15 percent of decisions, and information actions account for 12 percent. Thus ministry decisions result primarily in orders, directives, or warnings. On average, nine to ten signatures are required for the issuance of orders, directives, or warnings at high levels of ministry administration. Typically three to four officials participate

---

12 For a discussion of "signing off" see Fortescue, *The Technological Administration of Industrial Ministries*, Soviet Industry Science and Technology Work Group, Centre for Soviet and East European Studies, University of Birmingham, February 1986. Also see Kushnirsky, *Soviet Economic Planning, 1965–1980*, pp. 62–7.

13 Sergei Friedzon, "Top-Level Administration of the Soviet Economy: A Partial View," *Rand Memorandum*, January 1986, p. 101.

14 A former Gosplan employee explained that the *viza* process is used when, for example, Gosplan wishes to change a reporting form. The new form is distributed to all interested parties, and those opposed to the new form can write a memo. The affected deputy must agree to the new form. If there is sufficient disagreement, the matter can be discussed in the collegium.

15 V. A. Lisichkin and E. I. Golynker, *Priniatie reshenii na osnove prognozirovaniia v usloviiakh ASU* (Moscow: Finansy i statistika, 1981), Chap. 2.

in ministry decisions that result in orders or directives, whereas ten people participate in the less important informational decisions of the ministry. About 70 to 80 percent of ministry orders and directives are decided upon without a vote. When votes are taken, the vast majority are decided by a simple majority. Ministry votes are taken openly; there are no secret ballots.[16]

It takes various amounts of time to make decisions within the upper administration of ministries. Twenty percent of commands and directives are decided upon within an hour, 30 percent within a week, and 20 percent within a month. It also takes various amounts of time to carry out a directive or order. Eight percent are carried out in a day or less, 12 percent in a week, 14 percent in a month, 18 percent in six months, and 15 percent within a year.

Fifty percent of ministry decisions are made with the assistance of computers; 20 percent are made with pencil calculations. Ministry decisions are communicated primarily in the form of written orders (40 percent), letters or telegrams (22 percent), or protocols (10 percent) or are announced in the collegium (15 percent). Notification by telephone (8 percent) plays a relatively minor role.

The monitoring of fulfillment of production orders is done by the filling out of forms (30 percent), by requests for reports (25 percent), by investigative commissions (15 percent), or by reports to the collegium (15 percent). On supply directives, monitoring is done primarily by reports (40 percent) or telephone calls (25 percent).

Selection of subordinates

The Soviet *edinonachalnik* is constrained in two ways in the selection of subordinates. First, high-level subordinates have to be approved by superior organizations as part of the *nomenklatura* process. Second, the *edinonachalnik* may not be free to make personnel changes due to administrative regulations against hiring or firing.

On the matter of *nomenklatura*, respondents were not generally aware of cases in their organizations in which an unwanted subordinate was forced on a superior by higher authorities. Generally speaking, the organization head would be involved in the process and, most often, would nominate the person eventually confirmed for the position. The major exception appeared to be cases in which party officials would place unqualified friends and relatives in responsible positions. A large number of respondents told stories of such incidents,

---

16 Ibid., p. 50.

but this practice was regarded as a natural hazard of work in the bureaucracy, and others would have to cover for the defective work of the appointee.

Respondents generally agreed that the organization head was free to terminate subordinates. In fact, it appeared easier to terminate a subordinate in a responsible position than a common worker who fell under the protection of the trade union or labor legislation. If the subordinate had important political connections, the organization head would be less likely to attempt a termination.

The procedure of termination described by respondents resembles that used in Western bureaucracies. First, the subordinate is told that it might be better if he were to look for alternate employment. A voluntary departure would look better for all involved. In a number of reported cases, the organization head (working in conjunction with party officials) found the subordinate another position that gave the appearance of a promotion. If the subordinate was not willing to leave voluntarily, local party officials were called on to help execute the termination. A *glavk* official familiar with firing procedures in the ministry reported that the director first obtains approval of the unit's party secretary. If the subordinate occupies a high-level position, the ministry official will get the approval of local party officials. As described by this respondent, the local party organization plays a major role in the termination of high-level employees. When things go wrong, it is often the local party official who demands the resignation of responsible parties within the ministry's organization. The ministry often plays a passive role and tends to go along with party recommendations, particularly when the party has already selected a successor.

Respondents agreed that, if the organization head wishes to terminate a subordinate, it is always possible to find a way. He may, for example, eliminate the subordinate's position under the guise of cutting staff positions (*sokrashchenie shtata*) or assign tasks that he can demonstrate have been insufficiently carried out.[17]

Although the respondents agreed that the organization head has the authority to terminate subordinates, the degree to which the organization head can differentiate among subordinates according to financial rewards is less clear. The impression one obtains from the interviews is that premiums are shared throughout the organization according to the rules governing incentives and that it is difficult to

[17] One respondent told of the case of a factory director (whom the superior wanted to fire) who was terminated for the faulty placement of a crane.

penalize faulty work by withholding a premium from one subordinate while granting the premium to others. This impression is supported by the fact that, even within ministries (which are held responsible for final results), administrative and collective sanctions dominate economic sanctions as a means of penalizing poor work.[18]

One respondent who occupied a position of authority within a ministry told of attempting to withhold a bonus from a subordinate whose work was deficient. The subordinate appealed, and the process turned out to be so lengthy and time consuming that the respondent decided to grant the subordinate the bonus.

A surprising, but consistent theme among the respondents was the frequent use of verbal abuse by superiors. In fact, the Soviet economic bureaucracy appears to use verbal tongue-lashings much more readily than monetary sanctions. In view of the inability of superiors to differentiate monetary rewards within the organization, it may be that verbal abuse is the best substitute.

Responsibility in line and functional units

The Soviet literature on state administration states that *edinonachalniks* are responsible for final results, no matter what type of unit they manage.[19] To make *edinonachalniks* responsible, however, requires an ability to measure results. In some cases, the responsibilities of *edinonachalniks* are clearly defined (as in the case of a minister who is responsible for the combined results of his ministry's enterprises). In other cases, responsibilities are poorly defined and results are difficult to gauge. Many *edinonachalniks* are basically free to define their own duties and responsibilities.

The preceding chapter noted that staff and line organizations are likely to behave differently. In line organizations, there is a clear pattern of subordination and responsibility. The main administration of a ministry that handles the affairs of reinforced concrete plants is clearly associated with production outcomes. The manager of an industrial enterprise is held responsible for the results of that enterprise. The financial department of a ministry gives advice to the minister, monitors the financial health of ministry enterprises, and issues financial rules. The head of the ministry financial administration is not as clearly tied to the successes and failures of a particular line unit. Even if the ministry attempted to assess the finance department's

---

[18] Lisichkin and Golynker, *Priniatie reshenii*, p. 61.
[19] Averianov, *Funktsii i organizatsionnaia struktura*, pp. 91–3.

contribution to the success or failure of the ministry's program, it is doubtful that these results could be measured.

The *khoziaistvennik*

*Khoziaistvennik*s are administrators who occupy responsible positions in line administrative units and are held responsible for their results. They work under considerable risk: If the line unit does not complete its tasks successfully, a *khoziaistvennik* stands to lose bonuses, to receive a reprimand, or to lose his position. Examples of *khoziaistvennik*s are enterprise directors and their key deputies, heads of industrial ministry "line" main administrations (*glavks*) and their deputies, and ministers and their deputies.

Persons in responsible positions in state committees who work directly with line units (such as branch planning officials in Gosplan or in branch administrations of Gossnab) are not *khoziaistvennik*s, because they are not held responsible (except in rare cases) for the successes or failures of the branches they plan.[20]

The juggler analogy

Respondents describe the successful *khoziaistvennik* as an adept juggler. He is the Soviet counterpart of the capitalist entrepreneur, whose special skill is finding profit opportunities. Most likely, he is trained as an engineer; most of the issues with which he has to grapple are engineering issues.[21] The *khoziaistvennik* juggler knows where

[20] Respondents in "line" administrations of Gossnab reported that they were not totally immune from responsibility. When a ministry failed to reach a production goal, it could complain to the Council of Ministers that its failure was due to the poor supply work of Gossnab. Such complaints could lead to unpleasantness, but they appeared to be rare, perhaps because the ministry would not want to "spoil relations" with Gossnab. Gosplan could experience trouble if serious supply bottlenecks arose that threatened the national economic plan. The ministries could complain that this was the consequence of bad planning by Gosplan. When asked whether their departments were held responsible for their planning and distribution work, virtually all respondents replied that they were not. Only in circumstances of extreme failure would higher authorities look beyond the ministries for scapegoats within the state committees.

[21] Aron Katsenelinboigen, *Studies in Soviet Economic Planning* (White Plains, N.Y.: Sharpe, 1978), Chap. 1, discusses why bureaucratic managers tend to be engineers and how this affects Soviet bureaucratic thinking. Any number of respondents stressed the importance of being a good engineer and were scornful of those members of the economic bureaucracy who did not understand engineering matters.

the resources are, has connections that transcend ministry boundaries, knows how to secure powerful patrons, and is able to come up
with innovative solutions. If the *khoziaistvennik*'s construction project
requires extra bulldozers to be completed on time, he will figure out
how to exchange trucks for bulldozers. If plan completion is threatened by a labor shortage, he will charter a plane to transport workers.
The *kohziaistvennik* knows how to keep skilled personnel. He will find
them living quarters and make sure they always receive bonuses. The
juggler can persuade suppliers to ship supplies to him instead of
others who have a stronger legal claim to the materials.[22] The
khoziaistvennik is a tireless worker – a workaholic who lives, eats, and
drinks at his job.[23]

Knowing what superiors want

The *khoziaistvennik* knows how to complete those tasks that his superiors deem important. Part of his skill is the ability to sense what his
superiors want (and what he can get away with). As one respondent
stated, the *khoziaistvennik* knows how to juggle resources so that his
superiors always pat him on the back. The *khoziaistvennik* must work
with the rules, norms, and directives of functional agencies. The State
Committee on Labor and Wages tells him what pay he can offer, and
the Ministry of Finance dictates employment limits. The State Committee on Material-Technical Supply tells him that he cannot exchange materials with other administrative units. Local government
committees must sign papers that a construction project has been
completed. A functional department of the railway ministry sets a
rule that freight containers cannot be shipped until a certain weight
limit has been reached.

If the *khoziaistvennik* observed all these rules, he would find it impossible to please his superiors with his results. He therefore has to
break rules and even laws. The superiors of the *khoziaistvennik* tell him
to use any means possible to achieve success. That, in fact, is his job.
The Soviet literature stresses the inherent risks of being a *khoziaistvennik* and the need to break rules and laws.[24] These risks elicit the

22 All of these cases are actual examples of a good *khoziaistvennik* that were
   related by respondents.
23 Both the Soviet literature and interview respondents repeatedly emphasized the workaholic traits of admired *khoziaistvenniks*. For an example in
   the Soviet literature, see A. G. Zverev, *Zapiski ministra* (Moscow:
   Izdatel'stvo politicheskoi literatury, 1973), p. 229.
24 In his memoirs, *Uchitsiia upravliat'*, Paramanov clearly states that a good

systematic *khoziaistvennik* behavior patterns explained in the following sections.

Insurance

The *khoziaistvennik* runs two risks. The first is the risk of performing poorly. The second is the risk of being punished for wrongdoing. Wrongdoing can range from a technical violation (*narushenie*), for which the *khoziaistvennik* might be deprived of a bonus or reprimanded, to a violation of criminal law (*ugolovnoe delo*), for which he could be imprisoned.[25] If a law is broken (as in the common practice of paying fictitious workers to accumulate funds for higher pay for existing workers), the *khoziaistvennik* is subject to criminal penalties even if the money was used for the good of the unit. If the head of a ministry main administration authorizes higher prices for subordinate enterprises that violate existing pricing statutes (but allows the enterprises to reach called-for value targets), the official has violated established rules and can be punished. As respondents explained, it is virtually impossible to prove that illegal actions were taken for the good of the unit and not for personal gain. A former *khoziaistvennik* who had arranged incentive funds by paying fictional workers explained it as follows: "How would I have been able to prove that I had not taken the money for myself? It would have been impossible."

A skillful *khoziaistvennik* arranges insurance to guard against repri-

---

khoziaistvennik must be willing to take risks (including the risk of breaking rules and laws) to succeed (pp. 115–20). Paramanov taunts those who are unwilling to take risks and always run to higher authorities to cover themselves. The notion that line administrators must use innovative means (often of an extralegal nature) to achieve success is a clear trend running through the interviews. A typical example is to be tole by one's boss: "It is your job to get the materials (fulfill the plan) by using your own devices. Otherwise you are of no use to me." What counts is results, not excuses.

[25] Respondents reported on a formal system of reprimands. The first reprimand was called a *vygovor*. The second was called a severe reprimand (*strogy vygovor*). After receiving a severe reprimand, the administrator stood the risk of losing his job or worse if caught committing another violation. Respondents reported that some reprimands were indeed signals of serious trouble. Other reprimands were given on a more formal basis simply for the record. One *khoziaistvennik*, having been caught committing a violation, was given a reprimand by his superior, who then told him with a wink that the reprimand would be removed from his record in a few weeks.

mands, bonus losses, and prosecution. One insurance scheme is the practice of operating within a trusted circle of associates, all of whom are to some degree implicated in or dependent on the *khoziaistvennik*'s results. These associates occupy positions both subordinate and superior to the *khoziaistvennik*. They are recruited from old school friends, persons for whom past favors have been done, and persons whom the *khoziaistvennik* has bribed.[26] Some members enter the circle automatically through their hierarchical relation to the *khoziaistvennik*. These are administrators whose own performance depends on the performance of the *khoziaistvennik*. The *khoziaistvennik* of a main administration (*glavk*) of a ministry, for example, has a strong interest in having the administration's largest trust turn in a good performance. Local party officials have the same interest, because they are judged on the output performance of the largest enterprises in the region.[27] Such officials have a strong interest in avoiding scandals. If the *khoziaistvennik* were implicated in serious wrongdoing, they would be implicated as well for poor monitoring. The practice of the *khoziaistvennik* using a circle of associates to protect himself is well documented in the literature and is called a "collective guarantee" (*krugovaia poruka*).

Respondents gave numerous examples of how *khoziaistvenniks* use collective guarantees to protect themselves. Speaking of the intricate system of banking controls, a former banking official commented with disdain that external banking controls lose their effect because the parties responsible for enforcing rules usually belong to the same

26 Many respondents got their jobs through old school ties. A number of them obtained patrons in higher levels by writing dissertations for them (a surprisingly common means of obtaining patrons). Others recruited patrons by doing favors for them, of either a semilegal or an illegal nature. Bank officials could gain patrons by authorizing enterprises to buy material in stores with special accounts.

27 The protection of subordinates by higher-level bureaucrats is reported regularly in the Soviet press, often in an amusing form. For example, see the account of how ministry officials attempted to manipulate plan performance indicators in "Sprosim korrektirovat' plan," *Izvestiia*, September 2, 1986. One of the most common occurrences is for a local control committee (*komitet narodnogo kontrolia*) to uncover some incorrect or illegal practice and attempt to bring it to the attention of higher authorities. The higher authorities in turn try to quash the inquiry (by forming a fact-finding commission), and then the local committee brings the matter to the attention of Moscow authorities. For such a case, see "Diktuet vremia, zametki s zasedaniia komiteta narodnogo kontrolia SSSR," *Izvestiia*, February 11, 1987. For a case of a ministry covering up for one of its main administrations, see "Byla li pripiski?" *Pravda*, June 10, 1987 Also see "Pochemu ne kupish polyshubok?" *Izvestiia*, March 19, 1987.

party organization and socialize together. To expect one of them to side with an external authority is unrealistic.

Maintaining "good relations" is a second form of insurance. Collective guarantees provide protection against known risks but do not protect against unknown or unpredictable risks. Respondents emphasize that *khoziaistvenniks* operate in an environment of unpredictable risks. The trust director who has succeeded in wresting supplies from a supplier may be charged by the customer firm left without supplies. The ministry *glavk* head who redistributes funded goods from one enterprise to another may be accused of bribe taking by the enterprise that has had to sacrifice resources. If a deputy minister alienates a high local party official, the ministry official may find himself accused of some obscure offense. The *khoziaistvennik* can insure himself against unpredictable risks by staying on good terms with as many responsible persons as possible. Respondents repeatedly stressed the crucial importance of "not spoiling relations" (*ne isportit'otnosheniia*) because of the constant threat of complaints and retaliation.

One former ministry official who was involved in resource redistribution among enterprises indicated the care with which he handled such redistributions (so as not to "spoil relations"). It was best to work out a consensus for redistributions, offering the enterprise that was to lose resources some kind of concession. Although ministerial officials have broad powers to redistribute resources among enterprises, they nevertheless exercise this power with delicacy to maintain good relations with their enterprises. The Soviet press is full of accounts of enterprises that publicly complain about redistributions that they consider unfair and illegal.[28]

Maintaining good relations within one's own circle is also vital, because higher authorities dislike mediating disputes among subordinates. If a dispute cannot be handled internally and has to be referred to higher authorities, higher officials may decide not to worry about guilt or innocence, but to get rid of both parties.

A third insurance scheme is designed not to protect the *khoziaistvennik* from detection of violations, but to demonstrate innocence in case of plan failure. To achieve this goal, the *khoziaistvennik* prepares a meticulous "paper trail" to document his lack of responsibility for

---

[28] On this see "Nam ne nuzhen takoi glavk," *Izvestiia*, October 26, 1986. Ministry officials in charge of line operations even find it important to maintain good relations with heads of telegraph offices over whose lines confirmation of sales and plan fulfillment is transmitted. See "Prospekt Kalinina, 19. Pis'ma iz ministerstva."

failure. If the *khoziaistvennik* anticipates a reasonable probability of plan failure, he bombards the Council of Ministers, Gosplan, Gossnab, and ministry officials with letters and documents warning them of the dire consequences of their not meeting obligations to his unit. He writes to local party officials, to the central committee of the republic, and to the Moscow Central Committee to explain that if materials are not sent or if a promised factory is not completed, his obligations cannot conceivably be met. Respondents emphasized that a paper trail must exist. Telephone calls do not "fix" (*fiksirovat'*) the *khoziaistvennik's* case. The paper trail strategy also applies to personnel actions. An *Izvestiia* article reports that ministry officials are careful to go on record with a listing of potential problems with appointees when personnel actions are considered. If the appointee later makes a mistake, they can point back to their reservations.[29]

A fourth form of insurance is the practice of insuring oneself with one's superiors. Of all the insurance forms, this practice limits the flexibility of the *khoziaistvennik* most severely. Accordingly, it is practiced least by the successful *khoziaistvennik*. Insuring oneself with one's superiors means going to superiors to get approval for various actions. If being a good *khoziaistvennik* means having to be flexible and break rules, it is unlikely that a *khoziaistvennik* can maneuver well if he has to obtain the advance approval of superiors.[30]

What the khoziaistvennik does when caught

The insurance schemes do not provide absolute protection, and even the able *khoziaistvennik* is sometimes caught. A common strategy appears to be used in this situation. The clever *khoziaistvennik* looks his accusers in the eye, admits guilt, and assures them that the matter is being taken care of and will not happen again. Both the interviews and the Soviet press are packed with examples of this "admit and ignore" strategy. The *khoziaistvennik* can more safely follow the strategy if he knows that the disposition of the case lies within his circle of protectors.[31] If he has built a good protective circle, chances are that the matter will be referred to someone belonging to the circle.

One respondent who worked in a republican ministry told about a

---

[29] "Kadry. Pis'ma iz ministerstva," *Izvestiia*, December 19, 1986.

[30] Paramanov in his memoirs speaks derisively of those indecisive *khoziaistvenniks* who run to their superiors to get approval for every small decision.

[31] The Soviet press is full of examples of what happens when a *khoziaistvennik* is caught committing a wrongdoing. A typical case is as follows: Chemical

revision (*revizii*) of a trust that was prompted by a complaint filed with the Moscow division of the ministry. When asked whether the revision was particularly worrisome, the respondent replied that the revision was actually being directed by two officials from the republic office of the ministry. The Moscow representative had been included because the complaint had gone to Moscow. The respondent noted that the local ministry officials were able to manage the revision without any serious consequences to the ministry's trust.

A good strategist accepts his punishment if necessary to get the matter behind him. The worst possible strategy appears to be to fight against the charge. The *khoziaistvennik* who stubbornly fights can end up losing his position. One respondent told of an enterprise director caught clearly making a false claim to plan fulfillment by banking officials. The normal procedure would have been for the director to admit guilt, appear before local party officials for his reprimand (*vygovor*), and then return to his work. For some unexplained reason, this director stubbornly refused to admit guilt and ended up being fired in disgrace.

Efficiency costs

The efficiency costs borne by the *khoziaistvennik* are similar to the efficiency costs imposed by inflation. Rather than making an effort to discover better resource combinations or better products, the *khoziaistvennik* must devote time to avoiding detection and devote real resources to insurance. An illustration of this is the amount of time designers have to devote to preventing their designs from being vetoed.[32] Designs have to be submitted to superiors or to committees, and the safe action is to veto because there are few risks to saying no. When this mentality pervades the entire bureaucracy, it imposes substantial efficiency costs on society. The real resources devoted to creating paper trails cannot be measured, but judging from Soviet complaints, they may be substantial as well.

---

trusts were caught faking plan fulfillment figures so as to pay bonuses. This matter was brought to the attention of the ministry by the State Arbitration Committee (Gosarbitrazh). In this case (with the silent approval of the ministry), the guilty trusts admitted guilt but simply failed to pay the fines. Apparently, firms are often not required to ante up the fine by the responsible government commission. For this case, see "Dogovornaia rabota," *Gosudarstvo i pravo*, January 1985, pp. 23–6.

[32] "Stankostroenie i gibkie sistemy," *Eko*, No. 3, 1985, pp. 50–7.

The *apparatchik*

The *apparatchik* occupies a responsible position in a functional unit of the Soviet economic bureaucracy but bears little responsibility for final results. Examples of *apparatchiks* are directors of functional departments of a ministry or state committee, heads of financial departments of the Ministry of Finance, or department heads in Gosplan or Gossnab. *Apparatchiks* do technical documentation, norm setting, or output or supply planning.

Difficulty of evaluating performance

The preceding chapter pointed out the difficulty of tying the work of *apparatchiks* to final results. Some *apparatchiks* report to a number of superiors. The technical documentation work performed by various departments of the State Committee for Construction Affairs (Gosstroi) is done for a number of ministries and state committees. Work spread over different superiors is difficult to evaluate in its entirety. Even if the *apparatchik* reports to only one superior, the effect of the *apparatchik's* work on economic outcomes is difficult to establish.[33] The *apparatchik's* superior will be hard-pressed to determine whether the *apparatchik* has produced "good" norms, plans, or rules because these activities are not directly tied to specific, measurable economic outcomes. One former Gosplan employee stated the problem as follows: "Planning is a joint effort of the ministries and of the responsible Gosplan branch department. In the planning process, different people make suggestions, compromises are made, and the plan draft is altered many times. It is virtually impossible to associate a single individual or group of individuals with a specific plan outcome. Hence if the plan goes wrong, it is difficult to know whom to blame."

The *apparatchik's* work, although difficult to evaluate, is nevertheless important for economic outcomes. The *apparatchik* sets the rules and issues the directives under which the *khoziaistvenniks* operate. The *apparatchik* imposes transactions and insurance costs on the *khoziaistvenniks* by issuing restrictive norms, rules, and plans. In effect,

[33] Soviet texts distinguish between *shtatnoe* functional departments, which report to only one person (such as the finance administration of a ministry, which reports only to the minister), and functional departments, which report to various superiors. An example of the latter is the State Committee for Construction Affairs (Gosstroi), which reports to Gosplan, the Construction Bank (Stroibank), and the construction ministries. On this point, see Vyshniakov, *Struktura i shtaty*, Chap. 3.

the *apparatchik* sets the "rules of the game" for *khoziaistvenniks*. The efficiency with which *khoziaistvenniks* operate hinges on the working environment created by the *apparatchik*.

What does the apparatchik want?

The goal of the *apparatchik* is like that of the *khoziaistvennik:* to look good in the eyes of his superior. The *khoziaistvennik* impresses superiors by delivering good production results. The *apparatchik*'s superiors must consider other performance criteria. One is the extent to which the *apparatchik* formally complies with the instructions handed down by the superior. The *apparatchik*'s task may be to prepare scientific input norms, write rules for determining the effectiveness of capital investments, or draw up a material balance of coal resources or an operational plan for the distribution of cement. The *apparatchik*'s instructions give a deadline for completion of the task and supply a general description of the work to be done. The superior sets page targets to make sure that the *apparatchik* does not do a superficial job – a practice called "paper output" (*bumazhny val*).

The *apparatchik* must complete his assignments on time and in a form superiors find satisfactory. With established deadlines, it is easy for superiors to determine whether the *apparatchik* has completed his task on a timely basis. It is more difficult to decide if his work is well done. Superiors find it difficult to judge whether the devised rules or norms (such as rules concerning compensation or capital investment) are good or bad.

Respondents who worked at norm setting or rule setting had a jaded view of their work. One respondent reported a multiyear effort to set new rules that resulted in only a minor modification of the existing rules. When the rules were reviewed internally, it was discovered that there were sections that no one could understand. This did not prevent the rules from being passed.[34] Other respondents reported working out complex engineering norms for various industries only to find that in actual practice rough rules of thumb were being used in place of engineering norms. A ministerial official reported that the jargon of rules was so dense that he was able to interpret rules to his own benefit without being challenged.

---

[34] The Soviet press contains many similar accounts of rules being passed that no one can understand. See "Ne bez ogrekhov," *Eko*, No. 3, 1985, pp. 209–12, and "Kvartira za bumazhnym bar'erom," *Sotsialisticheskaia industriia*, May 21, 1987.

The preceding chapter pointed out that, the closer the functional unit comes to production outcomes, the easier it is for its work to be tied to the performance of line units. If the *apparatchik* is involved in planning outputs or inputs for line units, the superior could conceivably evaluate the *apparatchik*'s planning in light of final outcomes. If the *apparatchik* is in charge of allocating building materials and there are complaints from a number of construction enterprises about the maldistribution of building materials, the *apparatchik*'s superiors may determine that this is not a job well done.

When *apparatchiks* do work that can be tied to a production result, such as the preparation of feasibility studies for construction projects, they begin to act as *khoziaistvenniks*. The *apparatchik* prepares multiple variations of the design (to demonstrate that all eventualities have been considered) or insures himself with his superiors by means of frequent consultations on even small matters. Officials who worked in Gossnab's distribution departments could also make mistakes for which they could be held personally responsible (such as sending machinery to the wrong address). They too exhibited some of the behavior patterns of *khoziaistvenniks*.

Respondents who worked for Gosplan and Gossnab reported that there could be "unpleasantness" in the case of major branch plan failures or material distribution failures (in which they would be blamed specifically by the ministries), but under normal circumstances it was not necessary to look beyond the ministry for a convenient scapegoat. The plan outcome had to be disastrous before one would look inside Gosplan and Gossnab.

Respondents from functional units were asked how *apparatchiks* were evaluated and rewarded by their superiors. The most common response was that rewards (if any) were based on adherence to formal deadlines. Those individuals who worked in planning offices related that the offices worked under intense pressure to meet formal deadlines concerning planning balances and material allocations. Most respondents could remember distinctly the various phases of planning and the dates by which phases of their work had to be completed.

Respondents from functional units either did not remember the bonus system under which they operated or shrugged it off as unimportant. Their income was not tied to the results of their work.[35] In

---

[35] David Dyker, *The Process of Investment in the Soviet Union* (Cambridge University Press, 1983), Chap. 3, concludes from his study of ministry design organizations that their results are not tied to final results and that bonuses are not important.

general, respondents reacted with amusement to questions about how superiors judged their work. Apparently, this was the first time they had ever been asked to consider this issue.

Respondents emphasized that *apparatchiks* occupied privileged positions in Soviet society and that their prime concern was to keep their positions. A common expression was that everyone "feared for their chairs" (*boitsia za svoi stul*). To keep their positions, *apparatchiks* had to be steady performers and willing to carry out any task that their superiors handed them, no matter how impossible or senseless. Respondents repeatedly emphasized that the *apparatchik* gets ahead by saying, "Yes, it will be done" (*budet sdelano*), to all tasks handed down by superiors.

Respondents also spoke scornfully about the need to appear "progressive." An *apparatchik* could appear progressive by supporting new ways of doing things, such as trying out new management systems or devising new sets of rules. A number of respondents reported cases of *apparatchiks* supporting harebrained schemes simply because this would look good on their records. If the scheme failed to bear fruit, its failure would scarcely be recognized.

The technocrat

The Soviet economic bureaucracy has immense documentation requirements. The bureaucracy operates on an engineering mentality, which translates into the need for technical-engineering documentation of input–output relationships. The engineering mentality translates as well into a complex system of technical and financial norms and rules for line units. Disputes over resource limits are resolved in terms of engineering and technological arguments.

The technocrat is an experienced individual with professional training in engineering, science, or finance. The technocrat has accumulated many years of on-the-job experience, working either for a *khoziaistvennik* or for an *apparatchik*. The technocrat's job is to advise the *khoziaistvennik* on technical matters of production or finance or to assist the *apparatchik* in creating rules, norms, plans, or monitoring schemes.

Respondents (most of whom belonged to this group) emphasized that technocrats play an important role in decision making within the Soviet economic bureaucracy, especially if they have a reputation for professional integrity. Because most economic decisions within the planning system revolve around technical issues (How much coal is really needed to produce a ton of steel?), the opinions of reputable technocrats are valued by the planning apparatus. Respondents time and again related that only technocrats could "defend" a plan effectively, that is, "prove" a point to higher authorities. Respondents noted the disdainful attitude of higher authorities toward *khoziaistvenniks* whose job was to "prove" a point even if it were not justified from a technological point of view. Respondents emphasized the value of a technocrat's professional reputation. A technocrat's opinions would be respected by higher authorities as long as he had a reputation for professional integrity. A reputation of engineering integrity admitted technocrats to scientific councils of ministries and state committees, and their opinions were sought by high government officials. Several respondents reported being pressured by their immediate superiors to show branch "loyalty" – to support the position of their superiors even though that position was not technologically correct. Despite these pressures, technocrats expressed a great reluctance to sacrifice their professional integrity.

Technocrats, in turn, tended to evaluate their superiors according to their technical understanding and expertise. A superior would immediately lose face and credibility if he displayed a lack of understanding of technological matters.[36]

Technocrats are exposed to different degrees of risk in the Soviet economic bureaucracy. If they work in line activities, leading technocrats (chief engineers, chief technologists, chief architects, etc.) appear to be subject to many of the same risks as *edinonachalniks*. Technocrats who worked in functional organizations are not held responsible for the results of their work. They nevertheless could have an impact on the success or failure of line organizations. The way in which financial technocrats interpret bonus and compensation rules could determine whether a line unit is able to retain its professional labor force. Designers could exercise author's oversight (*avtorski nadzor*) with projects. Supply officials in Gosplan and Gossnab have to make tough choices as to which line organization will get materials. Architects and designers employed by city executive committees approve new construction and, hence, confirm plan fulfillment by line organizations.

[36] In his memoirs, Paramanov tells the story of a high ministry mining official whose credibility was ruined when he exhibited a total lack of knowledge of mining during an inspection trip. Respondents were quick to judge their superiors according to their knowledge of technical matters. Superiors were praised as "highly experienced engineers" or "experienced construction men." Superiors who lacked technological skills were looked upon with disdain.

Respondents revealed an unexpected source of technocratic power. A number of technocrats with advanced degrees employed by higher-degree-granting institutes reported assisting their immediate superiors in obtaining doctoral degrees. The doctoral degree, for example, would be on a technical issue (such as installing a new engineering-control system), and the respondent would either write the superior's dissertation or provide substantial assistance. *Khoziaistvenniks* desired a doctoral degree because the state was obliged to find academic appointments for advanced-degree holders. If a *khoziaistvennik* failed, the doctoral degree would guarantee another job.

Summary

The *khoziaistvennik* is the true risk bearer in the Soviet economic bureaucracy, and the risks involved dictate a distinctive pattern of behavior that is not shared by other economic bureaucrats. The *khoziaistvennik* conducts his affairs within a narrow circle of participants, because the transaction costs (in the form of creating the necessary insurance) of dealing outside the circle are high. The *khoziaistvennik* must devote a considerable portion of his efforts to cultivating friends and maintaining good relations. The *khoziaistvennik* devotes real resources to creating a paper trail to prove innocence in case of plan failure.

The *apparatchik* sets the rules of the game by which the *khoziaistvennik* operates. There appear to be no strong incentives for the *apparatchik* to create institutions that would allow the *khoziaistvennik* to operate more efficiently The practice of using the *apparatchik* to create the rules of the game while holding the *khoziaistvennik* responsible for final results creates problems. On the one hand, the system's directors do not wish to have line units operate unconstrained by rules and norms. On the other hand, it is recognized that rules and norms, if improperly devised, can reduce economic efficiency. Yet there appears to be no way to make the *apparatchik* responsible for the effectiveness of the rules and norms he constructs, and respondents provided no support for the notion that the *apparatchik* has a strong incentive to devise efficient rules. It is difficult to tie the *apparatchik*'s work to final results, and the system's directors may have reasons for not wishing to do so even if they could devise a monitoring system.

The technocrat supplies the economy with technical and financial information upon which the decisions of *khoziaistvenniks* and *apparatchiks* are based. Technocrats are listened to as long as their professional integrity is intact.

The Soviet system combines "dictatorship of rules and norms" with local discretion, because the system's directors need honest agents who have little incentive to distort the truth. The importance that technocrats attach to preserving their professional integrity is additional evidence of the importance the system's directors place in the testimony of honest agents. At the same time, the system's directors understand that the line unit cannot be directed by rules and norms imposed externally by functional units that bear little or no responsibility.

CHAPTER 5

Allocation

Dealing with scarcity

Every society must deal with scarcity. The Soviet economy is no exception. Claims on society's resources exceed its ability to meet them. Capitalist societies use market allocation to determine who gets scarce resources and how they are used. This chapter examines how the Soviet economic bureaucracy administers the allocation of scarce resources among claimants. Four key groups of questions are raised concerning Soviet resource allocation. First, how are output targets and resource limits determined in the actual planning process. How is it that one ministry or enterprise has easier targets and more abundant resources than other ministries or enterprises? What systematic patterns underlie the bargaining process? Second, how are output targets and resource limits "corrected" during the process of plan fulfillment? How is it that one ministry or enterprise can convince its superiors to lower its output targets or increase its resource limits whereas another ministry or enterprise is stuck with its original targets? Third, what formal and informal techniques, levers, and procedures do ministries and enterprises use to ensure the successful fulfillment of their tasks once they have achieved their "best deal" from their superiors? Fourth, how are financial resources – particularly wage bills – allocated among claimants?

This chapter is not a comprehensive account of Soviet planning.[1] It focuses on the bargaining and decision making that take place during and after planning. The available literature on bargaining focuses on enterprise–ministry relations. It shows how enterprises bargain with

---

[1] See Paul Gregory and Robert Stuart, *Soviet Economic Structure and Performance* (New York: Harper & Row, 1986), Chaps. 7 and 8; Alec Nove, *The Soviet Economic System* (London: Allen & Unwin, 1977), Chap. 1–4; Abram Bergson, *The Economics of Soviet Planning* (New Haven, Conn.: Yale University Press, 1964), Chap. 7; Herbert Levine, "The Centralized Planning of Supply in Soviet Industry," in *Comparisons of the United States and Soviet Economies* (Washington, D.C.: U.S. Government Printing Office, 1959).

ministries for their plans, how plans are corrected, and the procedures enterprises use to ensure plan fulfillment.[2] This chapter focuses on bargaining and planning decisions above the enterprise level.

Formal planning is only the first step of Soviet resource allocation.[3] What goes on after a plan is drawn up is as important or more important than the plan itself. Chapter 3 showed that Gosplan necessarily constructs unrealistic plans. Its plans must embody the economic objectives of the political leadership. Gosplan is not judged for the realism of its plans, but for implementing the leadership's economic policies. Gosplan must impose the leadership's growth targets on the industrial ministries, and it uses unrealistic productivity norms and assumptions of timely completion of investment projects to justify aggregate-plan targets that are not feasible.

Plans are unrealistic because production units do not have the materials, labor, or capacity required to achieve the plans' production goals. That production plans will have to be corrected is known by all participants. Respondents referred to formal plans as "mirages," "self-deception," and "full of air." People know that allotted materials will not be forthcoming and that funds are insufficient to complete investment targets on time. They know they cannot meet their "progressive" labor-productivity targets.

Unrealistic plans mean that the final allocation of resources will be different from that planned. How does the Soviet system deal with these deviations? One option would be to stick with authorized output plans and not attempt to manage the shortfalls in plan fulfillment that occur. Following this option would make the Soviet economy as much a "planned" economy as possible, because the actions of production units would presumably be directed by the plan. Yet planners have limited control over ultimate economic outcomes, because they do not manage who fulfills plans and who falls short. A second option would be to consider the plan only as a starting point. When operating units begin to fall behind in their output plans and supply plans are broken, the bureaucracy could shuffle resources around in a systematic

---

[2] Joseph Berliner, *Factory and Manager in the USSR* (Cambridge, Mass.: Harvard University Press, 1957); David Granick, *Management of the Industrial Firm in the USSR* (New York: Columbia University Press, 1954).

[3] Eugene Zaleski, *Stalinist Planning for Economic Growth* (Chapel Hill: University of North Carolina Press, 1980); Peter Rutland, *The Myth of the Plan* (LaSalle, Ill.: Open Court, 1985); J. Wilhelm, "The Soviet Union Has an Administered, Not a Planned Economy," *Soviet Studies, 37*, No. 1 (1985), pp. 118–30.

manner, lowering some targets, raising others. Although the plan serves as the starting point in this scheme, the administered shuffling of resources and output targets makes the economy more a resource-managed economy than a planned economy, especially when deviations from the original plan are large.

The Soviet economy combines planning and resource management. The authorized plan affects the course of economic activity, but the final shape of resource allocation is determined after the plan is authorized. Scholars have pondered why the Soviet planning system is set up in this fashion. Eugene Zaleski concludes that the Soviet leadership wishes to use the plan as a "vision of the future" that sets difficult and perhaps unattainable goals toward which society should strive.[4] Holland Hunter has argued that "optimally taut" plans force a greater volume of output from the Soviet economy.[5] Raymond Powell has argued that "taut" plans create important information on relative scarcities.[6] A taut plan creates frictions as enterprises, and ministries find they cannot fulfill their output targets. As they compete for more resources and for lower plans, superior organizations accumulate valuable nonprice information on relative scarcities, which enables them to make more rational decisions.

There is ample evidence that Soviet planners consider authorized plans to be only the first step in the resource-allocation process. State plans remain subject to numerous amendments during the course of plan fulfillment despite sixty years of planning experience.[7] This chapter shows why the Soviet economic bureaucracy cannot compile plans that do not require frequent amendments through resource management. First, economies are subject to exogenous shocks such as earthquakes, droughts, and embargoes. Perfect planning requires the ability to anticipate such events, and it requires that no mistakes be made throughout the system. If a key factory fails to meet its output targets or if a construction unit fails to complete a new factory, the plan will be thrown off. Second, data limitations require that planning proceed at a high level of aggregation. Resource limits must be stated

---

4 Zaleski, *Stalinist Planning For Economic Growth*, Conclusions.
5 Holland Hunter, "Optimal Tautness in Developmental Planning," *Economic Development and Cultural Change*, 9, No. 4, part 1 (1961), pp. 561–72.
6 Raymond Powell, "Plan Execution and the Workability of Soviet Planning," *Journal of Comparative Economics*, 1, No. 1 (1977), pp. 69–73.
7 I. S. Darakhovsky, *Organizatsiia upravleniia promyshlennym proizvodstvom* (Kishenev: Stiinsta, 1984), p. 100, reports that production and realization are changed two or three times a year on average and that one-half of the enterprises do not fulfill supply plans.

in tons; outputs must be designated in thousands of units or millions of rubles. Production units, however, produce distinct products and use specific materials. The planning bureaucracy is unable to plan at the level of aggregation at which the actual production units work. The planning apparatus cannot balance administratively specific goods and resources. Third, a planning system that allocates resources on a branch basis necessarily encounters territorial imbalances.[8] On a territorial level, planners are faced not only with aggregation problems but also with a lack of procedures for achieving regional balances.[9]

The ultimate source of plan unrealism is the imposition of unrealistic goals on the planning bureaucracy by the political leadership. However, even if this problem were removed, external shocks, disaggregation problems, and regional imbalances would make it difficult to construct plans that did not require frequent amendments.

Negotiating the plan

Soviet resource allocation is a complex bargaining process in which the participants seek to strike the best deals possible. Production units (ministries and enterprises) must negotiate with their superiors for output plans and resource limits. The political leadership, as represented by the Council of Ministers, wishes to achieve its growth objectives; Gosplan and Gossnab must compile plans that meet the approval of the Council of Ministers and Central Committee; the ministries want achievable targets that (when fulfilled) make them look good; the enterprises want plans that they can fulfill without undue risk. The different layers of the bureaucracy have divergent objectives when they bargain for plans. To understand planning outcomes, one must understand the rules of bargaining.

Determinants of bargaining power

Alice Gorlin has explored the bargaining framework in which ministries negotiate with their principals.[10] She has shown that, in any

---

[8] Gerhard Fink, *Gossnab SSSR – Planung und Planungsprobleme der Produktionsmittelverteilung in der UdSSR* (Berlin: Duncker & Humblot, 1972), pp. 16–31.

[9] Jerry Hough, *The Soviet Prefects: The Local Party Organs in Industrial Decision Making* (Cambridge, Mass.: Harvard University Press, 1969), argues that the local parties have had to intervene in economic affairs largely to correct the regional problems created by the branch planning system.

[10] Alice C. Gorlin, "The Power of Soviet Industrial Ministries," *Soviet Studies*, 37, No. 3 (1985), pp. 353–70.

negotiating process, outcomes are dictated by the relative strengths of the participants (by the cards they have been dealt) and by their negotiating skills (ability to bluff, knowledge of the other players). Ministries are not without bargaining chips; their principals (Gosplan and Gossnab) must consider their ability to retaliate for unfavorable plans.

The ministries are not only claimants vis-à-vis Gosplan or Gossnab; they are also suppliers of resources to their principals. A ministry's outputs serve as inputs for other claimants as well as inputs for the ministry's own agents.[11] Gossnab's own supply plan can be jeopardized if a key ministry experiences production shortfalls or if that ministry redirects its resources to its own enterprises. A ministry that produces basic inputs for other ministries and produces most of its own inputs is therefore in a strong bargaining position. The same principles hold for enterprise negotiations with their principals (the ministries).

The autarkic tendencies of ministries categorized in Chapter 3 as opportunistic behavior can be interpreted as well as strategies to increase ministry bargaining strength. Gossnab is noted for being careful with powerful ministries that can cut deliveries to supply organizations.[12] The penalties that central organizations can impose on ministries for breaking supply plans are less severe than those for breaking output plans.[13] Former ministry and enterprise employees confirmed the difficulty of enforcing supply plans. Whenever they complained about nondelivery, they were told they would have to wait their turn. Even complaints from high patrons to offending supply organizations were often met with indifference. Soviet press accounts confirm the difficulty of enforcing delivery plans and the loose sanctions for nonfulfillment imposed on suppliers.[14] The Soviet legal literature complains about the toothless fines that offending suppliers have to pay – fines that are often not even collected.[15] Autarkic

---

[11] Andrew Freris, *The Soviet Industrial Enterprise: Theory and Practice* (New York: St. Martin's, 1984), Chap. 2, notes that the majority of ministry supplies come from the ministry's own supply channels. Gossnab supplies less than half of the materials and controls only 12 percent of production inventories.

[12] Fink, *Gossnab SSSR*, p. 50.

[13] Freris, *The Soviet Industrial Enterprise*, Chap. 1; "Aktual'nye voprosy ukrupleniia distipliny postavok. Vstrecha za kruglym stolum," *Planovoe khoziaistvo*, No. 2, 1984, pp. 39–46.

[14] "Priniato k . . . neispolneniiu," *Sotsialisticheskaia industriia*, May 6, 1987.

[15] "Osleplenie 'firmoi,' " *Sotsialisticheskaia industriia*, May 7, 1987; "Dogovor

ministries therefore have considerable bargaining power. Punishments for withholding materials from the supply network are not feared; ministries can work out reciprocal deals with central supply organizations.

Another strategy for maintaining bargaining power is to avoid producing goods that create "hold-up" problems for suppliers, which occur when a unique item is produced that can be used by only one customer.[16] Many respondents knew of cases in which suppliers refused to produce unique equipment on the grounds that this would tie them to one customer. The problem appears especially severe in the area of precision machine tools. Soviet sources also give ample evidence of suppliers' fears of hold-up problems, which they believe will reduce their bargaining power.[17]

Large organizations (be they enterprises, trusts, or ministries) appear to be more effective bargainers than small organizations. Large organizations receive more attention and help from the local party, from their supervising *glavk*, and from the ministry's central apparatus. Because of their visibility, principals tend to be judged on the basis of the performance of large units. Large enterprises are noted for being able to obtain supplies more readily than small enterprises.[18]

Bargaining procedures and strategy

Ministries and enterprises participate in two bargaining negotiations with their principals. First, they bargain for favorable output plans and resource limits. Second, they bargain for favorable changes in plans during the course of plan fulfillment.

Input and output planning is a cooperative effort between Gosplan, Gossnab, the industrial ministries, and the enterprises. Gosplan works out the general outline of the plan in broad aggregates, and it is the job of Gossnab and the ministries to work out the actual details.[19] Gosplan sends down "control figures" to the ministries and works out

na stole arbitra," *Sotsialisticheskaia industriia*, June 18, 1987. These articles speak of the dictatorship of the supplier (*diktat postavchika*) and how suppliers can break supply plans with immunity.

16 For an explanation of the hold-up problem, see Benjamin Klein, "Contract Costs and Administered Prices: An Economic Theory of Rigid Wages," *American Economic Review*, 74, No. 2 (1984), pp. 332–8.

17 Fink, *Gossnab SSSR*, p. 94; "Kontrakty s defektom," *Izvestiia*, April 9, 1987.

18 Fink, *Gossnab SSSR*, p. 35.

19 In the 1960s, Gosplan constructed 2,000 balances for 120 fundholders, of

general resource limits for them. Gosplan's industrial departments work out a limited number of material balances of funded commodities at relatively high levels of aggregation. Gossnab prepares the assortment and supply plan from Gosplan's directives. Gossnab's branch departments work out a larger number of material balances. One respondent who worked for Gossnab told of receiving plans in tons of machinery from Gosplan. Gossnab had to turn Gosplan's general *"tonnazh"* directives into an operational supply plan with actual specifications. In effect, Gossnab determines the operational plan because it works closer to an operational level of aggregation. Gossnab draws up the assortment/supply plan that is the operational plan on which later corrections are made.

Gossnab is supposed to create a supply plan that is consistent with Gosplan's output plan. Gosplan's output plan becomes law; Gossnab's supply plan does not.[20] Respondents refer to Gosplan's output plan that is confirmed by the Council of Ministers as the "state plan" (*gosudarstvenny plan*). The state plan occupies a higher position than other plans, such as ministerial plans or supply plans, and it is more difficult to amend than other plans.

Gosplan serves as the arbitrator of disputes, and ministries can refer Gossnab actions to Gosplan for arbitration. One respondent noted, however, that Gosplan relies heavily on Gossnab in planning matters because Gossnab is better informed about operational details. This respondent claimed that Gosplan rarely overrules Gossnab in matters of operational detail.

Soviet planning law clearly states that Gosplan and Gossnab are to compile economic plans in conjunction with the ministries. Respondents confirmed that output and input planning are indeed cooperative efforts among the ministries, Gosplan, and Gossnab, with a great deal of the operational planning taking place in the ministry planning departments. Ministries work out material balances and distribution plans for their own product categories.[21] The material balances drawn up by the ministries are automatically accepted by Gosplan if

which the Council of Ministers confirmed 327. Gossnab planned 12,000 products centrally, and the ministries 25,000. In the 1980s, Gosplan worked out 410 balances for the Council of Ministers. Fink, *Gossnab SSSR*, pp. 42–4; M. Chistiakov (nachalnik podotdel Gosplana SSSR), "Novye metodicheskie ukazaniia k razrabotke gosudarstvennykh planov," *Planovoe khoziaistvo*, No. 7, July 1980, pp. 73–83.

20 Freris, *The Soviet Industrial Enterprise*, Chap. 2.
21 Chistiakhov, "Novye metodicheskie ukazaniia," pp. 73–83.

they avoid obvious material imbalances.[22] Although planning is a cooperative venture, it takes place in an adversarial situation with the defense (*zashchita*) of the plan carried out in an atmosphere of intense debate. When asked whether a ministry could blame Gosplan for a plan that went wrong, one respondent noted that the plan was formulated and approved by both the ministry and Gosplan; therefore, the ministry could not very well blame Gosplan for poor planning.

The most important plans formulated by Gosplan, Gossnab, and the ministries are approved by the Council of Ministers. The rest are approved at lower levels, such as the council of ministers of the republics or even within the ministry. Planning goes through a number of stages; the industrial ministries participate less in the early stages, when basic directives are set and investment projects are approved.[23] During the first "control-figure" phase of planning in early spring, Gosplan sets the main physical targets of the annual plan and works out general resource limits. This work must be completed in the first quarter, and ministry planning departments are scarcely involved. The purpose of the control-figure phase is to implement the economic strategies of the political leadership. Presumably, industrial ministers in their capacities as members of the political elite negotiate for their ministries, but little is known of this process. Control figures are worked out with the branch departments of the Central Committee.[24] The outcome of the first stage of planning is a set of control figures in physical units (often expressed as growth rates over the previous year's output), which serve as the basis for plan decisions in subsequent phases of planning.

During the draft-plan phase (July), which respondents referred to as the project of the plan (*proekt plana*), ministry targets are set. During this phase, enterprises and ministries must itemize targets and material requirements following the control-figure directives. Material balances are drawn up by Gosplan's industrial departments, and these balances are coordinated by Gosplan's summary departments.

The draft-plan phase is a period of intense struggle between Gosplan and Gossnab, representing the interests of the political leadership, which wants to push through growth targets, and the minis-

---

22 Freris, *The Soviet Industrial Enterprise,* Chap. 2.
23 Fyodor Kushnirsky, *Soviet Economic Planning* (Boulder, Colo.: Westview, 1982), Chap. 3.
24 Sergei Friedzon, "Top-Level Administration of the Soviet Economy: A Partial View," *Rand Memorandum,* January 1986.

tries and enterprises, which wish to have feasible targets. Both the respondents and the literature refer to the "siege of Gosplan" and the "defense of the plan" that take place during October.[25] Ministries and factory representatives descend on Moscow, and the "ministry officials and enterprise directors live and eat together." One respondent stated, "They try to beat you down and you resist." Another commented, "The main objective of the defense of the plan is to prevent increases (*chto by ne bylo bol'she*) and to get more wage funds."

As noted in Chapter 3, the interest of a ministry during this stage of planning is to obtain feasible output targets that are sufficiently progressive to enable the minister to advance. The minister also fights for key investment projects. The minister fights against output targets that are too difficult given the resources allotted. Respondents recounted cases of their minister appealing unrealistic targets to the Council of Ministers and to the Central Committee during his defense of the plan. Respondents noted that the interests of the ministry and its enterprises are the same during the defense of the plan, although enterprises may be more interested in easy output plans than are ministries.

Much of the defense of the plan revolves around technical arguments. The ministry, assisted by key personnel from its larger enterprises, engages in lengthy technical arguments and brings technical documentation for its Gosplan and Gossnab counterparts. Respondents uniformly emphasized the vital importance of engineering and technological expertise in the course of bargaining. One must make a good technical case in order to win. According to one respondent, "If you don't defend your resource requests well, you can't get anything. Every request has to be technically substantiated." Ministry officials take their most reputable engineers and technologists for the plan's defense, knowing that Gosplan and Gossnab are more readily swayed by engineering arguments from experts than by "self-serving" arguments from ministry officials.

Similar battles are carried out within a ministry between ministry officials and factory directors and their staffs. The plan defense occurs before the chief of the planning department and the wage department, often with representatives of Gosplan and Gossnab present.

"Scientific norms" of central organizations are not decisive in arguments over input requests. Those who worked on norms for central

---

25 Kushnirsky, *Soviet Economic Planning*, Chap. 3, describes the siege of Gosplan.

organizations understood the great variability in production conditions.[26] Norms on coal production varied by factors of more than five among coal producers owing to differences in natural conditions. The natural variability of norms allowed ministries or enterprises to argue that their situation required a substantial deviation from Gosplan or Gossnab's scientific norms. There was little incentive for ministries or enterprises to be truthful about norms. Exaggerated norms were welcomed as an opportunity to accumulate excess inventories to protect from supply risk.[27]

A respondent from a transportation trust planning department described the draft-plan phase as follows: The trust received only one control figure from the ministry – the number of tons to be transported. To calculate the trust's draft plan, the planning department used only this control figure plus an estimate of capacity. From these two indicators, the planning department compiled thirteen indicators broken down into quarters. The most important indicators were the production plan and the wage fund plan. The completed draft plan was then sent to the ministry for aggregation. At this stage, the indicators were still not regarded as a plan, but as a "projection." In October, the draft plan started to become an actual plan as the defense of the plan proceeded. Each branch would aggregate and defend its plan in a department of Gosplan. During the negotiations, the participants worked with lists of products in physical terms (that covered about 40 percent of the wide product categories), and the title lists of ministry investments were discussed. Inside the ministry, the trust administration had to defend its plan before the head of the ministry planning department and the head of the department of labor and wages. On matters of wages, the trust administration had to deal not only with the ministry but also with Gosbank and the Finance Ministry. The minister defended the plan before Gosplan and Gossnab with a large group of experts from the ministry and its major enterprises. The experts were needed to work out all the variations and to demonstrate why not enough resources were being allocated.

Although the defense of the plan is a serious business, participants in the negotiations recognize that the decisions made at this point are only "first bids" in the resource-allocation process. However, the plans that Gosplan submits to the Council of Ministers – such as the main

---

26 T. P. Grinchell et al., *Sovershenstvovanie upravleniia obshchestvennym proizvodstvom* (Minsk: Izd. BGU, 1983), Chap. 10; Fink, *Gossnab SSSR*, p. 41; "Sleduiut li nedra?" *Eko*, No. 2, 1985, pp. 131–47.

27 Fink, *Gossnab SSSR*, p. 41.

output indicators of ministries and the title lists of major investment projects – are regarded as relatively firm targets, as discussed later. They represent the most important tasks that the ministries must strive to meet.

Respondents were uniformly skeptical about the firmness of input limits negotiated during the draft-plan phase. The battle over resources was described cynically. What counts is not the resource orders (*nariady*) that are promised but the resources you can realistically expect to receive. The two are quite different because cuts are made in the course of plan fulfillment. It was recognized that the resource allotments (*nariady*) authorized by the supply plan gave enterprises the right to begin negotiations to draw resources. The question was not how to get all resource allotments filled but what percentage of resource allotments customers would actually receive. One respondent who occupied a high position in a construction ministry reported that he expected no more than 60 percent of the authorized resource allotments to be filled.

Gosplan's supplicants pursue a number of strategies during the defense of a plan. The first is to try to obtain a plan that is as general as possible. With a general plan (such as output plans stated in rubles), a ministry has room to maneuver. A second strategy is to accept unrealistic plans in the hope that corrections will be made in the course of plan implementation. Respondents reported being pressured by a ministry to accept ambitious output targets so that the ministry could justify higher resource limits. They were told to hope for adjustment in output targets later. The third strategy is to fight against assignments for unique equipment or supplies. Unique equipment or supplies can get units into trouble because they tie the unit to one customer and reduce the "dictatorship of the supplier" (*diktat postavchika*).

Surprisingly, respondents and the literature report that unfavorable contracts can be refused and that considerable negotiation goes on to persuade suppliers to take on contracts specified in a plan.[28] Refusing contracts is apparently a tricky business, because the supplier firm runs the risk of being held accountable for a nonfulfilled plan. Respondents told of efforts by the contracting firm to force suppliers to take on contracts with appeals addressed to Gosplan, Gossnab, and party organizations.

---

[28] Soviet sources confirm that suppliers do have the right to refuse contracts they regard as unfavorable. See "Dogovor na stole arbitra," *Sotsialisticheskaia industriia,* June 18, 1987.

How firm are plans?

Although production units hope to gain favorable plan corrections during the course of plan implementation, this hope applies more to enterprise plans than to ministry plans. It is known that there will be a great deal of flexibility within a ministry. Ministry enterprises regard the ultimate distribution of plan tasks as a zero-sum game. When one firm negotiates a plan reduction, another firm must take on a higher target. When one firm gains an increase in its wage fund, another ministry firm must lose some of its wage funds. Respondents spoke of plan corrections within the ministry as a *trishkin kaftan*, meaning that, with a limited amount of material, the tailor must reduce the length of one arm to increase the length of the other.

A ministry's plan itself is seen as not easy to correct. Respondents differentiated between the "government plan" approved by the Council of Ministers and the ministry plan. Any plan target approved by the Council of Ministers would be difficult to change because it involved high-priority items whose fulfillment would be closely monitored or cross-ministerial projects beyond the control of the ministry. It is for this reason that ministers expend their main efforts to get a "good" plan. Respondents familiar with the process felt that the minister would call in all his political chips during the draft-plan stage to get reasonable production targets. Middle-level respondents would have little personal experience with high-level negotiations over ministerial plan changes that had to be submitted to the Council of Ministers. What is clear from their observations, however, is that ministry plans are difficult to change, whereas the ministry has considerable flexibility in reshuffling plans among its enterprises.

It is difficult to assess the firmness of ministry plans on the basis of interview evidence. The literature on this subject has shown that ministry plans are firmer than enterprise plans, which are corrected frequently during the course of plan implementation. A number of researchers have examined the issue by comparing initial ministry targets with output levels ultimately achieved by the ministry. Some conclude that ministry targets are indeed firm and that output plans, although subject to frequent renegotiation at the enterprise level, are meaningful at the ministry level.[29] Other researchers have concluded

29 Proponents of this viewpoint are David Granick, "The Ministry as the Maximizing Unit in Soviet Industry," *Journal of Comparative Economics*, 4, No. 3 (1980). pp. 255–73; and A. C. Gorlin and D. P. Doane, "Plan Fulfillment and Growth in Soviet Ministries," *Journal of Comparative Eco-*

that even ministry output targets are "up for grabs" in the struggle for resources.[30]

Although the absolute firmness of ministry plans cannot be established, the pattern is clear. The higher up the ladder one goes, the more difficult it is to get plan corrections. The ministry plans approved by the Council of Ministers are those that enter into the national material balances. A ministry plan must at all times be "specified" in the sense that the sum of enterprise outputs must equal the ministry output plan. To allow significant amendments in such plans would disrupt balances in other sectors. How the ministries meet their output plans appears to be a matter higher authorities are quite willing to leave to the ministries. If ministries wish to reshuffle targets or material limits among enterprises, this is not a matter of concern for higher authorities.[31]

The plans for which ministries are held responsible belong to the so-called narrow product categories. They are expressed in physical units or in constant prices. The coal ministry must produce a designated number of tons of different types of coal. The chemicals ministry must produce a designated quantity of sulfuric acid and the like. There are any number of "assortments" that yield a fulfilled ministry plan. Ministries are judged on the basis of the broad aggregate targets approved by the Council of Ministers. The assortment plan is the actual operational plan of the economy. As noted earlier, it is constructed by Gossnab and the ministries. The assortment plan specifies the actual products that ministry enterprises are to produce and to whom they are to be delivered. The assortment plan becomes the supply plan of the economy when the outputs are assigned to different ministries and enterprises.

Patterns of negotiation

Ministries and enterprises battle for resources and favorable output plans. There are winners and losers in this struggle. Interviews with

nomics, 4, No. 3 (1983), pp. 415–31. In her study of Soviet factory managers, Susan Linz also concluded that ministry targets are regarded as firm by ministry enterprises whereas enterprise plans are regarded as flexible. Susan Linz, "Managerial Autonomy in Soviet Firms," *Soviet Studies*, 40, No. 2 (1988), pp. 175–95.

30 Michael Keren, "The Ministry, Plan Changes, and the Ratchet Effect in Planning," *Journal of Comparative Economics*, 6, No. 4 (1982), pp. 327–42.

31 *Spravochnoe posobie poizvodstvennogo obedineniia predpriiatiia* (Moscow: Ekonomika, 1977), Vol. 2 clearly states the rights of ministries to redistribute resources and plan targets among enterprises.

former members of the bureaucracy and published accounts of these negotiations suggest that outcomes are not random; rather they follow systematic patterns.

First, resources are allocated according to the strength of the bargaining party, not according to the task the bargaining party is to carry out. For example, a large defense manufacturer would have more bargaining strength if it had to manufacture shoes than would a sewing machine manufacturer who had to manufacture defense subcomponents. A powerful construction ministry building a recreation center would have more bargaining power than a local construction ministry building a manufacturing plant. People know who the powerful ministries and enterprises are. Respondents noted with envy that certain ministries consistently had better access to resources than others.

Second, bargaining strength (as noted earlier) is determined by a unit's control of resources. Ministries that produce materials for broad use in other ministries have more bargaining power than ministries that produce primarily for their own needs. Large diverse republics, such as the Ukraine, have greater bargaining power because of the diversity of resources located in the region. Gossnab has to treat ministries that serve as major suppliers carefully, because it fears spoiling relations with them.[32] Major suppliers would be the last cut in the case of material deficits.

Third, a well-understood system of priorities affects bargaining outcomes. The most obvious priority is defense, but respondents could cite other cases – such as pet construction projects of powerful party leaders – that enjoyed privileged bargaining status. Moreover, the priority system is difficult to manipulate. One respondent who worked in road building attempted to raise the priority of one of his projects by arguing that the road was heavily used by the military. The response was that everyone tries to play this game and that this ploy would not get him more resources.

Fourth, large units have more bargaining power. Within a ministry, large enterprises have more bargaining power because the success of the *glavk* depends on the success of its largest enterprises. Large territorial enterprises receive more assistance from local party officials because of their visibility. Even though small units may account for the lion's share of a ministry's output, they are less visible and, hence, have less bargaining power.

Fifth, all respondents agree that personal relations are decisive in

[32] Fink, *Gossnab SSSR*, p. 50.

determining bargaining power. Some respondents worked for *khoziaistvenniks* whose personal influence was so great that they could persuade suppliers from other ministries to favor them over enterprises from their own ministry.[33] Personal relations are an important wild card in the game of bargaining for resources. They can be sufficiently strong to overcome many of the systematic patterns described here.

Plan fulfillment

Plan fulfillment is a battle over two things. The first is who will get plan corrections; the second concerns who will get resources.

Plan corrections

The term "plan corrections" has a variety of meanings, ranging from permission to shift output targets from one quarter to another, to modifications of input allotments, to changes in the physical output targets of ministries. Plan corrections are a consequence of unrealistic plans and disruptions of supply plans. Plan corrections occur frequently (for enterprises they average two to three times per year). They tend to be concentrated at the end of the planning period. Production units, for the most part, can claim plan fulfillment at the end of the year despite beginning the year with an unrealistic plan.[34] Hence, most corrections appear to be granted near the end of the year. Perhaps, this strategy is designed to force as much output from enterprises as possible before relief is granted in the form of plan corrections.

There are different expressions that describe how plan corrections are used to adjust the plan to actual results. Soviets speak of "fulfilling the plan with the plan" (*vypolnit' plan planom*) or "pushing the plan down to the plan" (*podgonka plan pod distignuty uroven' vypoleniia*).

[33] One respondent spoke of his former boss with great admiration, declaring that he had his "hands in the party and in other ministries." When something went wrong, he could get on the phone and persuade enterprises belonging to other ministries or located in other regions to send him supplies that were supposed to go to other enterprises with a stronger legal claim.

[34] Kushnirsky, *Soviet Economic Planning*, p. 103, shows that the number of firms not fulfilling their plans in the eleventh month is large, whereas the number of firms not fulfilling the annual plan is small. Hence, corrections, timed to take place in the last month, lower plans so that enterprises can report plan fulfillment.

These expressions do not make it clear whether plan targets are simply shifted among quarters or among enterprises or whether changes in annual plans that affect overall ministry outputs are made.

Most ministerial requests for plan corrections come in after the twenty-fifth of the month.[35] After the twenty-fifth, officials of the Central Statistical Administration (the agency that formally receives ministry requests) can scarcely step out of their offices because of the rush of requests for corrections. Some ministries request that targets be shifted to a later quarter, and such requests are granted more readily than corrections of annual targets. The shifting of obligations to later quarters simply shifts pressure for plan fulfillment to the end of the year. Enterprises file requests for plan corrections almost immediately upon receipt of plans. Some enterprises even get plan corrections in advance to be used at the appropriate time during the year.[36] A number of situations are accepted as grounds for plan corrections. Delays in deliveries of funded materials or late receipt of designs and specifications qualify as excuses for quarterly corrections. As already noted, production units are reluctant to use nondelivery of materials as an excuse for corrections because of the risk of spoiling relations with suppliers.

Although quarterly corrections are granted more readily than annual corrections, there are costs even to quarterly corrections. Many bonuses and incentive payments require the fulfillment of quarterly plans. Gosbank can refuse to authorize wage payments if quarterly plans are not met. Corrections of quarterly plans can therefore jeopardize payments to workers. Good *khoziaistvenniks*, respondents noted, are able to arrange production and corrections so as not to lose incentive payments for workers.

In fact, much of the illegal manipulation of fulfillment reports done by production units is designed to show successful completion of quarterly targets. Unfinished goods are reported to be finished, and customers are willing to pay in return for gentlemen's agreements that they will be the first to receive goods in the next quarter. Goods to be produced in the next quarter are shifted to the current quarter. These statistical manipulations are well known from studies of enterprise behavior. It is important to recognize that such practices whittle away at the margin. Respondents agreed that truly large deceptions are not possible under normal circumstances. Authorities tolerate small deceptions, but they are unwilling to accept large ones.

---

[35] "Prosim skorrektirovat' plan," *Izvestiia*, September 2, 1986.
[36] Ibid.

The timely reporting of deliveries and speedy transmittal of payments are important for plan fulfillment. Ministry officials cultivate good relations with telegraph operators to ensure that plan fulfillment will not be threatened by communications breakdowns.[37]

Supply problems

The assortment plan becomes the supply plan when delivery designations, means of transport, and delivery dates are added. The outputs of one firm are the material inputs of other firms. Interviews with former ministry officials and enterprise managers reveal quite vividly the scope of the supply problem. Soviet surveys show that enterprise managers rate supply problems as their most prominent headache.[38] Susan Linz, in her study of Soviet managers, concurs that supply problems are a dominant concern of Soviet managers.[39] High-level ministry officials spend two-thirds as much time on supply problems as on production.[40]

Material-technical supply is such a headache at the ministry and enterprise levels because allotted resource limits are not sufficient to fulfill original production goals, even if the supply plan is perfectly carried through. To compound the problem, the supply plan is systematically sacrificed for output plans. The Soviet system rewards the fulfillment of basic output goals, not the fulfillment of the supply (assortment) plan.[41] The supply plan, as noted earlier, is not even a legal obligation of ministries and enterprises.

Authorities find it difficult to judge the fulfillment of supply plans.[42] A supply plan (*plan postavok*) is multidimensional. It specifies the assortment of goods to be produced, the means of transport, dates of delivery, quality specifications, and so on. It cannot be reduced to simple, measurable indicators like the ministry's output plan.

The actual balancing of material supplies and demands takes place when the actual fund distributions are made.[43] Fund distributions

---

[37] "Prospekt Kalinina, 19. Pis'ma iz ministerstva," *Izvestiia*, December 16–20, 1986.

[38] A. G. Aganbegian, *Upravlenie sotsialisticheskimi predpriiatiami* (Moscow: Ekonomika, 1979), p. 286.

[39] Linz, "Managerial Autonomy in Soviet Firms."

[40] V. A. Lisichkin and E. I. Golynker, *Priniatie reshenii na osnove prognozirovaniia v usloviiakh ASU* (Moscow: Finansy i statistika, 1981), p. 45.

[41] Freris, *The Soviet Industrial Enterprise*, Chap. 1.

[42] See "Aktual'nye voprosy ukupleniia," pp. 39–46.

[43] Fink, *Gossnab SSSR*, p. 50.

take place at a finer level of aggregation than that used by Gosplan or Gossnab; therefore, equilibria must be achieved through bargaining, negotiation, and other ad hoc means.

Gossnab is not held responsible for final results. All Gossnab has to do is make sure that goods are shipped in such a manner as to conform to the broad aggregates with which Gossnab works.[44] Under conditions of "dictatorship of the supplier" (*diktat postavshchika*), customer firms are unlikely to complain about late deliveries and accept deliveries that violate the planned assortment. Customers who do complain find that fines are inadequate and that the complaint only serves to spoil relations with suppliers.[45]

In addition to all these supply problems, respondents and the Soviet press point out a flaw in Soviet supply planning that creates imbalances. The planning system calls for enterprises to request their material inputs six months to a year before they know their output plans.[46] Accordingly, production units end up with material allocations not suited to their production plans. Respondents and the Soviet press describe the supply plan as a confused jumble. Enterprises receive materials that they do not know are coming and do not know how to return. Ministries cannot return unwanted materials to Gossnab.[47] Although there are formal procedures for returning unwanted goods (and even allowing their free sale), these provisions are so complicated that they are rarely used.[48]

Authorized supply plans call for the release of resource ration coupons (*nariady*) that permit production units to make claims on ministry funds. For major deficit goods (respondents persistently talked about the shortages of high-quality pipe and reinforced concrete), authorized allotments exceed the amount produced by the supplier firms. Claimants, with legitimate ration coupons, have to clamor for their "fair share" of the overauthorized resource. To buttress their claims, customers visit factory sites with their own supply agents and trucks.[49] They write letters of complaint to Gosplan and Gossnab, and

[44] Iu. N. Prudkoi, "Sovershenstvovat' sistemu snabzheniia," *Eko*, No. 12, 1986, pp. 91–9.

[45] Ibid.

[46] "Vmesto fondirovaniie," *Eko*, No. 6, 1987, pp. 22–59; "Aktual'nye voprosy ukupleniia," pp. 39–46.

[47] "Try – mne, Ia – tebe," *Sotsialisticheskaia industriia*, October 29, 1986. Prudkoi, "Sovershenstvovat' sistemu snabzheniia," *Gossnab SSSR*, p. 53.

[48] Fink, *Gossnab SSSR*, p. 53.

[49] A. Pydrin and V. Kichin, "Vstrechny plan i zakazy potrebitelei," *Planovoe khoziaistvo*, No. 2, February 1984, pp. 53–60.

in extreme cases, they complain to arbitration commissions. They also apply pressure on the local party. One respondent told a typical story of having to visit the central committee offices of a central Asian republic to fight for allotted supplies from a local enterprise (after having exhausted official supply channels). In this case, the search was successful, because the respondent elicited a phone call from the offending enterprise. The phone call, however, did not secure the allotment, but a "fair share" of the authorization. Respondents reported that they did not expect to get their promised allotment. The uncertainty was over what percentage they would receive.

From state committees to ministries and to enterprises, people fear "spoiling relations" with important suppliers. Numerous respondents said that for this reason they feared using a lack of supplies as an excuse for plan shortfalls. By not complaining, they could work out deals that would give them access to materials in the future.

Redistributions

Ministries must use their supplies of scarce resources to enable their enterprises to meet ministry output targets. Ministries are in a position to control resource flows among ministry firms because they are the official holders (*fondoderzhatel'*) of funded resources. In fact, the majority of rationed supplies are controlled by ministry supply departments and not by Gossnab. The only legal way for ministry enterprises to obtain funded materials is through the ministries.

Ministries have two plans. One is the state plan approved by the Council of Ministers; the other is what respondents called the ministry's operational plan. The operational plan, which serves as the "real" ministry plan, calls for enterprises to produce output in excess of the government plan. A ministry knows that some enterprises will fall short of output goals, but if enough meet the operational plan, the government output plan can be met. As some enterprises fall short, the ministry shifts output targets among ministry enterprises. By shifting materials, wage funds, profits, and output targets among its enterprises, the ministry maneuvers to achieve its most important plan targets.

The ministry's main lever to ensure plan fulfillment is redistributions among enterprises. All respondents who worked for ministries or for enterprises encountered ministry-directed redistributions. Ministry redistributions took a variety of forms. In some cases, output targets were shifted among enterprises.[50] There were also redistribu-

---

[50] *Spravochnoe posobie*, Vol. 2, p. 213.

tions of wage funds, capital or amortization funds, and profits among enterprises.[51]

Respondents regarded redistributions as a zero-sum game in which the gains of winners equaled the losses of losers. When enterprises succeeded in obtaining downward plan corrections or increased funds, respondents felt that the deficit had to be made up elsewhere. Corrections went both ways. A number of respondents worked in enterprises that had their targets increased to make up for shortfalls elsewhere.

Respondents were able to shed some light on the mechanics of redistributions within a ministry. All requests had to begin with the *glavk*. If the *glavk* was unwilling to go along with the request for a plan change, it would go no further. Enterprise directors were expected to exhaust all other means before requesting increased funds or plan reductions. Managers were told by the *glavk* to see what the local party could do for them or to fill the plan "by any means." Increased distributions would be granted only as a last resort after other channels had been exhausted.

Respondents reported that the *glavk* evaluated redistribution requests on the basis of the manager's long-term record. *Glavk* officials knew who had been successful over the long run and how often the manager had requested redistributions in the past. A director who came in too often could not survive. One respondent said, "You can go once, maybe twice, and then your reputation is ruined." When the enterprise was in a true bind, it was best to go to the *glavk* director and tell him frankly about the problem. If personal relations were good, the *glavk* director would try to help. Linz, for example, found cases of managers who preferred to go to the local party for assistance before appealing to the ministry.[52] Presumably, managers preferred to expend political capital on the local party than on their supervising *glavk*s.

Former Soviet enterprise management personnel recognized that they depended on ministry redistributions. However, they had a perception (correct or incorrect) that what the ministry gave to one enterprise it had to take away from another. From the enterprise's perspective, the ministry had a relatively fixed branch output plan and a fixed "limit" of key industrial commodities. If other enterprises were to have major shortfalls, others would have to take up the slack. Operat-

---

[51] "Khozrashchet: na dele i na bumage," *Trud*, May 6, 1987; "Ekonomika i demokratiia," *Izvestiia*, July 3, 1987.

[52] Linz, "Managerial Autonomy in Soviet Firms."

ing in a zero-sum world appeared to moderate somewhat their individualistic tendencies. Presumably altruistic tendencies (worrying about the ministry's interests) would be muted, but there would be an incentive to help ministry enterprises that were in trouble, knowing that the ministry may have to take from a profitable enterprise to help the struggling enterprise. A number of respondents reported that they had been asked to show "branch patriotism" – to do things that were for the good of the branch if not for the good of their unit.

Ministerial officials had to worry about "not spoiling relations" when making redistributions. Enterprises that lost resources were likely to complain about favoritism or fraud if they felt unfairly treated.[53] One ministry official explained that he was very careful to forge a consensus concerning redistributions. He would promise enterprises that were losing resources some favor in return so as to limit complaints.

Substitutions

Ministries use material substitutions as another means of plan implementation.[54] Ministry supply departments have surpluses of certain materials, such as heavy steels or low-quality cement, that they can distribute freely. When enterprises fall short of deficit materials, ministries ask them to substitute the surplus material for the deficit material. In many cases, the proposed substitutions are "irrational" in the sense that they are inconsistent with enterprise technology or with quality standards.[55]

Ministry enterprises accumulate inventories of funded materials as a consequence of supply planning errors, excessively liberal input coefficients, or the like. There are few incentives to return these materials to Gossnab or to ministry supply departments. In the Soviet literature, one can find bitter complaints from enterprises about their inability to exchange funded materials with other enterprises.[56]

Although ministry enterprises cannot legally exchange funded materials (zamena), they are allowed to exchange them within a general product profile. They can exchange five-inch steel pipe for seven-inch steel pipe, for example. This practice is subject to complaints

[53] "Nam ne nuzhen takoi glavk."
[54] Grinchell et al., Sovershenstvovanie upravleniia obshchestvennym proizvodstvom, Chap. 10.
[55] Ibid.,
[56] See "Aktual'nye voprosy ukupleniia," pp. 39–46.

because the substituted material may not fit with the technology of the enterprise. It is not clear from the interviews how strict ministerial control over such official exchanges is, but the bitter complaints about limited formal exchange opportunities suggest that enterprises are severely constrained.[57]

Informal exchanges

The literature on Soviet management has demonstrated the importance of informal material exchanges among Soviet enterprises. Enterprises employ material expeditors (*tolkachs*) to find deficit materials and arrange trades. The interviews reveal that enterprises can also trade plan fulfillment indicators. For example, one trust official explained that his trust had no difficulty in overfulfilling its physical output targets but was constantly short of wage funds. Hence, the trust traded output fulfillment for additional wage funds.

Interviews with former employees of ministries reveal that an informal trade network exists among ministries and between ministries and local party organizations. Former ministry officials said that deputy ministers arranged trades of funded materials on a routine basis and that procedures for such exchanges were well established. It was understood whether a *glavk* director or a deputy minister had to sign for particular exchanges. Moreover, local party officials had access to local resources (such as construction materials) and were willing to trade them for funded materials controlled by the ministry. Funded materials were traded for the use of trucks or bulldozers.

Allocation of financial resources

The battle for resources is for more than materials and equipment. The Soviet economic bureaucracy exercises strict control over wage funds, and ministries and enterprises must struggle for their share of the economy's wage funds. The defense of the plan consists of the battle for materials and equipment and for wage funds. Requests for wage funds must be presented both to the ministry and to Gosbank and the Ministry of Finance.

Respondents, especially those who worked in construction, spoke about "money" (*den'gi*) as a scarce, funded resource. The plan they worried most about was how many million rubles they were allocated. Closer questioning revealed that by "money," they meant wage funds.

[57] Prudkoi, "Sovershenstvovat' sistemu snabzheniia," pp. 91–9.

Credit funds were of lesser significance, and the lack of bank credit was never a reason for being denied real resources.

Financial monitoring

The Soviet system of financial accounting is designed to monitor closely wage fund flows. Although Gosplan and Gossnab work indirectly with enterprises through the intermediation of ministries, Gosbank and the Ministry of Finance work directly with enterprises. Gosbank monitors the flow of wage payments and credit through the economy, and the Ministry of Finance monitors the payment of taxes and the use of credits in the economy.

Respondents who worked for Gosbank or in enterprise accounting departments described a strict set of controls for wage payments. The main reason for financial controls was to keep a sharp eye on the cash accounts of enterprises and to prevent them from advancing each other credit. Bank inspectors compiled daily balances of cash inflows and outflows and checked plan fulfillment to determine whether bonuses and incentive payments should be paid. Enterprises were allowed to settle only very small sums of cash without Gosbank clearing. Enterprises fear bank inspectors and describe elaborate inspection procedures. Each bank inspector works with five to ten enterprises and is well versed on their dealings.

Gosbank enforced a strict order of payments on enterprises. Wages and social insurance had a first claim on enterprise revenues. Payments into the state budget had a second claim on financial resources. After these obligations were met, enterprises could pay their other bills. Payments for materials were not automatic. Ministry officials complain about problems of collection.[58]

If enterprise plans are not met, Gosbank has the authority to withhold wage payments. Not paying workers means the potential loss of the enterprise's labor force; a number of respondents knew of cases in which managers were not able to pay their workers, which was regarded as the most severe sign of managerial failure. Good managers make sure that their workers are paid wages and bonuses. Typically, when Gosbank threatened to withhold wage payments, local party officials were brought in to mediate.

Gosbank inspectors monitor enterprise payments down to checking bills of lading and confirming the actual arrival of goods. A strict payment discipline for self-liquidating credit was in force to prevent

[58] "Pis'ma iz ministerstva."

enterprises from advancing each other spontaneous credit. Interenterprise credit was limited to self-liquidating transactions (credit was advanced until the good was received, and then the accounts were cleared). If enterprises were caught cheating on self-liquidating credit, they faced a loss of bonuses but not legal sanctions. The threat of being deprived of bonuses was taken seriously.

The ability of Gosbank to convert bank credits into currency was strictly limited. A number of Gosbank employees had encountered cases of graft and corruption and had colleagues who have been sent to jail. In this profession more than in any other there appears to be real opportunities for graft, and graft in banking apparently carries severe penalties.

Control of the money supply

The six to seven thousand branch banks of Gosbank know the cash needs of their enterprises on a daily basis. Every day, regional and republican Gosbanks tally the wage payments that must be made on the next day and compare them with the currency flowing into their banks from the retail trade network and from social insurance contributions and saving. In Moscow, a special Gosbank commission checks the proceeds of the trade network on a daily basis.

If regional cash inflows into banks equal cash outflows in the form of wage and bonus payments, regional Gosbanks can authorize wage payments without permission from higher bank authorities. However, if cash inflows fall short of wage payments, permission is required from higher authorities to release into circulation currency held in Gosbank vaults. As one former regional Gosbank official put it, "Bank reserves belong to Moscow." A department of monetary circulation in Moscow is technically responsible for releasing currency into circulation, but this is a decision on which high political officials must be consulted.

Former Gosbank employees described the constant struggle to maintain a regional balance of cash inflows and outflows. If purchases from the trade network decline, the regional Gosbank falls short of cash to meet regional wage payments, and special permission has to be sought from Moscow to issue currency. The issuance of new currency, according to respondent reports, is decided at high levels. In the case of a regional imbalance, the first secretary of the republic has to appeal to his superiors in Moscow to cover the deficit. Republican party officials dislike making such appeals and prefer instead to place pressure on the retail trade network to increase their sales.

The pressure to maintain regional balances of cash inflows and outflows appears to be the procedure used by Soviet authorities to restrict the growth of the money supply. If regional inflows and outflows are equal in all regions, there is no expansion of the money supply. By referring imbalances to Moscow, control over the money supply is exercised by high political officials in the Soviet Union.

Former officials of Gosbank reported frequent contacts with local party officials because of the political significance of money supply issues. They tell of local party agitation among local enterprises for increased outputs of consumer goods so as to increase the cash inflows into regional banks. One of the key economic functions of local party officials was to ensure that balances between cash inflows and wage payments were maintained.

Payments to the budget

The Ministry of Finance monitors the use of credit and ensures the orderly payments of taxes and fees into the state budget. Gosbank acts as the Finance Ministry's agent by booking these transactions through Gosbank accounts. At the local level, Ministry of Finance officials are interested primarily in collecting profit taxes, fixed payments, and capital charges from enterprises; so they have a vested interest in enterprises achieving their profit targets.

The financial activities of the Ministry of Finance are also related to problems of money supply regulation. If state revenues fall short of state expenditures, currency must be issued to cover the wage and bonus payments of enterprises that are funded out of the state budget.[59]

It is perhaps noteworthy that no respondent occupied a responsible position in the Ministry of Finance. This suggests that this ministry plays a more important role in Soviet resource allocation than has previously been assumed. Sergei Friedzon writes that only the minister of finance is allowed to present an independent opinion on Gosplan's draft plans, which must be coordinated with the state budget.[60] According to Friedzon, the minister of finance has the same status as the chairmen of other state committees, although he is not a deputy chairman of the Council of Ministers. The USSR minister of finance

[59] Directorate of Intelligence, *USSR: Sharply Higher Budget Deficits Threaten Perstroyka*, SOV 88-10043U, September 1988.
[60] Friedzon, "Top-Level Administration of the Soviet Economy," pp. 144, 152.

is responsible in the Council of Ministers for the development and execution of the USSR state budget.

Summary

Formulating the operational plan is only the first step in Soviet resource allocation. Plans must be changed because of disaggregation problems, shocks, and the weakness of territorial planning.

In bargaining for input and output plans, bargaining power depends on personal relations, control of supplies, and the size of the organization concerned. Priority belongs to the organization and does not depend on the activity the organization is carrying out. Production units avoid contracts that tie them to specific customers to avoid hold-up problems.

The operational plan is worked out by Gossnab and the ministries. Gossnab works closest to an operational level of disaggregation. Gosplan tends to accept the opinions of Gossnab because of its greater understanding of operational details.

The defense of the plan is based on technical and engineering arguments in which ministry and enterprise specialists play an important role. The plan is regarded as a first bid in the resource-allocation process. Ministries and enterprises seek plans that are as general as possible, and they can reject unfavorable supply contracts. Economic plans tend to be firm at the ministry level, but they are corrected frequently at the enterprise and trust level as ministries scramble to achieve their plans.

The supply plan is hampered by difficulties of determining plan fulfillment, fear of spoiling relations with suppliers, and the need to state supply requests before output plans are known. Ministries use redistributions and forced substitutions as levers for plan fulfillment. Both ministries and enterprises enter into informal supply arrangements to ensure plan fulfillment. Redistributions allow ministries to achieve a high level of autarky.

The monitoring of wage payments is stricter than the monitoring of other financial flows. Growth of the money supply is controlled by requiring regional balances of cash payments and cash inflows.

CHAPTER 6

Construction

Introduction

This chapter discusses construction as a distinctive element of the Soviet planning system. Construction, with its unique locational, technological, and supply characteristics, creates special problems for the Soviet economic bureaucracy. Construction takes place in an atmosphere of severe overbidding for and overallocation of investment resources. This chapter explains the sources of overbidding and overallocation and its consequences. It discusses the problem of negotiating contracts between buyers and sellers and the monitoring solutions used, and it explains why so much construction is undertaken by nonspecialized organizations.

Overbidding for investment

The principle of Soviet investment planning is that new plant and equipment should be selected to yield planned output increases. Theoretically, each enterprise has a claim to sufficient new capital to meet the planned growth of its outputs. Consequently, a ministry has a claim to that amount of new capital that enables it to meet the planned growth of its production targets.

Investment hunger

The investment hunger of Soviet enterprises and ministries is well documented in the literature. "Investment hunger" means that the Soviet economy generates a demand for investment that far exceeds the resources available at established opportunity costs. Curiously, this demand is translated into permission by responsible authorities to carry out projects that far exceed real investment resources. As a consequence, Soviet investment in plants and structures is characterized by extraordinary completion delays. Soviet studies conclude that the total lead time between design assignment to capacity operation is from two to two and a half times what would be normal in Western countries.[1]

These facts raise two questions. First, why do Soviet organizations tend to overbid for investment resources? Second, how do they succeed in getting authorization for investment projects that far exceed real resource limits? Scholars who have studied the first question offer a number of explanations.[2] One is that expansions of firm size and capacity enhance incomes and reputations, not only of the affected enterprise or ministry, but also of regional party officials. A large automotive assembly plant raises the prestige and incomes of both enterprise officials and local party officials. As noted in the preceding chapter, large production units have higher priority in the scramble for resources.

Many respondents worked in investment and construction and were able to offer an explanation for the overbidding for investment resources. They described vividly the bitter struggles over plant site selection waged by regional party authorities. They confirmed that enterprise salaries and prestige were linked to the capacity of the enterprise. Enterprise managers operating large-scale plants belonged to a higher *nomenklatura* and received higher salaries and bonuses. Local officials benefited from large construction projects in the form of higher prestige, and their regions were placed on more favorable consumer-goods rations when large, important enterprises were located in their territory. A surprising number of respondents reported that party officials would plead for investment as a means of offering employment opportunities to constituents ("Our people have to have work").

Respondents who witnessed the negotiation of plants sites for major industrial projects reported that the Council of Ministers and Gosplan appeared to base their decisions on technical considerations, not on the power of the party officials involved. Local party officials are more likely to influence the selection of smaller projects. As will be pointed out later, party officials in large republics have considerable capacity to build their own plants and, hence, can exercise this authority rather freely.

[1] This conclusion is based on studies by V. Krasovski and V. Maevsky, cited in David Dyker, *The Process of Investment in the Soviet Union* (Cambridge University Press, 1983), p. 36.

[2] This phenomenon has been studied by Western political scientists and economists. See, e.g., Jerry Hough, *The Soviet Prefects: the Local Party Organ in Industrial Decision Making* (Cambridge, Mass.: Harvard University Press, 1969), Chap. 12, and David Dyker, *The Future of the Soviet Economic Planning System* (Beckenham, Kent: Croom Helm, 1985), Chap. 5.

A second explanation of investment hunger is the constant pressure to raise the level of output every year – the so-called ratchet effect. Enterprise and ministry officials know that every year planning officials will demand more output. Without persistent capacity increases, production units cannot conceivably satisfy the planners' demand for output increases. When asked about the source of investment hunger, most respondents pointed to this phenomenon. Respondents also confirmed the ratchet effect on investment demand. The constant pressure for higher output targets appeared to them to be the main source of investment overbidding. One respondent who worked in the investment-goods area was so taken aback by the question as to why Soviet enterprises fought so hard to get investment (the answer to which he felt was obvious) that he declared indignantly, "You obviously don't know much about the Soviet economy."

Respondents also emphasized the low risks of overdemanding investment, pointing out that it was easy to shift the blame if the project was not completed on time because of the formal certifications required. The failure to complete new capacities on schedule could be used as a justification for downward plan correction. As pointed out later, new capacities must be certified by a state commission, and if the commission does not certify them, it is clear that the enterprise has not received the necessary capacity increase. This view of zero risk reported by respondents may be oversimplified in view of the risks of having a new installation certified before its being operational. This problem is discussed later in this chapter.

A third explanation for investment hunger is that participants in planned economies have an investment-goods fetish nourished by the doctrine that socialism can be built only by concentrating resources on capital goods.[3]

Overauthorization

It is easier to explain the sources of investment hunger than the persistent overcommitment by planning authorities to more investment projects than can conceivably be handled by available resources. After all, title lists for investment projects are approved by high organs of state authority, which are able to maintain a more reasonable balance of authorized plans and productive resources for current output. There are a number of explanations. The first is the wide dispersal of authority to begin investment projects, ranging from the

[3] On this, see Dyker, *Investment in the Soviet Union*, Chap. 1.

Council of Ministers' approval of construction of a new city to a factory manager's authorization of the building of a new clubhouse. Moreover, these authorizations are carried out under intense political pressure from ranking republican and local party officials, who are able to pull appropriate strings in Moscow. Respondents who worked on construction projects that fell under the supervision of high state and party officials in the Ukraine or in the Moscow region related that these projects could be carried out largely on the basis of local resources. In large, economically powerful regions, the risks of construction fiascos could be reduced by the supplies of construction materials and equipment that could be marshaled by regional authorities.[4] Respondents, moreover, spoke of the pressure to keep the cost of the project low enough that it could be authorized at relatively low levels. In other words, Soviet investment planning may be an area that high political authorities have trouble controlling owing to the political egos and discretionary local resources involved.

A second explanation for Soviet planning authorities' overauthorization of investment projects is that this may be a rational course of action under conditions of extreme supply uncertainty.[5] Both the Soviet and Western literature agree that supply problems plague construction more severely than other branches of the economy. Construction sites change, making it difficult to establish routine lines of supply. There is greater dependence on a generally unreliable transportation network. Construction managers must deal with a mobile and unruly labor force. One bank official respondent characterized the plight of construction enterprises as follows: "When they have money for wages, they have no supplies. When they have supplies they have no money for wages. They have to constantly come begging." In this setting of supply uncertainty (where ministry officials do not know where and when labor and supplies will be available), it may be rational for a ministry to try to initiate as many projects as possible so that available resources can be applied to the most conveniently located project. The construction ministry may be simply following a queuing strategy that is not irrational under conditions of extreme supply uncertainty.

A third explanation is that high planning authorities may feel that they can regulate the basic direction of capital resources despite the

---

[4] A respondent who worked on pet construction projects of high party officials from one of the major republics reported that it was not difficult to fit even a mammoth project desired by the party leadership into the annual investment plan even if it was not in the five-year plan.

[5] This point is made by Dyker, *Investment in the Soviet Union*, Chap. 1.

overcommitment of investment resources. They set the resource limits on major projects, and they have a priority system that makes sense out of chaos. Respondents revealed that party officials would single out important projects as *komsomol'skie stroiki*. Once a project received this designation, it was clear to all that the project had priority. Respondents also spoke of investment projects that had a "green street" (*zelenaia ulitsa*), meaning a go-ahead from the party. Thus, Soviet officialdom most likely feels that it can make sense out of all this confusion and ensure that the most important projects are completed. Confidence that political authorities can control overcommitted construction resources is also reflected in the amount of high-level monitoring that key projects receive from Gosplan or Council of Ministers officials, who personally monitor (*kuriruet*) major projects.

A fourth explanation is that construction is indeed an area that can draw heavily on local resources, such as gravel, tar, and lumber. If Soviet authorities tolerate overbidding, projects of lower priority must exercise initiative in locating local sources of supply. Liberal authorization of construction projects means that local initiative will be unleashed to search out local resources.[6] In effect, construction may be an area in which taut planning does flush out hidden reserves. If construction planning were less taut, there would be much less local initiative.

Investment planning

Conceptually, investment plans are based on the output increases called for in the five-year plan compiled by Gosplan with the assistance of the ministries. Each enterprise has a "plan for the increase in output" (*plan uvelicheniia vypuska*). On the basis of this plan, enterprises calculate what new capacities are required to meet their projected output increases. On the basis of such calculations, which are often checked by outside agencies, the enterprises make their initial claim to the ministries for capital resources.[7] The ministries use their

---

[6] Respondents reported that much construction took place without the blessing of official authorization. Factories succeeded in building seven-story apartment complexes by themselves using their own resources. An official authorization, however, would make the task of uncovering local reserves easier.

[7] The author interviewed two respondents whose job it was to check the capacity calculations of enterprises or ministries used for making claims to investment resources. One worked in an independent scientific research institute, the other in Gosplan. This suggests that capacity calculations are checked by a variety of agencies.

design bureaus to work with enterprises in preparing and reviewing enterprise projects, and compile from these their claim for investment resources. Ministry claims are not general claims for investment resources, but listings of the investment projects that they wish to have authorized.

In the case of investment, higher planning authorities act on specific investment projects (especially if they involve large expenditures). There are detailed rules concerning what agency approves investment projects according to projected cost. The various claims for investment resources must be translated into specific projects, and this work is done by an army of design institutes, constructor's bureaus, and projecting organizations attached to the ministries, to state committees (such as the State Committee for Construction Affairs, Gosstroi), and to large enterprises. Almost 1 million persons work in the approximately two thousand design institutes of the Soviet economic bureaucracy.[8] Most design work is done by design bureaus associated with the ministries. In fact, about 35 percent of ministry decision making is devoted to scientific design and capital construction work.[9]

Designs for the largest investment projects (which are compiled by design bureaus from different ministries and state committees) are presented to Gosplan and to the Council of Ministers for approval after review of technical documentation by Gosstroi. Designs for intermediate-size investment projects are presented to the republican Gosplans and republican councils of ministers. Designs for small, local projects may be approved by the ministries themselves or by local organs of government. Given the large number of agencies involved in industrial construction, the process of early review is complicated and obscure to the outsider observer.

Authorization to proceed on an investment project comes when it is placed on a "title list" (*titul'ny spisok*) by a responsible superior organization, such as Gosplan for large projects. Four pages of details are required to specify what agencies can approve what title lists in planning handbooks. These matters are quite complicated but boil down to the simple fact that the Council of Ministers approves the most important projects with the advice of Gosplan. Intermediate-size projects are confirmed by the ministries with the consent of Gosplan. The most important republican projects are approved by the republican

[8] See Dyker, *Investment in the Soviet Union*, p. 51.
[9] V. A. Lisichkin and E. I. Golynker, *Priniatie reshenii na osnove prognozirovaniia v usloviiakh ASU* (Moscow: Finansy i statistika, 1981), p. 45.

council of ministers. Small local projects built with their own resources can be approved by enterprise managers.[10] Title lists authorize the organizations staking a claim to investment resources to proceed with the project. The title list is a nonbinding document that gives the location, general characteristics, and projected costs of the project. The overall cost of the project (*smetnaia stoimost'*) is determined primarily by ministry design bureaus, which follow general pricing regulations.[11] Respondents (and the Soviet literature) reported that there was considerable manipulation of projected project costs in order for the authorization to take place at a lower level.

A respondent who worked in a design institute of a republican ministry told of the tug-of-war between "Moscow" (Gosplan) and republican authorities over the projected cost of projects to be built in the republic. Moscow wanted the project to cost more than 3 million rubles so that it had to be approved and monitored from the center. Republican officials wanted it to be less than 3 million to "keep it at home." Surprisingly, the respondent claimed that the institute was under pressure to keep the cost below 3 million rubles during the construction phase. This implies that, if the actual cost overran the 3 million rubles, Moscow could come in and assert control.[12]

The authorization of the title list grants the "ordering" (*zakazchik*) ministry the right to enter into contracts with construction ministries or construction authorities.[13] The *zakazchik* can either build the project itself using its own resources or contract with a construction ministry or construction authority. In the case of large projects, the project will be built by a construction ministry (or a consortium of ministries) operating on a contract from the *zakazchik* ministry.

Negotiating between *zakazchik* and contractor

The negotiation of construction contracts sheds considerable light on the problems of the construction industry. Take a typical case of a

---

[10] *Spravochnoe posobie direktoru proizvodstvennogo obedineniia predpriiatiia* (Moscow: Ekonomika, 1977), Vol. 1, pp. 359–64.

[11] The rules for pricing construction projects are set by Gosstroi. Apparently Gosstroi is wary of ministries not obeying pricing rules and fears conspiracies by the ministries to price projects to their mutual benefit. See "Dogovr, a ne sgovor," *Sotsialisticheskaia industriia*, July 4, 1987.

[12] Dyker, *Investment in the Soviet Union*, Chap. 3, points out that the *zakazchik* has every incentive to understate the costs of a project.

[13] In the Soviet Union, much construction is carried out by construction enterprises subordinated to republican, city, or provincial governments.

machine-building ministry (the *zakazchik*) that has been authorized by the Council of Ministers to negotiate the construction of a new factory. The new factory has entered the title lists, which authorize the *zakazchik* to negotiate with a construction ministry, which will serve as the contractor (*podriadchik*). The *zakazchik* uses its design bureaus and outside consultants to prepare the designs and specifications of the project before approaching the ministry *podriadchik*.[14] The documentation prepared in-house describes the *zakazchik*'s project specifications. The documentation gives technical details concerning the frame, the equipment, the dates by which different phases are to be completed, and the costs.

The *zakazchik* enters into negotiation with the *podriadchik* with its in-house documentation. If the project is a large one, the documentation will be checked at an early stage by Gosstroi and at a later stage by Gosplan. If a contract can be settled upon, the *podriadchik* becomes the agent of the *zakazchik* – its principal. The principal would like its agent to build the project as designed and on a timely basis.

The agent wants to accept only those projects that it can complete without getting into trouble. According to what criteria will the work of the agent-contractor be evaluated? Construction projects cannot be reduced to a simple physical output indicator, such as tons of steel or cement. Rather, construction projects must be translated into a value expression, which is done by taking the designs and estimating the total cost of the project (*smetnaia stoimost'*). The agent's first success indicator will therefore be to build a construction project according to the specifications presented by the *zakazchik* at a cost of x million rubles. The fact that construction ministries thought in terms of value targets is confirmed by respondents who worked in construction ministries. They all spoke of orders to build a 10-million-ruble plant or an apartment house for 1.5 million rubles. Unlike steel or truck manufacturers, who thought in terms of physical units, construction officials talked exclusively of plans in ruble values. A second success indicator will be the dates by which specified phases of the project must be completed. A third success criterion will be how closely the *podriadchik* meets the *zakazchik*'s intent (i.e., how closely the designs are observed).

The negotiation between the *zakazchik* and potential *podriadchik*

---

[14] Respondents from construction ministries emphasized that the ministry *zakazchik* would come to them with completed designs and plans as a basis for negotiation. The construction ministry would not be involved in this process.

takes place over the total cost (which becomes one of the contractor's main success criteria), completion dates, technical specifications, and resources that will be made available for the project. According to the testimony of respondents (confirmed by the Soviet press), the *podriadchik* is not obligated to accept the contract offered.[15] The *zakazchik* and *podriadchik* negotiate about the design, the completion dates, the customer's projected input requirements, and so on.

One respondent who was highly placed in a construction ministry described the intensity of the negotiations over construction projects. He reported that the construction ministry was not obligated to accept what it regarded as an unfavorable contract. The ministry's main concern was that sufficient labor and materials be made available for the successful completion of the project. It would refuse to accept contracts that provided an insufficient material base. In the negotiation phase, the *zakazchik* would support the construction ministry's claims for centrally allocated materials, but once the contract was accepted, the *zakazchik* often would not be able to help the contractor further. Some respondents did, however, report that the *zakazchik* could help the construction ministry by transferring materials from its own funds.

Negotiating with Gosplan

Once there is an agreement in principle that the *podriadchik* is prepared to accept the contract, the *podriadchik* (with the backing of the *zakazchik*) negotiates for materials and labor with Gosplan and Gossnab. Officials from the construction ministry descend on Moscow to bargain for inputs. They document that they require so many workers, bulldozers, cranes, and so on, to complete the project according to specifications and on time. They document the harmful consequences of not receiving the labor and materials they are bargaining for in the process of agreeing on the plan (*soglasovanie plana*). This documentation is kept as insurance for the ministry (the ministry must insure itself: *ministerstvo strakhuet sebiia*) to plead for plan changes

---

15 The ability of the contractor not to accept contracts appears to be confirmed by Soviet press accounts of arbitration proceedings. See, e.g., "Dogovor na stole arbitra," *Sotsialisticheskaia industriia*, June 18, 1987. The issue of how, why, and with what consequences a contractor can refuse to accept an unfavorable contract can apparently lead to legal disputes between contractors and customers, especially if the contract is called for in a plan. It appears that the contractor who refuses the contract may be regarded as not having fulfilled his plan.

and approval of delays when plan fulfillment is threatened. The end result of these negotiations is a supply plan (*plan postavok*) that gives the *podriadchik* the authority to draw funded materials from the central supply organs.

When these negotiations are concluded, the construction ministry receives a plan from Gosplan that consists of a gross value of construction (e.g., to build a factory for 10 million rubles), authorizations to draw funded materials from Gossnab, a credit plan, and a wage fund.

One respondent emphasized that his construction ministry never received a "real" plan from Gosplan. Rather the plan consisted of a list of projects with general documentation, a financial plan, and general resource limits. The respondent felt that the meager plan handed down by Gosplan was surprising in view of the vast amount of planning and documentation work that the ministry planning department had passed up to Gosplan. The financial resources required to carry out the construction project are deposited in an account that is managed by the Construction Bank (Stroibank), which monitors its disbursement. About 60 percent of these funds are supplied by the *zakazchik* ministry out of depreciation accounts and retained earnings, and most of the rest comes from budgetary grants with a small residual from bank credits.[16] The construction ministry uses these funds to pay labor and acquire materials. The wage funds are transferred from the *zakazchik* ministry's accounts into the wage fund account of the *podriadchik* ministry.[17]

Plan fulfillment

The overcommitment of investment resources expresses itself clearly in construction plan fulfillment and in the authorization of more new investment projects than can be covered with available real resources. Both the Soviet literature and respondent accounts confirm the se-

[16] Respondents who worked in construction planning confirmed that the customer ministry supplies the credit and wage fund resources for the construction plan and must create accounts at the beginning of the construction period. These funds come out of ministry depreciation accounts and retained earnings and from budgetary grants from the state budget. Only a small portion is financed by bank credits. See Dyker, *Investment in the Soviet Union*, p. 30.

[17] Respondents confirmed that the customer ministry in effect pays the wage bill of the contractor ministry. In turn, if the contractor ministry requires subcontractors, it pays the wages of workers supplied by subcontractors out of its wage funds.

vere difficulties encountered by construction managers in obtaining material, capital, and labor inputs – what Paramanov (a former construction official) describes as the "battle over bricks."[18]

Battles over materials, equipment, and labor

Respondents who worked in construction ministries and trusts reported constant battles over materials and equipment. Although the construction supply plans are based on "scientific" input norms, experienced construction officials are aware of the fact that the authorized materials will not be forthcoming. One such official insisted that his ministry received, as a general rule, only 60 percent of the planned materials. Its material planning was based on the premise that it would get no more than this percentage of allotted materials. Moreover, construction officials know that materials are allocated in reality not on the basis of scientific norms, but by crude rules of thumb.[19]

Equipment authorizations are also not fulfilled, and construction firms have to juggle their available park of trucks, bulldozers, and cranes among construction projects. Often heavy equipment is handled by subcontractors, whose services are also overcommitted.

One experienced construction ministry official told of the problem of meshing the setting up of heavy equipment with the delivery of materials. He described one subcontractor of heavy equipment who refused to put his trench-digging equipment in place until all the pipe that he was supposed to lay was in place at the site. It was only through pressure from the local party that the contractor could be convinced to install the equipment before the pipe had arrived. The respondent noted that the story did not end well. The pipe did not arrive despite assurances, and the valuable heavy equipment stood idle.

Construction enterprises have to scramble for workers. Because construction projects are dispersed and labor must be moved from one site to another (often in difficult climates), construction work is one of the least attractive for Soviet workers. Official wage scales do not permit construction firms to attract sufficient labor, and hence official pay scales must be ignored by construction managers. Respon-

---

18 I. V. Paramanov, *Uchitsia upravliat'* (Moscow: Ekonomika, 1970), p. 139.
19 One respondent familiar with input planning in construction reported that supply organs used crude rules of thumb by "millions" of rubles. For each "million," one needed so much of this material, so many workers, etc. Despite the considerable work of devising scientific norms, the use of rules of thumb appeared to be more prevalent than calculated norms.

dents repeatedly emphasized that, no matter how poorly the work was going, the workers had to be paid their bonuses. Otherwise they would disappear to work at a rival construction site.[20]

Setting priorities

The main task of construction organizations is to obtain overcommitted resources that other construction organizations want. When respondents in construction ministries spoke of "the plan," they consistently referred to the input plan. In this type of setting, higher Soviet authorities must have some means of ensuring that priority activities win out in the battle for resources. This is particularly important in construction, for which key inputs, such as construction materials and labor, can often be obtained locally. Because the production of building materials like gravel and tar cannot be concentrated in a few centrally controlled locations (for technological and transportation reasons), it is difficult for central authorities to regulate the flow of construction resources. A number of priority-enforcing mechanisms can be detected from the Soviet literature and the interviews.

Komsomol'skaia stroika *and military projects.* Respondents reported that high party officials and the Council of Ministers could designate particular projects as a "*komsomol* building site" (*komsomol'skaia stroika*). Projects carrying this designation were given priority over other projects by party officials, who were often responsible for supplying labor and allocating local construction materials to sites. Within the ministry, priority designations were also applied, which set priorities among ministry projects.[21] Military construction was also accorded a high priority. Respondents who worked in supply organizations reported that material-allocation forms destined for the military bore special red markings that were clearly visible. Moreover, the military had its distinct channels of supply, which it could direct to militarily important construction sites.

---

[20] See Dyker, *Investment in the Soviet Union,* Chap. 4, for a discussion of the manpower problems of construction. Many respondents declared that they worked in construction because this was an industry in which Soviet Jews could rise to high positions in view of the general distaste for managerial work in construction.

[21] These projects were designated as a *puskovoi obekt* (starting project). Respondents reported bitter battles among construction ministry branches over which projects would get this priority designation.

High-level monitoring. The monitoring of key investment projects by the Council of Ministers, Gosplan, and high party officials was another means of imposing priorities on an unpredictable supply system. Respondents who worked on large-scale construction projects of national importance emphasized the amount of high-level monitoring by the Council of Ministers, Gosplan, and the *zakazchik* ministries that went into such projects. Interministerial commissions were formed under the supervision of the Council of Ministers and Gosplan in which both the participating construction ministries and the *zakazchik* ministries participated.[22] In such high-level projects, a number of state committees were asked to play a role. The State Committee on Labor and Wages helped plan for the manpower needs of the project. The State Committee for Construction Affairs coordinated the site planning and feasibility studies. The Ministry of Finance participated in the financing of the project. Gossnab participated in the implementation of the supply plan. The party assisted by marshaling local labor resources.

Local party intervention. Yet another means of imposing priorities on construction in a world of highly uncertain supply is the active intervention of local party officials. Western political scientists have emphasized the role of the party in construction, invoking the chaotic state of supply as the reason for this intervention.[23] Respondents who worked in construction in large cities were impressed by the amount of material support that could be arranged by local party bosses (who often exercised personal supervision of pet projects).

Intervention by local party officials has both benefits and costs. On the one hand, local party officials, who understand the national priority system, are able to impose some discipline on the uncertain supply system. On the other, local party officials have the authority to

---

22 One respondent reported that the amount of authority vested in the various *zakazchik* ministries depended on their contribution of resources to the project. The ministry that committed the most resources would have its deputy ministry chair the interministerial commission, which would meet on a regular basis under the supervision of Gosplan.

23 Hough, *The Soviet Prefects*, Chap. 10, argues that the local party plays a large role in construction because of the limited attention of planning officials to territorial planning. Investment funds tend to be allocated on branch principles, yet investments are carried out in a regional setting requiring regional coordination. The party is also active in construction affairs, because much civic construction is carried out on a "voluntary" basis with voluntary activities controlled by the local party.

override national objectives by diverting local resources to favored local projects. The Soviet literature provides examples of local party officials trying to divert resources from ministerial projects to their own uses.[24]

Supply problems as an excuse

Although it is difficult to generalize from such a small number of respondents, one gains the impression that failing to secure supplies through official channels is not readily accepted as an excuse for nonfulfillment in construction. This is curious in view of the chaotic supply situation in construction. A number of respondents indicated that one could point to late arrival of designs or weather problems but that it was the manager's job to arrange for supplies.

There are possible explanations. One is that allowing supply disruptions to serve as an excuse for nonfulfillment would open up a Pandora's box in construction, in which virtually all enterprises would suffer from severe supply problems. Construction is dependent on local supplies, connections, and ingenuity. If supply problems were accepted as a legitimate excuse for plan failure, this ingenuity might be applied less frequently. The typical response of a superior to the subordinate's complaint about supply problems is, "It is your job to solve these problems. Do not come to me."

Principal–agent problems

A *zakazchik* ministry's objective in entering a contract for a construction project with the *podriadchik* ministry is to receive a completed investment project by the specified delivery dates that implements its technical specifications. Completed construction allows the recipient to cope with the pressures of the ratchet. Construction agreements, the world over, are prone to severe principal–agent problems. Each construction project is unique. Each with detailed documentation, it is impossible to specify completely every action of the contractor. Exogenous events (such as bad weather) can influence the performance of the contract, and the contractor must make a number of independent decisions in the course of fulfilling the contract.

---

[24] Paramanov, *Uchitsiia upravliat*, pp. 131–47, gives a number of examples of conflicts with local party officials over investment resources in which the local party officials interfered with ministerial investment plans for the purpose of supporting local projects.

The relationship between *zakazchik* and contractor, in the Soviet case, is made even more complicated by the overcommitment of investment resources, the uncertain supply situation, and the peculiar reward system for construction organizations. Construction organizations complete their plans by building a project having the total cost called for in the plan. If the total cost of the project is 10 million rubles, this target is fulfilled by expending labor, material, and capital costs equal to this sum and completing the project on a timely basis.

The Soviet construction planning system gives construction organizations considerable flexibility in fulfilling their contractual obligations. This flexibility allows them to act in a manner inconsistent with the customer's goals. First, the "gross value of construction" target gives construction enterprises the incentive to substitute more expensive materials and more expensive labor, even when this is not required by the project's technical design.[25] Second, the uncertain supply system offers the construction enterprise the opportunity to make material substitutions that work contrary to the interests of the customer. Supply organs offer more readily available materials, such as heavy-metal castings or low-grade cement, for deficit materials. This process of offering substitute materials, *zamena*, allows construction enterprises to observe completion deadlines more closely, but it leads to the construction of projects that do not meet the requirements of the customer.[26]

One partial solution to principal–agent problems is the close monitoring of the agent by the principal. In the Soviet case, the *zakazchik* ministry appears to have an unusual monitoring opportunity. Ministry designers have the right of "author's review" (*avtorski nadzor*) over the construction process, which means that they, the ministry's own designers, legally ensure that their technical designs are being properly implemented.[27] Judging from the experiences of

---

[25] Dyker, *Investment in the Soviet Union*, Chaps. 2 and 3, focuses on the features of Soviet construction that lead to the use of expensive materials and expensive labor.

[26] T. P. Grinchel et al., *Sovershenstvovanie upravleniia obshchestvennym proizvodstvom* (Minsk: Izdatel'stvo BGU, 1983), pp. 163–5, point out that supply organs often ask their users to request "irrational substitutions." The use of irrational substitutions in construction has been emphasized in Helen Otto, "The Soviet Construction Industry," Ph.D. dissertation (University of Houston, 1985).

[27] A number of respondents were responsible for authors' control of construction and investment projects. They could therefore give firsthand accounts of their dealings with the organizations implementing their designs. No respondent spoke of antagonistic relations between the designer

large construction projects, the *zakazchik* ministry is entitled to head an interministerial coordination commission in which Gosplan or the Council of Ministers exercises a supervisory role. Moreover, the *zakazchik* ministry is assisted by other monitoring agents whose job it is to ensure the proper completion of construction projects. The other monitoring agents are Gosstroi (which concerns itself with technical documentation), Gosplan (which is charged with the general monitoring and reporting of plan fulfillment), Stroibank (which releases funds in accordance with instructions in the title list), and the "state accepting commission" (*gosudarstennaia priemnaia komissiia*), which must certify the completion of the construction project by signing an "act of acceptance" (*akt priem*).

The multitude of checks on construction gives the impression that construction ministries are under strong pressure to meet their agreed-upon contractual obligations. The massive documentation of completion delays and shoddy work suggests, however, that this monitoring system is not doing its job. The main reason for the failure of the system is that, with the massive overcommitment of investment resources, customers must take what they can get. The *zakazchik* ministry is anxious to get at least a portion of its new factory into operation. Part of a new factory is better than nothing. Moreover, the *zakazchik* ministry recognizes that it has nothing to gain by alienating a construction ministry to which it must turn for new construction in the future. Not "spoiling relations" with construction ministries is important because they have no dearth of potential customers. If good relations are maintained, a construction ministry may be favorably disposed to correct existing defects sometime in the future. If relations are spoiled, there is little chance that defects will be taken care of.

Respondents reported on the indifferent review exercised by most of the official construction-monitoring agencies. It may be, however, that the Construction Bank exercises a stronger supervisory role than other monitoring agencies.[28] The potentially strongest monitoring agency, the state accepting commission (which must certify the successful completion of construction projects), appears to be willing to

and the organization actually implementing the design. In fact, the designer would provide an extensive list of addresses and telephone numbers of whom to contact in case specific questions arose.

[28] Evidence for this proposition is put forward by Dyker, *Investment in the Soviet Union*, Chap. 1. Also see S. Lazareva, "Formirovanie i ispol'zovanie fonda sotsial'no-kul'turnykh meropriiatii i zhilishchnogo stroitel'stva," *Planovoe khoziaistvo*, No. 2, February 1984, pp. 31–8.

accept construction projects that are not ready for operation. A number of respondents spoke of accepting commission certification of factories without roofs, in which no equipment had been installed, and so on. Virtually every respondent who worked in construction had some such tale to relate.

The typical action of the accepting commission is to certify the construction project as being completed but with defects (called *nedodelki*). The construction organization agrees to the accepting commission's action and promises to remove the defects within a certain period of time. Respondents testified that no planned resources are made available from official supplies to take care of *nedodelki* and that it is very difficult to get workers and supplies together to deal with remaining defects. Accordingly, the defects tend to remain, despite their promised removal. Respondents reported that being placed in charge of removing defects is regarded as a form of punishment. They had no authorized supplies or special wage funds, and they received little or no credit for removing defects.

Why do accepting commissions fail to exercise stronger control? One possible answer is that accepting commissions, which are nominally answerable to Gosstroi, are dominated by local state and party officials, who want to show a successful record of completion of capital projects.[29] It is unlikely, however, that the accepting commission could flagrantly abuse the accepting process without the tacit consent of the *zakazchik* ministry. Soviet press reports indicate the amount of trouble that can be caused by the complaints of irate customers.[30]

Apparently, there is an implicit agreement between customers and construction ministries that customers will not complain about poor work and defects. A customer enters what respondents call a "gentlemen's agreement" that he will not complain in return for the construction ministry's promise to do its best to remove remaining defects. If the customer complains, the construction ministry will not willingly remove the defects and may not be inclined to enter into further contracts with the customer.

---

[29] Respondents reported that deals were made between the construction ministry and local party officials who controlled the accepting commission. One such deal involved the use of ministry equipment for the accepting commission's signature.

[30] In the article "Gladko tol'ko na bumage," *Kransnaia zvezda,* May 10, 1987, officers in charge of military construction projects were criticized for their failure to take care of construction defects as they had promised. Even though their superiors were trying to shield them, the article mentions the possibility of criminal punishment.

Self-supply in construction

One of the unusual features of construction in the Soviet Union is that a wide range of production organizations engage in some form of construction or another. This fact is reflected in the stories of respondents who worked in automobile repair works, light industry, and design institutes and who reported working on construction activities for their enterprises.

According to the rules of Soviet investment, small investment projects can indeed be carried out "in-house" (*khozposobom*) by the organization itself. The sources of investment funds are the various incentive funds set aside for decentralized productive investment or for investment to improve the welfare of workers.

A number of respondents who found themselves unwittingly working on construction projects of their own enterprise commented on the foolishness of carrying out one-time construction projects for which they had no special skills, when professional construction organizations were located around the corner. Respondents even reported that they did their own design work rather than use a centralized design agency (which they said was slow moving because of its monopoly position).

Building construction projects *khozposobom* has severe disadvantages. The organization is not specialized in construction and makes a number of beginner's mistakes. The organization does not have access to funded construction materials, but must make do with local materials.[31] Moreover, the organization must register the construction project with central authorities (respondents reported that the project became part of their plan), and they would often be judged on their construction work using the same standards applied to professional construction organizations.[32] The fact that so much construction is carried out by organizations nonspecialized in construction underscores the unsatisfactory solution of the principal–agent problem that exists between customers and specialized construction organizations in the Soviet Union.

Summary

Soviet construction is characterized by investment hunger and an acute tendency to overcommit investment resources. Investment hun-

---

[31] Respondents noted that, although local party officials could help with nonfunded materials and labor, they had little influence over funded materials allocated by the ministries. The party official could only petition the ministry.

[32] For such a case, see "Kvartira za bumazhnym bar'erom," *Sotsialisticheskaia industriia*, May 21, 1987.

ger is a product of the ratchet effect. The only way to keep up with the ratcheting up of output targets is to install new capacity. Although planners can keep a rough balance of materials in the industrial sector, they are unable to do so in construction. The overcommitment of construction funds is explained by the ability of local and regional units to authorize investment funds at relatively low levels, the extensive use of local resources, and by the fact that this may be a rational strategy in a system of uncertain supply. Moreover, Soviet officialdom probably believes that it is in a position to ration construction resources according to established priorities by high-level monitoring and the ability to set priority designations for projects.

Soviet construction projects are negotiated between the *zakazchik* ministry and the *podriadchik* ministry. Typically the *zakazchik* ministry draws up plans and designs, which are presented to the *podriadchik* ministry. The contractor ministry has the right to refuse to take on a project. The actual construction plan consists of the title list, total cost, and material limits. Respondents who worked in construction viewed the construction plan more in terms of the supply limits and total cost of the project than in terms of the technical design.

In any economy, construction creates a substantial principal–agent problem because of the problem of specifying the end product. Although the Soviet system sets up an extensive monitoring system in construction, the system appears to be ineffective. Its ineffectiveness is explained by the desire not to spoil relations and the implicit deals struck between the customer and contractor concerning the elimination of defects. The extent to which there is self-supply in construction attests to the strength of the principal–agent problem in construction.

CHAPTER 7

The party

The economic functions of the party

The Communist Party is heavily involved in Soviet economic affairs. Although little is known about how the Central Committee and its apparatus works, the committee is known to set general priorities, which are implemented through its executive arms, the Council of Ministers and Gosplan USSR.[1] The Central Committee is organized into branch departments that supervise industrial ministries but are not held responsible for the ministries' results. The committee plays a key role in high-level staffing decisions through its cadres department. Western literature and Soviet autobiographical sources reveal that Central Committee involvement has gone beyond policy setting and appointments to include direct intervention in operational economic decisions. The micromanagement by high party officials has been chronicled since the trouble shooting by war communism commissars. Stalin and Molotov were known for their micromanagement of the economy, and the agendas of the Central Committee focused on operational matters during the early 1980s.[2] Respondents reported numerous cases of micromanagement by high-ranking party officials of the Central Committee and republican central committees. The preoccupation of the Central Committee with economic affairs is evidenced by the fact that more than half of all its decrees deal with economic matters.[3]

---

[1] Fyodor Kurshnirsky, *Soviet Economic Planning, 1965–1980* (Boulder, Colo: Westview Press, 1982), has written most authoritatively about central committee–Gosplan interactions. The most comprehensive account, based largely on personal recollections is that of Sergei Friedzon, "Top-Level Administration of the Soviet Economy: A Partial View," *Rand Memorandum,* January 1986.

[2] See Tatjana Kirstein, *Die Rolle der KPdSU in der Wirtschaftsplanung, 1933–1953/54* (Wiesbaden: Harrassowitz, 1985), and A. I. Iakovlev, *Tsel' Zhizni (Zapiski aviokonstruktora)* (Moscow: Izdatel'stvo politicheskoi literatury, 1972).

[3] See Rutland, *The Politics of Industrial Stagnation in the USSR* (Cambridge

The Central Committee stands at the apex of the Soviet party structure. The local party apparatus occupies the middle level of the party organization. The term "local" (*mestny*) party apparatus is misleading because the "local" level encompasses party organizations ranging from the central committees of powerful regions and the city committees of Moscow or Leningrad at the top to small regional organizations (regional committees, or *raikomy*) at the bottom. First secretaries of local party organizations (such as the first secretaries of the Leningrad or Moscow party committees) are usually members of the Central Committee and are members of the Soviet Union's top political leadership.

Soviet references do not mince words on the economic responsibilities of local party officials. Soviet law clearly states that party organizations are responsible for plan fulfillment and the implementation of the Central Committee's economic policies. Specifically, local party organizations are charged with overseeing plan fulfillment, enforcing centralized priorities, formulating regional policy, devising scientific policy, resolving conflicts, overcoming departmentalism, and handling appointments to key positions that are not filled by the Moscow cadres department.[4] Because construction does not lend itself well to centralized direction, the local party is authorized to play a prominent role in the direction of construction. The party's role is especially prominent in consumer-goods production and food output.[5]

The local party derives its authority for involvement in operational economic matters from the party's general responsibility to lead (*rukovodit'*) and educate (*vospitat'*). Although the planning structure does not formally include a role for the local party, local party involve-

University Press, in press), Introduction. The Leningrad party organization reports that its subordinate party bureaus dealt with more than one thousand questions related to economic plans in 1976. From their emphasis on this number, it appears that a major portion of party bureau matters involve economic plans. See *Partiinoe rukovodstvo na uroven' sovremennykh trebovanii: iz opyta paboty Leningradskoi partiinoi organizatsii* (Leningrad: Lenizdat, 1978), pp. 44–5.

4 Merle Fainsod, *How Russia Is Ruled*, rev. ed. (Cambridge, Mass.: Harvard University Press, 1964); Peter Frank, "Economic Activities and the Intermediate and Lower Levels of Party Organization," in Hans-Hermann Hohmann, Alec Nove, and Heinrich Vogel (eds.), *The Economic and Politics in the USSR* (Boulder, Colo.: Westview Press, 1986), pp. 79–80; *Partiinoe rukovodstvo na uroven' sovremennykh trebovanii*, pp. 44–46; *Partiiny kontrol' deiatel'nosti administratsii* (Moscow: Izdatel'stvo politicheskoi literatury, 1977).

5 Rutland, *The Politics of Industrial Stagnation*, Chap. 4.

ment in economic affairs is justified by the party's responsibility to supervise all aspects of Soviet social and economic life. In theory, the local party is supposed to limit its activities to supervision, leaving the state apparatus and enterprises to deal with actual resource-allocation directives.

Local party organizations are known for their interference in the operational affairs of the economy. Party interference is called *podmen,* which denotes the party's practice of issuing concrete directives concerning economic tasks. Examples of *podmen* are the issuing of compulsory joint decrees with state bodies or issuing direct orders to enterprises or trusts.

Why local party organizations get involved in resource allocation is no mystery. The leaders of local party organizations are held responsible for economic results, normally measured by the achievement of territorial plan targets and the percentage of territorial firms that meet their targets.[6] Party officials, who are held responsible for territorial results, have found it hard to draw the line between excessive intervention and too passive supervision.

Do the supervision and intervention of the local party improve or retard Soviet economic efficiency? Jerry Hough has argued that without the trouble shooting of local party officials the Soviet economic system would be reduced to chaos.[7] In fact, Hough refers to local party officials as "prefects," who correct local and regional disequilibria. Party trouble shooting is required because the Soviet planning system is organized on functional lines rather than on regional lines. With weak regional planning, it is up to the party prefect to cross functional boundaries and ensure a more rational regional allocation of resources. In a similar vein, Raymond Powell has argued that Soviet political authorities serve to sort out information about relative scarcities in a planned economy. The Soviet party boss injects economic rationality into the system through an understanding of local relative scarcities.[8] Gregory Grossman has maintained that the party can improve economic efficiency by its ability to deal with externalities, which cannot be handled by the ministerial system.[9]

[6] Ibid., Chap. 2.
[7] Jerry Hough, *The Soviet Prefects: The Local Party Organization in Industrial Decision Making* (Cambridge, Mass.: Harvard University Press, 1969).
[8] Raymond Powell, "Plan Execution and the Workability of Soviet Planning," *Journal of Comparative Economics,* 1, No. 1 (1977), pp. 51–76.
[9] Gregory Grossman, "The Party as Manager and Entrepreneur," in Gregory Guroff and Fred V. Carstensen (eds.), *Entrepreneurship in Imperial Russia and the Soviet Union* (Princeton, N.J.: Princeton University Press, 1983), pp. 284–305.

The frequent criticisms of *podmen* in the Soviet press, official warnings against the practice from high party circles, and Soviet efforts to reduce local party intervention in economic affairs suggest that local party authorities are perceived to harm rather than raise economic efficiency.[10] Peter Rutland, in his assessment of the economic activities of the local party, concludes that party intervention in economic affairs actually makes matters worse.[11]

This chapter examines how the local party affects Soviet resource allocation. The main issue is whether the party makes things better or worse. There are no clear tests for this, and large-scale surveys of former Soviet citizens fail to yield a consensus on whether the party raises economic efficiency.[12] Despite the lack of a measuring rod, we are nevertheless interested in the general impressions of informed persons on this matter – in this study, former members of the Soviet economic bureaucracy.

Emigrants as sources of information about the party

Interviews with former members of the Soviet economic bureaucracy appear to be an unlikely source of information on the economic role of the party. Few emigrants, if any, were members of the party and hence able to talk firsthand about party activities. Persons who occupied the highest positions in the state bureaucracy either did not want to leave the Soviet Union or were not allowed to for reasons of state security. As noted in Chapter 1, former economic bureaucrats worked in the middle and lower bureaucracy. The most highly placed worked as deputies to heads of ministry main administrations, as subdepartment heads in state committees, or in high-level technical positions in ministries, state committees, trusts, and large enterprises. Few occupied high positions in central

---

10 For example, *Partiiny kontrol' deiatel'nosti administratsii*, pp. 258–9, warns party bureaus against engaging in *podmen* and petty tutelage. They are advised to let the experts deal with the technical operational details.
11 Peter Rutland, *The Myth of the Plan* (LaSalle, Ill.: Open Court, 1985), pp. 259–69.
12 The Soviet Interview Project survey of almost three thousand former Soviet citizens revealed that most respondents felt the party did not make any difference with regard to enterprise performance, but a minority of about one-quarter felt that the party made things better. See Paul R. Gregory, "Productivity, Slack, and Time Theft in the Soviet Economy," James Millar (ed.), *Politics, Work, and Daily Life in the USSR; A Survey of Former Citizens* (Cambridge University Press, 1987), p. 250.

institutions. More occupied responsible positions in the republican bureaucracies.

Interviews with former middle-level economic bureaucrats have shed light on the economic role of the party. Because economic bureaucrats are in formal charge of resource allocation, party intervention in economic affairs necessarily takes place through the bureaucracy. Although middle-level bureaucrats lack firsthand information on the internal workings of the party, they are eyewitnesses to party actions that work through the bureaucracy and are thus able to report on the interactions between the party and the bureaucracy.

Responsibility for economic performance

Former members of the Soviet economic bureaucracy take it for granted that local party officials are held responsible for local results. This fact of Soviet life seems so obvious that little is gained by pursuing this topic in interviews. Respondents do add important shadings to our understanding of local party responsibility. The extent to which respondents who worked in republican organizations remembered republican first secretaries depended on how much cotton or oil or wheat production had increased in the republic during the secretary's tenure. The practice of judging the republican party according to the republic's major product appears not to have changed since the 1930s, when Smolensk party officials were judged according to the output of key agricultural products to which Moscow paid close attention.[13]

Respondents reported that city party officials were judged according to enterprise results within the city; *oblast* party officials were judged according to the showing of *oblast* enterprises. A former ministry official summed up the consensus of respondents with the remark that the first secretary of the *obkom* is primarily an "economic worker [*khoziaistvenny rabotnik*] from whom the central committee expects as much as from the ministry." Preoccupation with the economic affairs of the region is reflected in the dominance of economic matters in local party bureau agendas, decrees, and orders.[14]

That local party officials are held responsible for the economic

[13] Merle Fainsod, *Smolensk Under Soviet Rule* (Cambridge, Mass.: Harvard University Press, 1958), pp. 69–72.

[14] *Partiinoe rukovodstvo na uroven' sovremennykh trebovanii*, pp. 44–5, and evidence presented by Rutland, *The Politics of Industrial Stagnation*, show that economic affairs dominate party bureau work.

results of local enterprises is well established in the literature. Rutland provides numerous examples from the Soviet press of the problems local party officials encounter when their territory fails to fulfill a plan.[15] The interviews simply supplement what can be found in the Soviet press. They confirm that local party officials attempt to present plan fulfillment in the most favorable light possible and that they try at times to distort reports on plan fulfillment to central authorities.[16] The interviews also show that local party officials tend to favor policies from below that make them appear progressive in the eyes of the Moscow leadership. Respondents reported on a number of cases of selling ideas on experiments and changes to local party officials because being progressive was part of their job.

When plan failure threatens, local party officials have been known to take direct control of enterprises. In fact, failure to take control can result in censure of the party organization.[17] When this direct intervention is successful, it is proudly publicized by the local party organization.[18] As Hough notes, the worst thing that can occur is for something to go wrong without the party having done something. A failure that takes place without any evidence of party action (of either a positive or negative nature) is taken as a sign that the local party is not doing its job.[19]

The interviews generally confirm Rutland's finding that the highest local party officials rarely lose their positions for territorial plan failures.[20] Unlike enterprise managers, who find it difficult to avoid

---

[15] Rutland, *The Politics of Industrial Stagnation*, Chaps. 2 and 3.
[16] One respondent who had worked as a consultant for Gosplan uncovered false reporting in a major heavy-industry enterprise in a Central Asian republic after regional party authorities had attempted to stifle his investigation. Other respondents reported that they were told that they should be "local patriots" in preparing reports for central authorities even if it meant distorting reality.
[17] Rutland, *The Politics of Industrial Stagnation*, Chap. 2.
[18] For example, the Leningrad *obkom* uses the successful example of the Kaliniski *raikom*, which is creating a special staff to coordinate construction work on large industrial construction projects.
[19] Hough, *The Soviet Prefects*, Chap. 7.
[20] Rutland, *The Politics of Industrial Stagnation*, Chap. 2, finds that high local party officials are not fired for major plan shortfalls. They are usually able to find convenient scapegoats. Respondents confirmed the general scapegoat phenomenon in Soviet society, starting at the enterprise level and going all the way to the top. For more on the scapegoat phenomenon, see Leonid Khotin, "The Distribution of Responsibility Within the Soviet Union: The Soviet Manager Between the Ministry and the Obkom," Soviet Interview Project Report, December 1987.

sanctions by passing blame to enterprise subordinates, the highest local party officials appear to be able to find scapegoats for failures. This testimony is consistent with Rutland's finding that senior *obkom* officials are rarely dismissed for poor economic performance. Rather, junior officials are singled out for blame.[21]

The local party and the higher levels of the bureaucracy

Studies of Soviet enterprise management analyze how responsibility for economic results leads party officials to intervene in enterprise affairs. They show how local party officials and enterprise managers form family networks to protect themselves from failure and how the local party can both assist and hurt the enterprise.[22]

Writers on the party emphasize the dilemma of the local party.[23] The local party organization, headed by its first secretary, is responsible for the economic results of local enterprises. Yet the local party organization operates in a strongly centralized system that restricts its ability to influence plan outcomes. The local party is held responsible for results that it cannot fully control. The enterprise manager is, theoretically, the *edinonachalnik* – the one-man boss of the enterprise. The *edinonachalnik* manager is supposed to be a strong, independent figure who makes the enterprise decisions and is held responsible for enterprise performance.

The most important local enterprises are subordinated to union ministries, upon whom they depend for supplies and relief from excessive output targets. Typically, only the less important local enterprises are directly subordinated to local authorities. Those subordinated to union republican ministries have complex dual loyalties.

The union ministries are the major distributors of materials and parts, and regional authorities are residual claimants to centralized materials and supplies.[24] Changes in output or input plans must be obtained from ministries or state committees.

---

21 Rutland, *Politics of Industrial Stagnation*, Chap. 2.
22 Joseph S. Berliner, *Factory and Manager in the USSR* (Cambridge, Mass.: Harvard University Press, 1957); David Granick, *Management of Industrial Firms in the USSR* (New York: Columbia University Press, 1954).
23 William J. Conyngham, *Industrial Management in the Soviet Union* (Stanford, Calif.: Hoover Institution Press, 1973), Introduction.
24 Industrial ministries are "fund holders" (*fondoderzhateli*). In some instances, state executive committees that direct construction organizations and local industry have fund-holding authority as well. Only these organizations are legally entitled to distribute funded resources. Even Gosplan and Gossnab do not have these powers.

On a formal level, the local party appears to occupy a weak position relative to central institutions. The Soviet planning system appears to place local party officials in a dependent position to central institutions like the ministries.[25] The local party has the formal power to direct only local resources to the enterprises. It does not control the key centralized materials, nor does it have the authority to grant reductions in output targets to enterprises.

Despite its weaknesses, the local party has weapons of its own to bring to bear against central institutions. The true balance of power between the local party and central bureaucratic institutions depends on relative bargaining strengths.[26] In any bargaining process, the ministries, on the one hand, can use their control of funded materials and their power to redistribute plan targets among enterprises as bargaining weapons. They can also use their autarkic sources of supply to reduce dependence on outsiders (*chuzye*). Local party organizations, on the other hand, can use their access to local materials and labor, their influence with higher political officials, threats of exposure to the press, and even the withholding of approval required by the ministries as their bargaining weapons.

Local party and ministries

Local party officials cannot issue orders to enterprises that are subordinated to union ministries, because these enterprises are already subordinated to higher party control. Local party authorities do exercise greater control over "local industry" (*mestnaia promyshlennost'*), whose enterprises are legally subordinated to regional authorities, but even in these instances respondents reported cases of centralized control.[27]

Ministers as members of the pravitel'stvo. Respondents supported the principle that ministries are part of the central apparatus and hence are subject to the control of higher party organs. They referred to

---

[25] William J. Conyngham, *The Modernization of Soviet Industrial Management* (Cambridge University Press, 1982), Chap. 1.

[26] Alice C. Gorlin, "The Power of Soviet Industrial Ministries," *Soviet Studies*, 37, No. 3 (1985), pp. 353–70.

[27] For example, an enterprise subordinated to the local ministry of local economy may be called upon to produce goods that fall under the *nomenklatura* of higher bodies. Respondents reported that, when this happens, the enterprise is expected first to meet the targets of the higher *nomenklatura*.

ministers as the "government" (*pravitel'stvo*) or as members of the "ruling elite." If ministries are directly responsible to the highest party organs, they are not required to obey orders or honor requests from lower party organizations. If a minister is a surrogate for higher party authority, he need not answer to local party officials.

Respondents offered scattered bits of information that support their view of ministers as surrogates for higher party authority. A respondent who worked for a regional branch of Gosbank, for example, related that no party representative attended the meetings of its collegium, contrary to other banks. The head of the bank was a former minister, and hence the interests of the *pravitel'stvo* were automatically represented.

Another sign that ministers are part of the government is the lack of supervision of ministries by ministry party committees. Respondents spoke of the weakness of the ministry party organization, whose activities were limited to routine personnel matters and political education. One knowledgeable former ministry official did not even know who the secretary of the ministry party organization was. Party publications and Soviet press accounts support the respondents' view of the independence of the ministries from party supervision. Ministry party committees often copy the agenda of the ministry collegium, and they are officially told that they should stick to education and cadre matters.[28] Rutland could find no cases in the Soviet press in which a ministry party committee had punished or sanctioned ministry officials and found that efforts to increase the independence of ministry party committees have failed.[29]

This evidence suggests that ministerial status places one in the inner sanctum of the Soviet ruling elite – a status that does not allow monitoring by lower bodies – and that it is difficult to differentiate party from state at this high level. Local party officials, therefore, would not be in a position to issue orders to the ministries. If they wanted to influence the ministries, they would have to use other means.

Friedzon's account of high-level relationships between regional party bosses and Council of Ministers officials appears to confirm the view that the highest state officials represent the interests of the government. Republican secretaries, according to Friedzon, occupy a lower position than the chairman of the Council of Ministers. Were this not so, there could be no single party line, and powerful regional figures might succeed in exceeding national resource limits.[30]

28 *Partiiny kontrol' deiatel'nosti administratsii*, pp. 250–60.
29 Rutland, *The Politics of Industrial Stagnation*, Chap. 2.
30 Friedzon, "Top-Level Administration of the Soviet Economy," pp. 97–8.

Petitions and deals. In describing the working relationship between local party officials and ministries, respondents supplied accounts of interventions by local party officials with a ministry on behalf of local enterprises. Respondent accounts confirm that most of the dealings between local parties and the ministries revolve around the same "battles over bricks" referred to in Chapter 6.[31] A local enterprise, experiencing supply problems, turns to its *obkom* to assist it in obtaining increased supplies. Some of these supplies can be obtained locally from the local party's own material inventories. If these are not sufficient, the local party is expected to use its good offices to appeal to the ministry for help. In its appeal it would cite the failure of suppliers to meet their obligations to the beleaguered enterprise or some exogenous misfortune that had befallen the enterprise.

In this "battle over bricks," local party officials (even highly placed ones) could not order a ministry to supply "bricks." The local party could only petition for increased allotments of funded commodities; it could not demand. The local party could pressure the ministry for early release of funded commodities, but respondents agreed that the annual distribution of funded commodities was a decision of the ministry and ministry alone.

Respondent accounts of local party dealings with ministries is consistent with the account presented by Rutland.[32] From press accounts, Rutland concludes that local parties approach ministries as petitioners. They can be pesky and irritating, flooding offending supply ministries with hundreds of telegrams and telephone calls and even mustering support from high party officials in Moscow. They can accuse ministries of planning delays and for treating enterprises that fail to meet their supply plans too lightly. They can also accuse ministries of ignorance of local conditions and of favoring their own enterprises (departmentalism). Rutland concludes that, although there are cases of good working relations between local parties and the industrial ministries, on balance the relationship is antagonistic. Rutland can find few cases reported in the Soviet press in which the local party is victorious over ministerial departmentalism.

Local party officials approached the ministries for things other than materials. According to respondents, local party officials had to approach ministries for supplemental wage funds and "corrections" in enterprise output targets. The number of times that respondents mentioned local party intervention to obtain additional wage funds

---

[31] I. V. Paramanov, *Uchitsiia upravliat'* (Moscow: Ekonomika, 1970).
[32] Rutland, *The Politics of Industrial Stagnation*, Chaps. 2 and 3.

was substantial. Although interventions for wage funds were not as common as those for materials, the lack of wage funds appears to be a constant irritant for local party officials. Frequently, they argue that the ministry will have to increase wage fund allotments or else the enterprise work force will depart. Chapter 5 pointed out that local party officials must intervene to convince Moscow to issue currency to cover regional monetary imbalances.

It is difficult to generalize from respondent accounts about what types of local party petitions are granted and what types are denied. In allocating their resource "limits," ministries must juggle resources to ensure fulfillment of their own ministerial production targets. The importance of an enterprise to the ministerial plan could obviously be different from its importance to the fulfillment of regional plans.

How do ministries decide which local party requests to grant? The most common thread that runs through the interviews is that resource allocations depend on the personalities involved. Respondents often referred to officials as "strong" or "weak," where "strong" meant an official with strong connections and strong convictions and who could act on the merits of a case. A number of respondents spoke with respect of superiors who were able to stand up to political pressure from important petitioners. Local party officials would often take technical experts with them to a ministry to prove the technical value of their petition. Like enterprise directors, it was the job of the local party officials to request additional resources. This was expected of them, and ministerial officials would discount their testimony for that reason. A common theme throughout the interviews is the importance of technical documentation by specialists to support requests to ministries and state committees. The interviews reveal that most individuals who occupied responsible technical positions had frequent contact with the ministries. This contact occurred in most cases by the expert being taken along by a local party official to provide technical support for supply requests.

High local party officials were involved in considerable operational detail in their dealings with ministries. A respondent who worked in a ministry main administration reported that *obkom* first secretaries would come to the main administration to discuss detailed technical matters, but would deal with the minister on more general matters.

Former ministry officials reported barrages of requests from local party organizations. Some requests could be granted; most could not. These officials knew that the local party organization could appeal up its chain of command and that the enterprise might appeal to some state committee. One stated reason for granting specific requests from the local party was to avoid the nuisance of having to answer to questions raised by higher-ups in response to complaints local party officials had directed to Moscow.

Respondents disagreed on the relative powers of ministers and local party officials. Their answers depended on whether the individuals they had known in ministerial or local party positions were strong or weak.[33] One experienced respondent cogently argued that the organizational setup of the planning system gave ministers an important advantage over local party officials. Ministers can deal directly with central bureaucratic institutions like Gosplan or Gossnab. Local party officials, however, must deal indirectly with the central bureaucratic institution through the appropriate central committee instructor. Ministers therefore have more direct and reliable access to the central economic bureaucracy than do local party bosses.

An enterprise manager who wants to overturn Gosplan or Gossnab decisions can do so through the local party.[34] The local party has the formal right to request information and to petition in a virtually unlimited fashion. The local party official can contact the local central committee, and the appropriate instructor of that committee can then issue a request to the state committee. The state committee can then determine whether it is possible to act on this request.

Local party officials do not always deal with ministries as empty-handed petitioners. Respondents reported cases in which local party officials came to negotiations with something to offer in exchange. Only a few respondents were privy to deal making between local party officials and ministerial officials, but the stories they told were logically consistent.

Respondents agreed that local party officials have an impressive command over local resources. In the case of republican officials in large, resource-rich regions, the party commands a resource base that rivals that of any minister.[35] The ministry has materials needed by the region; the region has resources needed by the ministry. Opportunities for mutually beneficial exchange are high, and it would be

---

[33] For example, at one time the manager of the Magnitogorsk metal combine was a member of the Central Committee. As such, he could go directly to the highest political officials. See Peter Frank, "Economic Activities," pp. 77–91.

[34] Chapter 3 pointed out that some large enterprises and trusts are "line items" in national plans. These enterprises can appeal directly to Gosplan.

[35] In fact, one former ministerial employee recalled being told by his minister to go to the *obkom* for supplies. The minister said something to the effect that it was the *obkom* that had all the valuable materials.

surprising not to find many quid pro quo deals between the local party and the ministry. Local party–ministry deals need not always involve an exchange of resources. One respondent told of trading ministerial resources for local party "acceptance" of an unfinished project needed to fulfill the ministry's plan.

Nomenklatura. The Western literature speculates that the local parties and ministries feud over appointments.[36] It is logically argued that local parties are responsible for results that they can poorly control; therefore, they seek to protect their interests by placing their own people in key positions. Once an individual is appointed to a high industrial administration position, that person is immune to political pressure from local party authorities.[37] Local parties must therefore select their nominees with care. Ministries, in contrast, want qualified individuals who are loyal to the branch and not to regional interests.

Most respondents were able to talk knowledgeably about *nomenklatura* appointments in their organizations. Their descriptions of *nomenklatura* contain few outright surprises. High-level positions in ministries, state committees, and large enterprises are approved by the Central Committee, but nominations can be initiated by either the party or the bureaucratic unit. Lower-level appointments are approved by the cadres departments of local party organizations, but at lower levels the nomination typically comes out of the unit itself.

Personnel matters are discussed at meetings of the ministry collegium with the minister, the deputy ministers, the heads of main administrations, and important factory directors. Eyewitness accounts from the Soviet press capture the "insuring" that goes on in such personnel meetings. If an appointee later makes serious mistakes, his supporters can be penalized.[38] Accordingly, discussants publicly express their reservations about the candidate in order to have a written record of their objection to fall back on if the appointment proves to be a bad one.

The general rule that appears to emerge from respondent descriptions of appointments is that the more technical the position, the more likely it is to belong to the *nomenklatura* of the bureaucratic unit (like a ministry). For example, managers of large enterprises, heads of

[36] Hough, *The Soviet Prefects*, Chap. 7.
[37] This point is made by Hough on the basis of data on tenure of high industrial administrators. *The Soviet Prefects*, Chap. 7.
[38] One such meeting is described in the *Izvestiia* series on the Soviet ministry. See "Kadry. Pis'ma iz ministerstva," *Izvestiia*, December 19, 1986.

ports, and heads of ministry main administrations (and all higher ministerial positions) are in the *nomenklatura* of the Central Committee. The chief engineer of a large enterprise, the main architect of a port, and the head of ministry subdepartments are all in the *nomenklatura* of the ministry. Respondents spoke of personal *nomenklatura*s, such as "The head of the computing center was in the *nomenklatura* of Director Ivanov." By this, they appeared to refer to the positions that could be filled by the head of the organization.

The most notable point that emerges from these discussions is that no cases were cited in which a bureaucratic unit's nominee was not accepted by the party or vice versa. Respondents emphasized that there is no way to be nominated for a high position unless one gets along with the party (and mention was made of qualified individuals who were not acceptable to the party for one reason or another). Persons were selected for responsible industrial administration positions with little rancor, judging from the lack of anecdotes on disputes between the parties and the ministries. It appears that all the actors understand the rules of the game so well that unacceptable candidates are implicitly not brought forward.

The lack of rancor does not mean that enterprises, trusts, and ministries are consistently satisfied with persons nominated by the party. Many respondents reported cases of unqualified persons with high party connections who had to be accommodated, but this was accepted as a fact of life. Respondents also reported cases of party officials who had been involved in scandals (that made a further party career impossible) being placed in responsible positions of industrial administration.

The overall impression that one gets from discussions with respondents who had witnessed the *nomenklatura* process is that it works on the basis of consensus rather than conflict. If conflicts between the ministries and local parties over key personnel matters were common, this fact could scarcely have been overlooked by respondents, many of whom were anxious to relate interesting gossip. The respondents' silence on the question of conflict over *nomenklatura* matters is evidence that such conflict was not strong.

Firing. Respondents who worked in ministries, trusts, and large enterprises consistently noted the active role of the local party in the firing of industrial administrators. This theme is not particularly surprising in view of the formal responsibility for firing that is accorded the party.[39] Former ministry officials confirmed that the first step in

---

[39] *Partiny kontrol' deiatel'nosti administratsii* specifically states (p. 264) that the

firing an industrial administrator is to clear the firing with the organization's party committee. If the position is high (such as manager of a large enterprise), ministry officials clear it first with local party officials. There appears to be agreement that officials in the bureaucracy can indeed fire management subordinates if they so desire without fearing party resistance, unless the subordinate has high party connections. In that case, his superior would know better than to initiate firing proceedings.[40]

According to the respondents, the internal party committee plays a rubber-stamp role in such firings. The active role is played by the local party. A number of respondents reported that enterprise managers fear the local party more than their ministry superiors because the local party typically originates proposals to fire managers. As described by respondents, the local party organization is quicker to fire enterprise managers, preferring to get a new manager on the job rather than give the current manager another chance. One respondent reported that the local party often has the replacement selected before the firing even takes place. Whether the enterprise manager is indeed fired depends on his support within the ministry. Apparently that support must be strong to withstand local party pressure to remove the enterprise manager.[41]

If the impression gained from the interviews that the local party initiates firings of industrial administrators is true, it raises an interesting question: Why is the local party more willing to fire industrial administrators than their immediate superiors in the ministry? One answer may be that the ministry values industrial experience more highly than the local party, which must be viewed as "doing something" when things go wrong.

Dealings of local party with state committees

Respondents who worked in state committees such as Gosplan or Gossnab occupied middle and lower positions in those committees.

party committees of ministries and state committees are responsible for presenting proposals to the collegium to remove responsible persons from their positions.

[40] One respondent who occupied a very high technological position reported not being able to withhold a bonus from a lackluster subordinate because the subordinate had a strong patron in the party. Such accounts were common in the interviews.

[41] One respondent told the story of an extremely successful manager who made an enemy of a high local party official. Despite the enterprise manager's excellent reputation, the local party official succeeded in having him removed for a minor safety violation.

They were not privy to high-level discussions, so their frame of reference is limited. Despite this limitation, former employees of Gosplan and Gossnab shed some light on dealings between local party officials and state committees.

Output and investment planning. Former middle-level employees of Gosplan and Gossnab reported extensive contact with local party officials. There was regular contact during the process of planning. Respondents, who participated in the "defense of the plan" from both sides, spoke of the siege of Moscow by ministries and by regional state and party officials. The defense of the plan is a rough-and-tumble tug-of-war over resources in which enterprises and ministries attempt to keep what they have – to keep the cuts to a minimum – rather than to get more. Regional state and party officials, who sometimes adopt contradictory positions, employ a variety of arguments to head off resource cuts. They cite the importance of the region, the need for employment, recent natural disasters, and the like.

The active role played by local party authorities in the defense of the plan is not surprising and is well known. Rutland has documented available press accounts of local party lobbying efforts.[42]

Many respondents worked in construction – an area in which regional authorities are known to play an active role. Respondents were able to describe the bitter disputes over major investment projects and the intense pressure brought on the state committees by regional party officials. Respondents who dealt with major construction projects in a technical capacity seemed to feel that major investment decisions were decided on the basis of merit. Major expenditures of resources were not decided on political grounds.

Local party officials pressured design institutes to plan centralized investment projects to be as big and expensive as possible. This pressure could come from two sources: Regional party officials used their influence with the Central Committee, which jointly with the Council of Ministers decided major investment projects. Regional state officials used their influence with the appropriate state committee (such as the State Committee for Construction) to make projects bigger and better.

Respondents also described the maneuvering of regional state and party officials to maximize the number of construction projects that could be approved at the local level. Construction projects that fell below established ruble limits could be approved by local authorities;

---

[42] Rutland, *The Politics of Industrial Stagnation,* Chap. 2.

respondents who "projected" construction projects reported being pressured by local officials to hold the projected costs below the sum that required centralized approval.

Respondents who worked on "prestige" construction projects reported that regional party officials were able to direct ample resources to them, especially in resource-rich republics like the Ukraine. They reported as well that high-ranking republican party officials had sufficient clout to include major republican construction projects in the annual plan (which required inclusion in the "title list" of construction projects) even though the project was not included in the five-year plan.

Supplies. The channels through which local party supply requests reach central bureaucratic organs such as Gosplan or Gossnab are informative. According to respondents, enterprise managers (even of the largest Soviet enterprises) have no choice but to petition through their local party. Any attempt by an enterprise to appeal over the heads of the immediate superior (such as a trust or a ministry main administration) would be thwarted because the ministerial bureaucracy does not condone bypassing channels. Petitions that circumvent an immediate superior are automatically returned to that superior.

Memoranda "for the record" from industrial managers are not regarded as circumventing the bureaucratic chain of command. Virtually all respondents spoke of the use of memos as personal insurance. When a supply problem threatened, industrial managers would begin a furious campaign of writing memos demonstrating that if X happens, the enterprise cannot conceivably meet targets Z and V. Such insurance memos are sent to the appropriate ministry and local party officials, to appropriate state committees officials, and even to the Central Committee.

Former state committee employees reported frequent direct contacts with local party officials concerning supply requests. Such requests typically come in written form so that they become part of the written record. Local party officials also appeal to the Central Committee. Respondents report that such appeals are considered by the appropriate instructor of the Central Committee, who transmits the committee's action requests to the appropriate state committee through the Council of Ministers.

As noted in Chapter 5, the receipt of a written order signed by the highest Soviet officials does not guarantee favorable action. The number of high-level requests exceeded Gossnab's ability to act. One Gossnab respondent reported that his superiors in Gossnab were remarkably unimpressed by requests received in the name of high officials. If supplies were not there to meet all these requests, nothing could be done.

Money and wages. A number of respondents formerly worked for Gosbank in regional and Moscow branches. They reported a surprising degree of involvement of local party authorities in matters of money circulation. Regional Gosbank offices were required to report on a daily basis balances of regional cash outflows (through regional wages payments) and cash inflows (through the receipts from regional retail trade). If the outflow exceeded the inflow, Gosbank officials would report this imbalance to local party authorities.

One of the major responsibilities of local party authorities, according to the accounts of former Gosbank employees, is to deal with regional currency imbalances. Local party officials deal with these imbalances by jawboning officials in charge of retail trade (trying to get them to sell more), bargaining for increased supplies of consumer goods, and pleading for currency injections from currency-surplus regions. If all these measures fail, the first secretary of the republic is required to contact the Central Committee for permission to issue uncirculated currency in the vaults of regional Gosbank offices. Apparently, republican first secretaries were quite reluctant to request permission to issue new currency because the Central Committee regarded this as a sign of regional mismanagement.

Gosbank officials reported frequent contact with local party officials on the matter of wages. Local party officials apparently feared the loss of labor and became quite worried when lagging enterprises were threatened with inadequate funds to pay their workers. Bank officials reported being invited to meetings with the first secretary of the *obkom* to discuss particular enterprises. They also reported being harassed by local party officials for lack of local patriotism when they did not honor *obkom* requests for supplemental wage funds. Rutland confirms, from Soviet press accounts, the involvement of local party officials in labor force matters.[43] Local party officials can set quotas when labor shortages threaten a region and can influence supplies of qualified labor through the local educational system.

Local party officials were reported to promote equalization among local enterprises, much as the ministries equalize profits among their enterprises by redistributing profits from high- to low-profit enterprises. They fear that if one local enterprise becomes too successful

---

[43] Ibid.

(offering higher compensation to its workers), workers will move to that enterprise, jeopardizing the plan fulfillment in other local enterprises. Although respondent accounts are few, it seems logical that local party officials would worry about the optimal distribution of labor among local enterprises. They would prefer to have as many local enterprises as possible fulfilling their plan targets as opposed to having a few highly successful enterprises and many unsuccessful enterprises. This is not the first finding of regional redistribution among regional enterprises. According to Fainsod, the Smolensk party consistently redistributed output targets among its regional enterprises.[44]

Information sharing. Respondents who worked for central bureaucratic organizations dealing in matters of regional planning reported a few instances of the withholding of information by local authorities. One former Gosplan employee told of an attempt to conceal distorted plan reports (*pripiski*) by regional officials. Another respondent told of the efforts of regional authorities to withhold accurate industrial capacity information from Gosplan.

The withholding of information by local party authorities from central bureaucratic institutions comes as no surprise. It is assumed that ministries do so routinely with respect to ministerial enterprises. As long as local party officials are held accountable for regional results, they will be tempted to present regional economic results in the most favorable way and to make it difficult for central bureaucratic institutions to uncover *pripiski*.

The local party and local enterprises

Berliner and Granick have chronicled the relationship between local party officials and Soviet enterprises.[45] No major new insights have come out of these more recent interviews with former members of the Soviet economic bureaucracy, but such interviews do add to our detailed knowledge of local party–local enterprise interactions.

Respondents who had occupied responsible positions in large Soviet enterprises and trusts viewed the local party with two minds. On the one hand, the local party could help out in rough times by order-

---

44 Fainsod, *Smolensk Under Soviet Rule*, p. 80.
45 Berliner, *Factory and Manager in the USSR;* Granick, *Management of Industrial Firms in the USSR.* Also see Khotin, "The Distribution of Responsibility."

ing a dragnet for materials, which could cross territorial boundaries if the party official was clever and well connected. There are countless tales of the first secretary of the *obkom* intervening on behalf of the enterprise – finding extra workers and materials, obtaining permission to shift output from one period to the next, and so on. In such matters, the local party and the enterprise worked cooperatively. Cooperation appeared to be particularly great during the period of the plan project (*proekt plana*), when the local party and the local enterprise campaigned cooperatively for more materials and more reasonable outputs.

Respondents reported that not all local enterprises were treated in the same way by local party officials. The successful enterprise that consistently met its targets "by any means" (*liuboi tsenoi*) appeared to be left alone by party officials. If caught in a transgression, local party officials might read a formal reprimand but then privately tell the manager that everything was in order and the reprimand would be quietly removed from his record. Respondents noted that the success or failure of a construction project hinged to a great extent on party interest in the project. In construction, many materials can be obtained by the first secretary's dragnet; hence, the first secretary is in a position to determine the fate of local construction projects.

When things were not going well with enterprises, enterprise managers are more likely to be reprimanded by local party officials than by their ministerial superiors. Respondents reported that local party officials attempted to keep up to date on enterprise plan fulfillment, and bank officials reported being called in to discuss the finances of enterprises at the first sign of trouble. Gosbank officials would be warned about the serious effects on employment if the troubled enterprise did not meet its wage bill, and local party officials would appeal to the patriotism of local bank officials to supply short-term wage credits, thereby enabling the enterprise to survive its temporary liquidity problems.

The local party was especially useful in arranging transportation and finding additional workers for peak-load problems. Enterprise respondents confirmed that the local party was not as helpful in obtaining funded materials.

Although enterprises stood to benefit from local party intervention with their superiors, respondents voiced a number of objections to such intervention. A frequent complaint was the disruptive effect of local party assignments outside an enterprise's formal plan responsibilities – such as building a new silo or helping out with the construction of an apartment building. Notably, if the task assigned by the local party was outside the area of the enterprise's formal responsibility, the ministry could be totally bypassed. When asked whether the enterprise could cite these extra obligations as an excuse for non-fulfillment of plan activities, respondents replied that they could not use them in this manner. Judging from the number of complaints, the assignment of extra tasks by the local party was a source of considerable irritation. Regular plan tasks had to be set aside; orders were frequently nonsensical or irrational.

The issuing of extra tasks to enterprises is not the only source of friction between local enterprises and local party officials. A former Gosplan employee told of an enterprise manager who had been forced by local party officials to accept a factory as completed when no equipment had yet been installed. When asked why he had agreed to this, the manager responded that local party officials needed "acceptance" of this building to meet their investment targets and that the local party had promised that the equipment would be speedily installed.

On the details of working relationships, respondents reported that the key figure in the local party organization was typically the second secretary. If the region produced primarily industrial products, the second secretary was in charge of industry. If the region was agricultural, the second secretary was in charge of agriculture. The degree of intervention into enterprise affairs appeared to vary. Successful enterprises tended to be left alone, except when the party assigned extracurricular tasks. Troubled enterprises were monitored regularly, and (as noted earlier) the local party frequently initiated firing proceedings. Some respondents emphasized the constant meddling of the party in enterprise affairs, citing several meetings per week with the relevant party secretary. Others reported that the local party gave general advice and left the enterprise to its own devices.

One respondent who had frequent contact with local party officials felt that the constant meddling and clamor for reports was an attempt by party officials to "make work" for themselves, that they were simply going through the motions. This view of the party is consistent with the picture painted by Hough, who maintains that much party activity is a form of insurance. If a problem arises and the party cannot demonstrate that it was concerned and involved, party officials can end up being blamed.

Summary

We have no definitive answer to the question raised at the beginning of this chapter: Does the local party "prefect" make matters better or worse? The answer appears to depend on time, location, and circumstances. The local party provides a frontline defense against ministry departmentalism, but it substitutes its own "localistic" tendencies. The local party both helps and hurts its enterprises. Personalities appear to be crucial. Time and again respondents reported that outcomes depend as much on personalities as they do on positions.

The dealings of local party officials with central bureaucratic institutions are governed by distinct rules of the game. The most important is that the central bureaucratic institution answers to the highest party authorities and is not obliged to answer to local party officials. This principle is seen in the inability of local party officials to control funded commodities.

Local party officials petition central bureaucratic institutions on behalf of local enterprises for supplies, plan corrections, and increased wage funds. Their bargaining strength lies in their nuisance value, political connections, and their ability to offer local resources in return. Mutually beneficial deals are struck between ministries and local party officials on this basis.

Enterprises that wish to press claims to central bureaucratic institutions cannot circumvent formal lines of authority within the ministry system. Their only recourse is appeal to the local party, which can petition the Central Committee directly on virtually any issue. Ministers appear to have an advantage over local party officials because they can address central bureaucratic institutions directly. Local party officials can address central institutions only indirectly through the relevant instructor of the Central Committee.

Central bureaucratic institutions cannot respond favorably to all resource-allocation requests from high party officials, because the number of requests exceeds their ability to meet them. This imbalance gives central bureaucratic institutions leeway to make their own decisions.

The interviews fail to reveal evidence of conflicts between the ministries and the local parties over appointments. They do indicate that the local parties play an active role in initiating firing proceedings for industrial administrators.

Local party officials have an active influence on the distribution of investment resources, although major resource-allocation decisions appear to be based on merit. Local party officials argue for "bigger and better" centralized investment projects but try to keep other projects small enough so that they can be approved locally.

The local party plays a prominent role in matters of money circulation and wage funds. The responsibility for control of the money supply appears to rest heavily on republican first secretaries.

The interests of local party officials diverge from those of central bureaucratic authorities. This fact is expressed in the tendency of local party officials to withhold information from central authorities. Local parties both help and hurt local enterprises. They assist in obtaining supplies, wage funds, and plan corrections. They hurt by assigning extracurricular activities that drain enterprise resources, and they force enterprises to take actions that favor the locality but harm the enterprises.

CHAPTER 8

Reform

Restructuring the bureaucracy

Without the support of the bureaucracy, Gorbachev's *perestroika* (restructuring) program cannot be implemented. Western experts presume that distinct elements of the Soviet bureaucracy oppose *perestroika*. They fear that bureaucratic opponents will pay it lip service, while quietly sabotaging it. This chapter attempts to anticipate how the Soviet economic bureaucracy will respond to *perestroika* and to determine whether the widespread fears of bureaucratic sabotage are justified.

The Western literature often presents a black and white picture of Soviet bureaucratic thinking: Bureaucrats above the enterprise level are presumed to oppose reform because they fear loss of jobs, loss of power, and reduction of perquisites. In contrast, enlightened managers are presumed to favor reform that gives them increased freedom of action. They want to be free from the petty tutelage (*opeka*) of the ministries and intervention by the local party (*podmen*) to run their enterprises efficiently. This chapter shows that this categorization of the reluctant bureaucrat and enthusiastic manager obscures important undercurrents. An understanding of how the Soviet economic bureaucracy works – its rules of the game, its goals, and its methods – sheds light on the bureaucracy's probable reception of *perestroika*. The Soviet economic bureaucracy is diverse – much depends on personalities, assessment of responsibility and risk, and institutional affiliations – and consequently its reactions to *perestroika* will not be uniform. Nevertheless, how each person and bureaucratic organization deals with *perestroika* will determine, in the long run, its success or failure.

Bureaucratic features of *perestroika*

The main features of *perestroika* have been discussed at length.[1] Many of the ideas – direct links, full economic accounting, wholesale mar-

---

[1] See, e.g., Joint Economic Committee, *Gorbachev's Economic Plans* (Washington, D.C.: U.S. Government Printing Office, 1987), Vol. 1, Part 1.

146

kets, profit incentives, and increased freedom to contract with other parties – have been recycled from the 1960s.[2] However, the attention to sociological, foreign, and political factors and the serious intent of the Soviet leadership make *perestroika* a truly interesting social experiment.

Perestroika has five basic thrusts. The first is the technological restructuring of the Soviet economy, the objective of which is to modernize Soviet industry so that it meets world technological standards. Insofar as attaining world technological levels without the active participation of the outside world would be difficult, *perestroika* calls for an opening of the Soviet economy to the industrialized capitalist world. Soviet enterprises are to be granted increased freedom to deal directly with foreign firms, and the authority of the foreign trade monopoly is to be reduced. More flexible joint-venture arrangements are to make it easier for Soviet firms to deal with foreign partners.

The second thrust is the improvement of worker morale and discipline, goals to be achieved through improvements in consumer-goods availability, greater worker democracy and an increased worker stake in enterprise affairs, and discipline campaigns. There is to be a greater tolerance of private economic activity. More flexible cooperative arrangements are to be encouraged in light industry. Farm families are to be allowed to execute long-term leases with the state. In general, more emphasis is to be placed on the quality of goods produced by state enterprises for consumer markets.

The third thrust is increased initiative and responsibility at the enterprise level. It is this feature that stands to affect most significantly the way the Soviet economic bureaucracy works. The amount of tutelage (*opeka*) exercised by state committees and ministries over enterprises is to be reduced. Ministries, instead of overseeing the routine input and output operations of enterprises, are to concern themselves with long-term planning and with investment and technology policy. Gosplan is to concern itself with long-term planning and technology policy (the five-year plan is to become the dominant operational plan). The number of compulsory targets is to be reduced, leaving more leeway for enterprises to select their own output mixes. A system of state orders (*goszakazy*) is to replace compulsory output targets (although the distinction between state orders and

---

[2] For a general discussion of *perestroika* see Paul Gregory and Robert Stuart, *Soviet Economic Structure and Performance*, 4th ed. (New York: Harper & Row, 1990), Chap. 14.

compulsory targets remains unclear), and enterprises are to have increased freedom over the production and disbursement of goods and services produced above state orders. Higher-quality outputs are to be ensured by a system of state inspectors (*gospriemka*) who answer to higher authorities rather than to enterprise management.

The reduction of tutelage should reduce the volume of bureaucratic tasks. Hence, the size of bureaucracy will be reduced; scarce labor is to be shifted from bureaucratic tasks to enterprises. All actors in the Soviet economy are to be held accountable for final results. *Perestroika* will presumably number the days of *apparatchiks*, who are allowed to make bad decisions for which they are not held accountable.

To encourage enterprises to take on ambitious targets and to eliminate the ratchet effect, enterprises are to be judged on the basis of long-run plans and normatives. Instead of being given a series of compulsory input targets, enterprises should make more of their own decisions as long as they remain within norms set by the planning apparatus.

The freedom of enterprises to engage in deal making is to be increased. Enterprises are to be allowed to trade goods among themselves, although the use of middlemen will be discouraged. Interenterprise contracts are to play a more important role. Goods that are exchanged on a negotiated contractual basis are to be exchanged at prices agreed to by the exchanging parties. Enterprises are to conclude output and delivery contracts, and the delivery plan (*plan postavok*) is to become one of the enterprises' prime success criteria. Enterprise efficiency is to be improved by allowing enterprises to retain profits for managerial and worker rewards and for capital accumulation.

Both enterprises and ministries are to be placed on full economic accounting (*pol'ny khozrashchet*), which means that enterprises must cover their costs to remain in business. The old system of automatic subsidies for loss-making enterprises is to be replaced. In recognition of the long-standing practice of unplanned material exchanges among enterprises, such exchanges are to be made legal, and more private economic activities are to be legalized, although strict restrictions on the use of hired labor are to remain in effect.

The fourth thrust of *perestroika* is political reform. To gain public support for *perestroika*, Soviet society is to become more open (*glasnost'*). The relaxation of censorship will allow society to discuss more openly political and economic problems and facilitate the search for solutions. Workers are to be given more rights within their enterprises – even playing a role in determining the enterprise director. Widespread political reforms, intended to make the party more a policy-making body than an operational body in economic affairs, are to be implemented. As the party retreats from routine economic decision making, state bodies (ranging from the elected Supreme Soviet to the city executive committees) are to acquire more authority in economic affairs.

The fifth thrust is experimentation with new forms of socialist property rights. People are to be allowed to organize producer cooperatives; farm families are to be given long-term leases of state land; employees are to be allowed to buy shares of the enterprises for which they work; and foreign companies are to be permitted to own shares of joint venture enterprises.

Perestroika's social and political programs are at a surprisingly advanced stage of implementation. Its main economic programs, however, remain largely on the drawing boards. It is therefore germane to consider the potential obstacles to economic reform – in particular the reaction of the Soviet economic bureaucracy.

Bureaucratic responsibility

Perestroika aims to make every actor in the economy responsible for "final results." Enterprises that fail to cover costs will run the risk of bankruptcy. Workers whose work is shoddy will find themselves without jobs. Bureaucrats are to be made responsible for their decisions. No longer will vital resource-allocation decisions be made by individuals who bear no responsibility. Although it is easy to understand how enterprise managers and workers can be held responsible for final results, it is more difficult to see how a system can be created in which bureaucrats share responsibility and risk.

Chapter 4 distinguished between two Soviet bureaucratic types. The *apparatchik* issues instructions, devises norms, and makes rules. The "resource allocator," or *khoziaistvennik,* makes the actual resource allocations of the economy in the framework set by the *apparatchik.* The *khoziaistvennik* makes resource allocations at the microeconomic level, as a manager of an enterprise or trust; at intermediate levels, as a manager of branch resources in a ministry or as a local party organizer of construction projects; or at the national level, as a politburo member who decides major resource allocations and is held responsible for macroeconomic performance.

Soviet planning terminology provides a convenient discriminator between *apparatchik* and *khoziaistvennik* functions. Individuals who have the authority to move scarce resources – the fund holders (*fon-*

doderzhateli) – largely make up the *khoziaistvennik* group. Ministries, enterprises, and trusts have this authority. *Apparatchik*s are not fund holders. They prepare rules, norms, and laws for organizations that have fund-holding responsibilities. *Apparatchik*s influence the behavior of resource movers by setting the rules of the game under which *khoziaistvennik*s operate.

The key distinction between *apparatchik*s and *khoziaistvennik*s is the degree of responsibility for final results. As resource allocators charged with achieving a set of measurable directives, *khoziaistvennik*s are held responsible for the results of their actions. The directive-issuing and rule-making *apparatchik*s, in contrast, are not held responsible. Ministry officials occupying line positions, enterprise managers, and local party officials are held responsible for plan fulfillment. Officials occupying functional positions either in line organizations or in functional committees are not and cannot be held responsible for final results.

This book has shown why it has not been possible (and perhaps not desirable) to hold *apparatchik*s responsible for final results. First, the work of *apparatchik*s is difficult to tie to economic outcomes because of its joint nature. How would one establish to what degree the Gosplan materials balancer, the Finance Ministry budget planner, or the ministry norm setter has contributed to or detracted from plan fulfillment? Second, higher-level decision makers require honest information brokers. Holding *apparatchik*s responsible for their rules, laws, and norms creates principal–agent problems and, hence, a loss of honest information. The leadership may wish to keep *apparatchik*s separate from actual production units so that they will work honestly in the interests of the leadership. This book has shown that accountability for final results causes individuals to form alliances that work opportunistically against the interests of the principal. If *apparatchik*s were accountable for final results, a whole new set of principal–agent problems would emerge.

Perestroika plans to compensate for the loss of centralized control over enterprises by increasing the role of rules, laws, and norms – the kind of work done by *apparatchik*s, who cannot be held responsible for final results. As one Soviet planning official declares: "The battle for easy plans will be replaced by a battle for easy norms."[3] Enterprises will be allowed to enter more freely into supply contracts (in place of centralized supplies) but at prices that conform broadly to pricing

[3] "K voprosu o planirovanii" (V. Stetsiura), *Planovoe khoziaistvo*, No. 9, September 1987, pp. 95–100.

rules established by *apparatchiks*. The materials they buy will have to conform to the engineering input norms of *apparatchiks*. Enterprises will be allowed to retain profits according to formulas compiled by *apparatchiks*.

Paradoxically, any switch from direct tutelage to norms and rules reduces rather than increases responsibility for final results, given the difficulty of linking norms and rules to final results. It also provides an argument against trimming the size of the bureaucracy. As one *apparatchik* asked, "Who is going to do all the necessary work on rules, norms, and laws?" In effect, the "rules of the game" created by *apparatchiks* would gain considerably in importance. Rather than being the empty exercises criticized by many of the respondents in this study, rules, laws, and norms would actually direct resources to alternative uses.

A deeper question concerns the ability of Soviet economic bureaucrats to devise rules, norms, and laws that are economically efficient. In effect, a real transition from commands to norms, laws, and rules would mean that the established "rules of the game" would have significant effects on economic outcomes. Price-setting rules, tax systems, and rules concerning labor–management relations would have real effects on resource allocation.

Perestroika asks Soviet economic bureaucrats to create new rules of the game within a very brief period of time by historical standards. In Western capitalist societies, the prevailing economic rules of the game are a product of centuries of trial-and-error development. They are the outcome of constitutions, common law tradition, legislation, and court rulings, and they have been molded by constitutional guarantees of private property.

It is unclear whether the norms and rules devised by Soviet *apparatchiks* would promote or harm economic efficiency. Whether the devised rules of the game are efficient does not really depend on good intentions. In fact, it may be difficult for the rule writers to divine the common welfare. Rules that harm vocal groups of producers or consumers may promote the general welfare. Binding rules and norms would have distributional effects that benefited one group while harming another. Procedures and standards must be devised for evaluating norms and rules, so as to eliminate those that harm general economic welfare. Will these evaluations be carried out by the executive or judicial branches of Soviet government? What standards will be used to determine whether a rule or norm is in the public interest?

The task of creating efficient economic rules of the game within a relatively brief period of time is a daunting one. If the Soviet leadership is serious about moving from directives to rules, the outcome of *perestroika* will depend on how well the rules of the game are devised. There are few guideposts that mark the path to efficient rule making in a socialist economy. Will the rules of the game be devised for special interest groups? How well will invisible social interests be reconciled with special interests?

Petty tutelage of ministries

A paradox of *perestroika* is its aim to reduce the responsibilities of the ministries – bureaucratic agencies that *are* held responsible for final results. This book has emphasized the pivotal role of the ministries in Soviet resource allocation. The reduction of ministerial tutelage is a cornerstone of *perestroika*. In fact, the ministries have clearly been singled out for attack because it is the ministries, more than any other bureaucratic organization, that intervene in the affairs of enterprises.[4] The reduction of ministerial tutelage was also a cornerstone of the failed 1965 economic reform. In both reforms, the ministry was supposed to cease exercising routine day-to-day control over enterprises and restrict its involvement to long-term matters, like interbranch coordination and technology. Both reforms called for a reduction in ministerial employment as decision-making authority passed from the ministries to enterprises.

It is useful to review the forms of ministerial tutelage and ask why ministries might resist a reduction in ministerial tutelage. First and foremost, tutelage is exercised through ministry controls of the distribution of funded commodities among ministerial enterprises. Higher planning organs distribute resources to the ministries, not directly to the producing enterprises. In the absence of working wholesale markets, the ministries have assumed the role of distributor of industrial materials. Second, the ministries distribute the financial resources placed at their disposal by state committees, including wage funds. Third, the ministries redistribute profits among their enterprises. Fourth, the ministries prepare the actual operational plans of enterprises by disaggregating the ministry targets handed down by

[4] The attack on the ministries was initiated by the unofficial release of Tatiana Zaslavskaia's memo on the ministries in the early 1980s, which blamed the ministries for the economy's deteriorating economic performance. For a more recent statement of Zaslavskaia's views, see T. Zaslavskaia and V. Efimov, "Slomat' mekhanizm tormozheniia," *Sovetskaia Rossiia*, March 24, 1987.

Gosplan and approved by the Council of Ministers. Once operational plans are prepared, the ministries change enterprise output and input targets to ensure ministry plan fulfillment.

As noted above, the *perestroika* reform places great emphasis on holding every agent responsible for "final results." Ministries (and regional authorities with fund-holding authority) have been held accountable for the physical output targets of the unit's main product profiles. This book has shown that reputations of ministers and regional authorities depend on the fulfillment of physical indicators. Whereas enterprise managers are held accountable for the results of their enterprise, ministers are held responsible for the combined results of their enterprises.

The reform leadership remains undecided on how to judge ministers and ministry branch officials under the new system.[5] As long as ministry officials continue to be judged by traditional means, they have an interest in retaining the levers they use to ensure ministry plan fulfillment. Profit redistributions keep high-cost ministry enterprises in operation. The ministries' bargaining power depends on the extent to which they are independent of "foreign" producers. Ministries produce "foreign" goods at high cost relative to the main-supplier ministries, and ministry enterprises that produce foreign goods must be propped up by the profits of its other enterprises.[6] If ministries were no longer allowed to redistribute profits, they would be unable to continue their drive for autarky.

The ministries, in their capacity as the fund holders for enterprises, exercise considerable control over enterprise operations. Gosplan and Gossnab do not allocate materials directly to enterprises (except for a few major enterprises); rather they allocate "limits" to the ministries. It is not clear how *perestroika* intends to change this system, although there is a clear intent to make enterprises more responsible for their own supplies. In the past, ministries have kept free reserves that could be shifted to troubled enterprises. As long as ministries continue to be held responsible for final results, they will not want to give up the supply lever.

Gosplan and Gossnab must continue, in most cases, to plan at levels of aggregation too high to be operational. In fact, *perestroika* appears to be pushing them in the direction of even higher levels of planning

---

[5] At the date of this writing, Soviet authorities had yet to pass a new ministry law. It can therefore be assumed that ministries have continued to operate according to the old rules.

[6] I. M. Egorov, "Remont na uroven' sovremennykh trebovanii," *Eko*, No. 3, 1985, pp. 23–33.

aggregation and longer planning horizons. *Perestroika* does not plan to do away with "funded" goods – rather, it intends to reduce their number. Basic industrial goods and equipment will remain funded, and the ministries will continue to be the operational fund holders.

As long as the ministries remain responsible for producing physical output targets and serve as the economy's fund holders, they will want to remain in the business of petty tutelage. It should be emphasized that the distinction between petty tutelage and necessary intervention will remain difficult to draw. Even enlightened ministry officials tend to view problems that others regard as "petty" as major problems that demand administrative attention. The failure of one firm to meet its supply obligations can idle most ministry enterprises and threaten an entire ministry plan.[7] This "for want of a nail, the kingdom was lost" thinking makes it very difficult for ministries to refrain from petty tutelage.

New rules for ministries

Ministerial officials report that the political leadership has not changed its rules of the game.[8] Ministries are still judged on the basis of aggregated physical outputs in the same detail as before.

Unless *perestroika* alters in a fundamental way the manner in which ministries are judged, ministries are unlikely to change their dealings with enterprises, even if they are formally told to do so. Ministry officials argue in the Soviet press that, if they are to continue to have compulsory targets, they must continue to assign compulsory targets to ministry enterprises and use measures to ensure their fulfillment.

Perestroika's designers have not enacted a new ministry law because of the extreme complexity of the ministries' role. The ministries have traditionally held the key to Soviet centralized resource management. They have allocated the economy's funded goods and have produced the goods that enter into the economy's centralized material balances. The ministries have been the operational planners of the economy. They work at the operational level of the economy. Under *perestroika*, the ministries must continue to perform many of these functions. They must retain their arsenal of weapons to ensure that they can complete their tasks, yet the enterprises are to be autonomous! The new ministry law must somehow bridge this contradiction. How is

---

7 "Prospekt Kalinina, 19. Pis'ma iz ministerstva," *Izvestiia*, December 16–20, 1986.
8 "Pis'ma iz ministerstva," *Izvestiia*, December 16, 1986.

ministerial input–output planning to be done in an environment in which enterprises have considerable autonomy over what they produce, how they produce, and with whom they deal?[9]

Full economic accounting

Full economic accounting (*pol'ny khozrashchet*) is another cornerstone of *perestroika*. It is regarded as a key to the improvement of enterprise operations. It is the Soviet leadership's weapon for eliminating the "soft budget constraint," which Janos Kornai maintains is the prime source of scarcity in planned economies.[10] Without full economic accounting, enterprises can spend beyond their revenues so as to meet their physical plan targets. With a soft budget constraint, enterprises can demand labor, capital, and material resources beyond those they could afford with a hard budget constraint.

If enterprise survival depends on making a long-run profit, enterprises must become both cost and quality conscious. If full economic accounting makes enterprises cost minimizers, wholesale markets in industrial goods will become feasible, because enterprises will cease overdemanding inputs. Enterprises will become quality conscious because unsold output will pile up as excess inventory and draw down enterprise profits.

Full economic accounting is likely to be resisted by elements of the Soviet economic bureaucracy for a number of reasons. Full economic accounting would reduce ministry autarky because enterprises manufacturing products outside a ministry's main product profiles would be unprofitable. Full economic accounting would also affect Soviet labor markets. Traditionally, a major motivation for profit redistributions has been to limit labor turnover. Managers emphasize that their workers leave on a moment's notice if bonuses are not paid. Ministries, enterprises, and local party officials fear the loss of labor force, and the failure to reach profit and bonus targets means that labor cannot be paid their opportunity costs. Full economic accounting would be resisted by ministry officials, enterprise managers, and local party officials in high-risk enterprises, in construction, and in activities that require lengthy research and development cycles.

Even in capitalist countries, full economic accounting tends to be resisted by those who stand to lose. Closures of unprofitable plants

---

9 "Perestroika i planirovanie. Pervy zamestitel' predsedateliia Gosplana SSSR otvechaet na voprosy korrespondentov Izvestii," *Izvestiia*, August 19, 1987.

10 Janos Kornai, *The Economics of Scarcity* (New York: North Holland, 1980).

are resisted on grounds of harm to the local economy, loss of jobs, or the loss of votes in the next election. Similar resistance to full economic accounting would be expected in the Soviet Union as well.

Full economic accounting raises fundamental issues concerning the optimal industrial organization of the Soviet economy. *Perestroika*'s critics note that some organizations, such as research and development organizations, inherently cannot cover their costs; yet they perform functions that enable other organizations to be profitable. Other organizations provide positive externalities (such as educational institutions or transportation enterprises) but cannot be operated on a cost-covering basis. Moreover, even capitalist economies must deal with "hold-up" situations in which producers avoid producing unique goods that tie them to a single buyer.[11] Situations that call for one organization to do business with another typically involve transaction costs; high transaction costs can dictate an autarkic supply or sales structure that may appear inefficient at first glance.

Capitalist economies deal with these problems through vertical or horizontal integration and through public subsidies. *Perestroika*'s designers must determine which organizations provide sufficient positive externalities to merit budget financing. They must also create a fluid organizational structure that permits the optimal degree of integration to be established.

The most fundamental problem raised by full economic accounting is that profitability ultimately depends on input and output prices. If these prices reflect relative opportunity costs, full economic accounting make sense. If input and output prices are unrelated to relative scarcities, profitability reflects the organization's luck of the draw in obtaining favorable prices rather than its economic value to society.

The balance mentality

The balance mentality of Soviet economic bureaucrats poses an obstacle to *perestroika*'s implementation. Soviet planners have been brought up on the notion of balances in which prices and quantities are independent. Former members of the Soviet planning hierarchy made it clear that resource allocation proceeds independently of prices. Branch Gossnab and Gosplan officials typically have little or no knowledge of the prices of the goods whose limits they set. That

11 For example, General Motors had to acquire Fisher Body because it proved impossible to get the body manufacturer to produce equipment that was suited only for General Motors.

prices are divorced from resource allocation is an indication of the "engineering mentality" of Soviet planners, who view resource distributions in technological rather than economic terms.[12]

This book has emphasized that most Soviet resource-allocation decisions are based on technical-engineering considerations. To secure resources, one has to make a good technical case. To change output targets, one must show why the current target is technologically not feasible.

That equilibrium prices are to substitute for physical balancing is foreign to the mentality of Soviet economic bureaucrats.[13] In fact, *perestroika*'s designers remain uncertain of the role that prices are to play in the allocation of scarce resources.

The transition years of *perestroika* will most likely see gross imbalances in producer-goods markets. *Apparatchiks* in charge of planning these sectors will be alarmed by the perceived chaos. Demands will not be restrained until enterprises become convinced that full economic accounting will be strictly enforced. How participants react to the initial dislocations of *perestroika* will be crucial, because the natural inclination will be to reintroduce centralized allocations when trouble appears.

Apparatchiks will be troubled as well when equilibrium prices are perceived as unfair. *Perestroika* will inevitably create economic rents for those fortunate to produce goods that sell at high multiples of cost.

The lack of understanding of the equilibrating function of prices could lead to a replay of the NEP period of the 1920s when material balances were first introduced for goods in persistent excess demand. The pressure to recentralize material balances should be most intensive during the early transition to the *perestroika* system. Whether this pressure can be resisted remains to be seen.

If *perestroika* is implemented as designed, the distribution of cash balances will be radically transformed. This book has shown that the current system calls for balancing cash inflows and outflows on a regional basis. Regional imbalances are dealt with by central banking authorities using administrative measures at the highest political levels. The high-level planning of cash balances is part of the state's anti-

[12] Aron Katsenelinboigen, *Studies in Soviet Economic Planning* (White Plains, N.J.: Sharpe, 1978).

[13] For a conservative statement of the balance mentality, see "K voprosu o planirovanii," pp. 95–100. The balance mentality permeates all books on Soviet planning methodology. Such books prescribe a series of balances that planners must achieve.

inflation program. Under *perestroika*, cash balances will come to depend on the unplanned activities of enterprises. Enterprises that earn substantial profits will receive unplanned cash balances; those incurring losses will be unable to draw cash balances to cover their labor costs. There is no serious talk of a capitalist credit market to equate supplies and demand for money and credit.

Perestroika's designers must give careful thought to how the new system is to manage monetary growth. The prevailing system makes the growth of the money supply an administrative decision based on regional cash imbalances. Whether this system is consistent with decentralized decision making remains to be seen. *Perestroika*'s designers will have to consider the appropriate role of central banking and credit markets in the new economic setting.

Dictatorship of the supplier

Perestroika elevates the supply plan (*plan postavok*) to a key indicator of enterprise performance. As with prior reforms, one indicator is selected to be the hallmark of the new reform. In this case, it appears to be the supply plan. However, the Soviet press is full of reports of rejection of the supply plan by various levels of the bureaucracy. Enterprises that have an abysmal record of supply plan fulfillment continue to receive bonuses and medals.

There are a number of reasons why it will be difficult to use the supply plan as the prime performance indicator. First, the supply plan is very complex and does not reduce to a single indicator. Gosplan officials, in fact, wonder how to measure fulfillment of the supply plan.[14] The multidimensional supply plan consists of consignments, delivery locations, quality descriptions, and dates. It does not reduce well to several measurable indicators.

Rutland has documented the difficulty that local party officials have interpreting a complex set of plan indicators. He finds that they are able to deal at most with two or three indicators.[15] The difficulty already caused by interpretation of the supply plan (to which one can find virtually daily references in the Soviet arbitration literature) will render it one of the most dense plan targets. A system that proposes to judge performance on the basis of an indicator that few know how to measure appears to be a troubling feature of *perestroika*.

[14] "K voprosu o planirovanii;" "Perestroika i planirovanie."
[15] Peter Rutland, *The Politics of Industrial Stagnation in the USSR* (Cambridge University Press, in press), Chap. 2.

Basically, fulfillment of the supply plan under *perestroika* will come to depend on whether the parties to supply agreements have fulfilled the terms of their contracts. The Western experience shows that contract enforcement is carried out in the courts and in arbitration. Have suppliers shipped the goods they agreed to in the contract? Have they done so on a timely basis? If the contract has not been fulfilled, what compensation should be paid? The Soviet legal system has to this point not dealt effectively with such issues. If the supply plan is to be taken seriously by enterprises, the Soviet legal system must be placed in a position to make appropriate settlements.

Although centralized distribution of key industrial materials is to continue under *perestroika*, there is to be increasing use of negotiated exchanges among enterprises on the basis of negotiated prices. Presumably, centrally planned exchanges would take place at state prices according to state distribution plans, but above-plan production would be distributed according to negotiations among firms. *Perestroika*'s designers have given little thought to how these negotiated exchanges are to take place and how they are to mesh with centralized distributions. Enterprises are to receive the authority to sell unused inventories to other enterprises –probably in recognition of the fact that this has been taking place informally.

Chapter 5 noted that the current system actively discourages the production of specialized materials and equipment that can be used by only one buyer. Presumably, suppliers of materials who are prepared to enter into contracts would possess monopoly power and could use this monopoly power to extract monopoly prices and engage in price discrimination among buyers. If *perestroika* works, monopoly pricing will replace accounting pricing in many instances.

With full economic accounting, negotiated prices have a substantial effect on enterprise profits. Even in capitalist societies with a long tradition of market negotiated exchanges, attention is paid to the "fairness" of prices. In the Soviet case, there will be an even greater spotlighting of prices that appear to be unfair, especially in a country brought up on the labor theory of value. Negotiated exchanges will likely take place within a set of strict price guidelines set by the *apparatchiks*. There is already evidence that outside-of-guideline prices will be challenged by disgruntled customers.[16]

16 The Soviet economic press contains numerous articles of enterprises that have had their negotiated prices cut by functional planning authorities because they break some pricing rule.

Quality controls

To raise the technological level of the Soviet economy to world standards, enterprises must become more interested in manufacturing products of higher quality. *Perestroika* calls for increasing the power of the State Certifying Commission (Gosspriemka) to ensure that product quality improves. The commission is to be given broad authority to reject low-quality output and to impose penalties for failing to meet quality standards.

The State Certifying Commission will operate in an environment of "dictatorship of the supplier" (*diktat postavchika*). Previous efforts to raise quality standards by imposing external standards have failed, because customers feared spoiling relations with suppliers. Moreover, there are intense reactions whenever goods are rejected by outside quality control organizations. This means that supply plans cannot be fulfilled, bonuses cannot be paid, and ministry plan fulfillment is threatened.

Moreover, the Soviet economic bureaucracy has yet to create an organization that acts as a true "outside auditor" in the interests of society. Quality-control departments within an enterprise depend on the enterprise manager for salaries and bonuses. The supposedly independent state bank auditor is pressured by the local party and by local enterprises to overlook certain transgressions. As one former banking official put it: "The state bank devised elaborate procedures to ensure that regional bank officials would operate at arm's length from the enterprises. But what it all came down to was that the most important local officials belonged to the same party organization. They ate and drank together, and it was hard for anyone to look after the national interest."

Long-term planning

Although five-year plans have always received considerable attention, they have never been operational. Unlike the annual plan, the five-year plan is not broken down into actual ministry targets and it is not coordinated with the budget.[17] *Perestroika* calls for the five-year plan to become an operational plan.

There are important reasons why the five-year plan has never been operational. Plans are not constructed with knowledge of the future;

---

[17] "K voprosu o planirovanii," Pis'mo v redaktsiiu (V. Stetsiura), *Planovoe khoziaistvo*, No. 9, September 1986.

things change over a five-year period; and it would be foolhardy to set a plan in concrete for an entire five-year period. Annual plans are more appropriate for this purpose, and even annual plans have had to be revised routinely (up to several times per year) in the course of a year.

It is unclear how a dynamic economy (and *perestroika* is supposed to increase the dynamism of the Soviet economy) is to operate with such a long planning horizon, when in the past even quarterly plans have had to be amended frequently.

The five-year plan is intended to eliminate the pressures of the ratchet. Enterprise managers can reveal their potential over a five-year period (subject to stable normatives) without fear of their plans being ratcheted upward.

The very nature of the Soviet planned economy has dictated that quarterly and annual plans be the operational plans of the economy. A number of previous reform efforts have attempted to elevate the role of long-term plans but without success. Whether five-year plans actually gain in significance will be an important bellweather of the current reform. As long as ministries are required to meet production quotas and funded resources are allocated administratively, it is likely that quarterly and annual plans will remain the operational plans of the economy.

Superministries and turf protection

It is presumed that self-interested bureaucrats oppose changes that result in a reduction in their domain of authority. This view is supported by the fact that the importance and perquisites of Soviet officials depend on the scale of their operations. It is also supported by the autarkic tendencies of ministries, which build up extensive supply systems to ensure plan fulfillment. Soviet bureaucrats may also oppose change for a more simple reason: Change may result in a reduction of positions, and the Soviet press is indeed full of complaints about the bloated bureaucracy.

Bureaucratic reshuffling has been a hallmark of Soviet economic reform since the 1930s. *Perestroika*, in its early years, called for the amalgamation of ministries into superministries for the purpose of enhanced cooperation within major project groups or among regions. The superministries were supposed to eliminate the problems caused by narrow "branch patriotism" and localism.

The view that bureaucrats automatically resist a reduction in their domain of authority may be too simplistic. The tendency of new ministries to be created out of a single ministry suggests that there is an inherent tendency among high-level bureaucrats to give up domains of authority. Interviews with former Soviet economic bureaucrats who had witnessed the creation of new ministries suggest that these divisions took place with the consent and support of the minister who stood to lose enterprises and resources to the newly created ministry.

A loss of domain can result in a reduction of bureaucratic headaches. If a new technology emerges that is foreign to a ministry, it may be more comfortable to let the former branch go its own way and become a ministry.

The empirical trend has been toward disaggregation of technological tasks, not toward agglomeration of tasks. *Perestroika* seeks to reverse this trend by creating superministries and territorial complexes that are to overcome the problems of localism and branch parochialism. This feature is likely to be resisted by the bureaucracy because it, more than others, threatens status and perquisites. It is noteworthy that Gorbachev's first major initiative in the area of superministries proved to be a failure. The agricultural superministry – Gosagprom – was disbanded in March 1989. By the late 1980s, there was little talk of the creation of further superministries.

Fear of the transition period

A remarkable feature of the 1965 reforms was that most enterprises did not welcome a new management system that was designed to increase their freedom of action. Becoming part of the new system meant changing well-known rules of the game, which managers had learned to manipulate. Moreover, a change of rules meant a fairly long period of confusion and uncertainty in which a whole series of bureaucratic organizations would have to learn and interpret new rules.

The Soviet press cites many instances of bureaucratic confusion and misinterpretation of *perestroika*'s new rules of the game.[18] A change of rules creates so much confusion that higher bureaucratic organizations disagree among themselves on how the rules are to be applied and interpreted. To Soviet enterprise managers, probably the most forbidding feature of *perestroika* is learning how to live under the

---

18 For an example of the numerous complaints one finds in the Soviet press about enterprises operating under the new system not being allowed to follow the new rules, see "Neumestnye ambitsii," *Sotsialisticheskaia industriia*, May 6, 1987.

the new rules. Will normatives actually be held stable as promised? Will exchanges be allowed at prices that allow profits to be earned? Will ministries actually refrain from redistributing profits? Will outside inspectors be more loyal to enterprises than to a higher authority? Moreover, enterprise managers will have to divert managerial staff from actual production decisions to learning the new rules. Enterprise funds will have to be spent on hiring outside consultants. Many Soviet enterprise managers will resist *perestroika* for these reasons alone, much as they resisted the 1965 reforms on these grounds.

Respondents who worked in enterprises affected by the 1965 reforms expressed negative attitudes toward this reform. They had to battle with superiors who did not understand the new rules. They had to hire outside consultants to teach them the new rules. One respondent reported the trouble he had to go through to document that his enterprise was entitled to bonus funds. Respondent accounts echo current Soviet press reports of enterprises that must battle superiors concerning the interpretation of the new rules.[19]

Perhaps the most serious challenge to *perestroika* is whether it will be allowed to continue during the difficult period of transition to the new rules. A reduction in measured output may be the product of the confusion that accompanies the early years of reform.

Price formation

It makes little sense to allow decisions to be made by enterprises and trusts if these decisions are based on prices that do not reflect relative scarcities. Price reform is obviously one of the most thorny issues facing *perestroika* designers, and their failure to confront the issue of price reform attests to its difficulty.

A number of price formation problems can be cited. The first is the issue of the extent to which prices should be formed on the basis of voluntary contractual agreements among consenting parties. With a prevailing dictatorship of the supplier, industrial wholesale buyers may be quite willing to pay monopoly prices. What price-formation

---

[19] For Soviet press accounts of these problems, see P. G. Bunin, "Eksperiment na distantsii," *Eko*, No. 2, 1985, pp. 4–16; "Neumestnye ambitsii," *Sotsialisticheskaia industriia*, May 6, 1987; "Kvartira za bumazhnym bar'erom," *Sotsialisticheskaia industriia*, May 21, 1987; "Perestroika i planirovanie. Pervy zamestitel' predsedateliia Gosplana otvechaet na voprosy korrespondentov Izvestiia," *Izvestiia*, August 18, 1987; "Vyvody iz opyta paboty obedineniia v noyykh usloviakh," *Planovoe khoziaistvo*, No. 12, December 1986, pp. 31–8.

rules should be followed when the seller possesses considerable market power? How is market power to be measured? These questions raise the general issue of antitrust legislation and price regulation in a socialist economic system.

The second issue is the extent to which prices are to be determined by voluntary exchange agreements or by rules. As already noted, how prices are set will have important distributional effects in an economy based on full economic accounting. If buyers are prepared to pay prices that are five times unit costs, are such markups to be allowed by price-setting rules?

The third issue is the frequency with which prices are to change. Historically, prices have been changed infrequently because of the administrative complexity of price reform and because fixed prices have made quantity planning easier. If prices are to be set by voluntary exchanges, they will be free to change whenever a voluntary exchange agreement is consummated. If prices are set administratively, then administrative action will be required to change prices. The flexibility of prices under *perestroika*, therefore, will depend on the relative volume of voluntary exchanges and on the frequency of administrative price changes.

The fourth issue is the extent to which relative prices will be allowed to guide entry and exit decisions and on the extent to which entry and exit barriers are present in the economy. Monopoly prices will have a less deleterious long-run effect if they promote entry into the industry in which monopoly profits are being earned. Moreover, prices must be sufficiently flexible to be driven down by the entry of new producers. If, for example, a monopoly price is fixed administratively and is not lowered in response to entry, the beneficial effects of entry will not be felt by buyers.

The fifth issue is the manner in which economic bureaucrats will deal with price differentials between state and private sectors. If higher prices exist in wholesale markets for above-quota goods, producers will be tempted to shift resources out of the state sector. *Perestroika* calls for the retention of significant volumes of planned deliveries (based on the state order, *goszakazy*, system). As producers realize that higher profits are to be made in private markets, the state will find it difficult to make its planned purchases. How the state sector will react to price competition from the private sector remains to be seen.

Who will lose?

This book has cautioned against lumping all Soviet economic bureaucrats into one group. Some are intimately involved in producing and marketing goods and services and bearing risks; others are relatively immune from risk and from real production and allocation responsibilities. If the basic goals of *perestroika* are indeed realized, who stands to lose and who stands to gain?

Perestroika would appear to benefit those who know how to produce and market goods and services. Individuals who have managed industrial enterprises, who have worked in ministry main administrations or in trusts, have the technical and engineering know-how to survive in a more market-oriented environment. These are the *khoziaistvenniks* of the Soviet economic bureaucracy. *Khoziaistvenniks* have learned how to marshall resources in a hostile environment, relying on personal networks and a judicious assessment of risks. The major adjustment cost that such individuals would have to bear would be the cost of adjusting to the new rules of the game. They would lose the advantages gained by understanding how to work the traditional system. They would have to rely less on engineering skills; they would have to develop more marketing skills. In any case, the individuals who eventually benefit from the changes of a successful restructuring of the Soviet economic system would most likely be drawn from the ranks of the *khoziaistvenniks*.

The probable losers of a successful restructuring of the Soviet economic system would be the *apparatchiks*. The *apparatchiks*' work is divorced from actual production and resource-allocation decisions. They have not formed extensive personal networks. They possess skills that would prove to be less valuable in a restructured Soviet economy.

Successful Soviet economic reform would have serious distributional effects. Persons who command highly rewarded skills under the old system would find these skills less valuable in a different environment. Just as the distributional losers oppose changes that cause relative income losses in capitalist economies, so would the distributional losers oppose a successful restructuring of the Soviet economy. Soviet economic bureaucrats who stand to lose relative income through a successful restructuring would be just as rational in opposing reform as would a capitalist textile producer who stood to lose favorable tariff protection.

There may be rational reasons even for the potential winners to oppose *perestroika*. A long-time observer of the Soviet reform scene may be inclined to conclude that the likelihood of devising and carrying through a successful restructuring is too small. Hence, the expected value of the potential gains from *perestroika* is too small to warrant the personal support even of the potential winners, particularly in view of the transition costs that must be borne whether the reform succeeds or fails.

Summary

This chapter shows that reform of the Soviet economic bureaucracy is a very complex matter. The ministries' role is hard to redefine because of the complicated blending of administrative allocational and enterprise freedom that *perestroika* requires. The elevation of the supply plan requires a revamping of the Soviet legal system. The system must have the flexibility to select its optimal level of horizontal and vertical integration. Equilibrium prices must be found in a system that has operated over the years on a soft budget constraint.

The complexity of the task emphasizes that Soviet economic performance is not to be improved by passing decrees that require interested individuals to go against their self-interest. Telling ministries to cease their petty tutelage without changing the rules of the game for them will most likely have little effect on ministry behavior. Nor will putting bright, progressive people in responsible positions solve problems.

Soviet enterprise managers' fears of the confusion that will accompany the transition period, during which they will not know the new rules of the game, are justified. The degree to which different members of the bureaucracy will support or oppose *perestroika* cannot be easily generalized. Obviously, the leadership of the Soviet Union stands to benefit most from a successful restructuring. Both the ministries and the enterprises stand to lose, as do regional authorities. Both the ministries and enterprises have learned to live comfortably with the old rules, and the new rules introduce new uncertainties into their lives.

Soviet authorities have not determined the role of the ministries under the new economic system. The ministries must continue to perform many of their previous functions and will continue to be held responsible for final results. As long as they are held responsible, they will not be willing to give up their levers for plan fulfillment.

There are a number of factors that will create pressure for recentralization: the balance mentality of Soviet planners, the lack of understanding of equilibrium prices, and the difficult implications of full economic accounting.

The most challenging task of *perestroika* is to devise, within a very brief period of historical time, an entirely new set of rules of the game that will promote economic efficiency. This task would not be easy under any circumstances, but the fact that *perestroika* will have important distributional effects makes the process even more complex. It would be personally irrational for the potential losers from a successful restructuring to work in *perestroika*'s favor. In view of the past failures of the Soviet economic system to reform itself, it may not be personally rational for the potential winners to favor *perestroika* either.

Appendix: interviewing former Soviet economic bureaucrats

Former Soviet bureaucrats as a source of information

This study uses in-depth interviews with former members of the Soviet economic bureaucracy as an important source of information. Interview information must be treated differently than quantitative statistical data for reasons that will be discussed here. This appendix describes the collection, use, and interpretation of interview data.

Emigrants as expert informants

Studies of Soviet life based on the experiences of former Soviet citizens are of two types. The first involve interviewing a large number of former Soviet citizens on general issues of life in the Soviet Union (such as earnings, employment, political activities, and perceptions of quality of life) in order to gain insights into the characteristics of a referent Soviet population. In this type of large-scale survey research, respondents are selected on the basis of sampling criteria (such as age or educational background) that make the emigrant sample as similar as possible to the referent population. Western scholars have studied Soviet emigrants to acquire valuable information on work, politics, and daily life in the Soviet Union.[1]

The second type of research involves the selection of a relatively limited number of respondents who had special backgrounds and experiences in the Soviet Union. For example, respondents who worked as factory managers, statisticians, or lawyers in the Soviet

---

[1] Among the many research projects that have surveyed the "third" Soviet emigration are the Soviet Interview Project, headquartered at the University of Illinois, James Millar, director; the Family Budget Surveys conducted in Israel by Gur Ofer and Aaron Vinokur; and the Second Economy Surveys conducted by Gregory Grossman and Vlad Treml. See James R. Millar (ed.), *Politics, Work, and Daily Life in the USSR* (Cambridge University Press, 1987).

Union have been studied to shed light on selected Soviet professions or institutions.[2]

The present study falls under the second category of research. It uses interviews with former Soviet economic bureaucrats to study how the Soviet economic bureaucracy works. The respondents are used as "expert informants" to describe the workings of organizations with which they are familiar through personal experience.

Because expert informants provide testimony on a specific social institution (the economic bureaucracy), it is not necessary to use scientific sampling to reflect a referent Soviet population. For example, if we wanted to learn about the U.S. tax system, we would not need a representative sample of tax accountants. Instead, we would want to interview the most highly informed experts on the subject.

The former Soviet economic bureaucrats interviewed in this study do not represent a "sample" of former Soviet economic bureaucrats.[3] For this reason, this book refers to a "group" of respondents, rather than to a "sample" of respondents.

Biases

Studies that use respondents from the third Soviet emigration have to consider sources of bias.[4] First, these respondents have chosen to

---

[2] A number of studies of special target groups of former Soviet citizens have been conducted. Among them are studies by Steven Shenfield on Soviet statistics, Susan Linz on Soviet managers, Kenneth Gray on the food complex, Rasma Karklins on the camps, and Peter Solomon on the Soviet legal profession. See Stephen Shenfield, "The Functioning of the Soviet System of State Statistics," Soviet Interview Project Working Paper No. 23, July 1986; Susan J. Linz, "Managerial Autonomy in Soviet Firms", Soviet Interview Project Working Paper No. 18, April 1986; Susan J. Linz, "The 'Treadmill' of Soviet Economic Reforms: Management's Perspective," Soviet Interview Project Working Paper No. 39, August 1987; and Peter H. Solomon, "Soviet Politicians and Criminal Prosecutions: The Logic of Party Intervention," Soviet Interview Project Working Paper No. 33, March 1987.

[3] Chapter 4 deals with behavior patterns of Soviet economic bureaucrats, and for this purpose a sample of respondents drawn from some conceptual sample of the Soviet economic bureaucracy would have been appropriate. Such a sampling is obviously not possible because of the highly restricted number of former economic bureaucrats and their skewed distribution. Moreover, we know relatively little about the characteristics of the referent population.

[4] For discussions of how to deal with these bias issues, see James Millar, "Emigrants as Sources of Information about the Mother Country: The Soviet Interview Project," Soviet Interview Project Working Paper No. 5, December 1983.

leave their home country (and are automatically atypical in that respect). Second, the third Soviet emigration has been an emigration of small minority groups of the Soviet population, namely, of Jews, Armenians, ethnic Germans, and a small number of dissidents (and, again, may be atypical). Although emigrant bias is a serious issue when emigrants are used to draw inferences concerning a referent home population, it is less worrisome when expert informants supply information concerning the workings of Soviet institutions.

Respondents can be asked to report factually on their functions, responsibilities, and activities in the Soviet economic bureaucracy. They can be discouraged from making unfounded generalizations, and they can be encouraged to describe dispassionately the routine workings of their bureaucratic organization. Respondents can be requested to use concrete examples rather than to generalize about bureaucratic processes. Moreover, they can report on how their careers and outlooks were different from those of others – for example, in matters of discrimination.

The more troublesome problem associated with emigration is the restricted scope of the bureaucratic positions represented in the universe of potential respondents. The bulk of potential respondents are of Jewish origin, and they were excluded from the highest positions in the bureaucracy. They tended to congregate in certain professions, such as construction, and they often occupied positions below their educational and professional capacities. Relatively few were privy to high-level decision making.

Interviewing

Potential respondents were located either through informal networks within the Soviet emigrant community or through the National Opinion Research Center, which conducted the abstracting and field research for the Soviet Interview Project.[5] Networking proved to be the most efficient method of finding respondents who had quite specialized employment backgrounds.

Interviewing began in 1982 and continued on an intermittent basis through mid-1988. The bulk of the interviews were conducted in the United States under the aegis of the Soviet Interview Project, but a number of interviews were conducted independently in Israel and in

5 See Esther Fleischman, NORC project director, *Methodological Report on the Soviet Interview Project*, National Opinion Research Center, Chicago, 1986.

the Federal Republic of Germany. Several interviews were conducted in the Soviet Union to gain general background information.

The interviews were conducted in Russian in almost all cases. For most interviews, a native-speaking co-interviewer was present. Several interviews were conducted jointly with another scholar, studying another aspect of the bureaucracy.[6] One session of roundtable interviews was held with a group of respondents. With only a few exceptions, the interviews were taped and transcribed. Because of the diversity of the respondents' backgrounds, it was not possible to use a structured questionnaire. Each interview covered the respondent's educational background, employment experiences, and major jobs. Once the respondent's employment history was known, it was possible to hone in on issues on which he could be informative. A free interview format allowed unanticipated topics to arise, which could be pursued spontaneously. In this manner, serendipitous material was collected that would have been overlooked in structured interviews.

Few potential respondents refused to be interviewed. In fact, most seemed pleased to discuss their work in the Soviet Union with an interested American scholar. A number expressed concerns about possible harm to relatives who had remained in the Soviet Union, but most were satisfied with the confidentiality procedures. The basic confidentiality safeguard was that respondents would not be identified in any resulting publications, either by name or through the disclosure of information on position, location, or organization that might permit identification by inference.[7]

The most important lesson learned in the course of the early interviews was the incredible complexity of the Soviet economic bureaucracy. Large enterprises may have quasi-ministerial status, appearing as line items in plans and budgets. Republican ministries may be more powerful than their union ministry. Individuals occupying purely technical positions can be privy to important allocation decisions and may have considerable dealings with superior organizations. Institutes (some with obscure hierarchical relationships) can perform important planning and resource-allocation functions. Individuals who had worked in Moscow appeared to be particularly well informed.

6 Leonid Khotin and Konstantin Miroshnik were the native speakers who were present at most of the interviews. The joint interviews were conducted with Donna Bahry.
7 The tapes and transcripts and written notes of this project are to be archived, with access limited according to confidentiality procedures established by the Soviet Interview Project and this researcher.

The early interviews indicated an unexpected fluidity in the Soviet economic bureaucracy. New organizations are constantly being created. Republican ministries, set up to meet republican requirements, sometimes outgrow their markets and may be incorporated in the central distribution system. One of the most frequent claims of respondents was that the importance of the Soviet bureaucratic organizations depends as much on personalities as on an organization's formal position in an organization chart.

Early interviews showed that valuable testimony could come from unexpected sources, particularly from individuals who had occupied responsible technological positions, who had worked in large enterprises in Moscow, or in institutes subordinated to state committees or ministries.

Confidentiality

The need to preserve confidentiality complicates the presentation of results. The limited number of highly placed respondents makes it more likely that they may be identified through a description of their position, mention of the location of their work, or the recounting of specific incidents and anecdotes. Considerable care has to be taken to veil the identities of all the respondents. Only general descriptions of position, branch, and region are given. In no case is the gender of the respondent divulged. All respondents are identified as "he."

The need to mask the identities of respondents introduces imprecision. Even the masking of seemingly innocuous things such as gender reduces the information content in view of male–female differences in executive positions. The most severe loss of information is that contained in the rich anecdotes provided by the respondents: In many cases, their retelling even in modified form might reveal the identity of the respondent. This book tends to generalize from such anecdotes and to limit quotes to relatively generic renderings of respondent statements. The importance of protecting confidentiality, however, more than justifies the loss of information.

Interpreting results

The scientific method requires that hypotheses be stated, data gathered, and the hypotheses tested for consistency with the data. Two researchers, working with the same data, should draw the same conclusions. Qualitative information and the small number of respondents explain why hypothesis testing is extremely difficult in this type of research.

Interviews with former Soviet economic bureaucrats yield *qualitative* information that does not lend itself to conventional hypothesis testing. Respondents occupied different positions within a complex hierarchy, and very few occupied comparable positions that would have allowed their experiences to be contrasted across some other dimension. Questions appropriate for one respondent were frequently inappropriate for another. Interviews had to follow an improvisational format. No two pair of respondents answered the same set of questions, and skilled coders would not have been able to reduce these interviews to a standard set of machine-readable answers.

Can meaningful conclusions be drawn from qualitative data? The classic works on Soviet management have dealt with similar problems, and the fact that their conclusions have held up over the years establishes their scientific credibility.[8] Safeguards can be used to ensure that research results are not simply the impressionistic imaginings of the researcher.

The first safeguard is to limit "conclusions" to cases of clear repetitions. This procedure is direct, simple, and powerful when repetitions are strong. Repetitions occur when a number of respondents, drawn from different walks of life, tell similar stories about bureaucratic behavior. As repetitions occur without contradiction from other respondents, the researcher eventually becomes convinced that a real Soviet bureaucratic behavior pattern has been uncovered. For example, too many respondents mentioned the importance of not "spoiling relations," of justifying plan corrections by the need to "ensure worker bonuses," of the "investment hunger" of regional party officials, of the importance of connections, and of the career advantages of being a "yes-man" for these not to be real Soviet bureaucratic phenomena.

The use of published Soviet sources to confirm interview accounts is another safeguard. If a respondent describes a particular bureaucratic action, reference to the same bureaucratic action in published

---

[8] Joseph Berliner's classic study of Soviet management, *Factory and Manager in the USSR* (Cambridge, Mass.: Harvard University Press, 1957), has withstood the test of time. Berliner had to deal with the same methodological problems as confronted here, but with even less opportunity to use confirming evidence published in Soviet sources. David Granick's comparative studies of managerial behavior have also been based on interview material. See David Granick, *Managerial Comparisons in Four Developed Countries: France, Britain, United States, and Russia* (Cambridge, Mass.: MIT Press, 1972).

Soviet sources confirms that the respondent has reported something real. Examples of evidence confirmed by the literature are the misuse of "experimental" enterprises, the "overinsurance" strategies of bureaucrats, disputes over ministry redistributions of profits, the problems caused by the early ordering of inputs, and other phenomena too numerous to mention at this point.

The fact that interview testimony can be confirmed by published Soviet sources does not necessarily detract from the value of interviews. An interview often gives a better feel for the context, provides more detail, and explains the motivations of the actors, and the respondent can volunteer an opinion on whether practice is rare or common. Accordingly, an interview can considerably supplement the knowledge obtained from published sources.

The third safeguard is the use of logic and common sense in evaluating the respondents' testimony. Logic and common sense are required even in the case of repetitions or confirming published evidence, but they are most important in the case of nonrepetitive, unconfirmed testimony. Unfortunately, it is this type of testimony that is most important because it comes from the rare, highly placed expert-informant for whom no counterpart respondent exists. The respondent's testimony may be unique, and it may be about matters on which the Soviet press is totally silent.

Respondents have provided unique testimony about informal exchange procedures among ministries, about the relationship between overlapping party and Gosplan organizations, about the ability of high regional party officials to influence the distribution of funded materials, and about the procedures used to create new ministries.

A number of simple ground rules can be applied to uncorroborated, unique testimony. These ground rules, however, require that the researcher make a number of judgments and even guesses about the reliability of the respondent's testimony and about its meaning. First, the researcher must decide whether the respondent is providing informed testimony. Was the respondent in a position to have accurately observed the reported phenomenon? This judgment is not easy; respondents have a natural inclination to want to impress the interviewer. Second, the researcher must determine whether the story makes logical sense. Is this the way a rational Soviet bureaucrat would act in this set of circumstances? Third, and most difficult, it may be important for the researcher to decide whether the practice described is common or rare.

Three examples illustrate the problems of dealing with nonrepeated, unconfirmed testimony. First, a former Gosbank official claimed that Gosbank keeps books on even informal exchanges among enterprises. Although this respondent appeared to be well informed, his testimony was rejected on the grounds that it would be illogical for Soviet enterprises, which had to go to considerable trouble to arrange informal transactions of questionable legality, to enter these transactions in Gosbank's official books.

Second, a former Gosplan consultant claimed that all Central Asian investment projects were approved in one Central Asian republic. No other respondent had experience in this area; the respondent's testimony appeared to be informed; and there was no reason to doubt the testimony on logical grounds. The fact that this type of practice took place at all is sufficient grounds for reporting it. Although it would be interesting to know how prevalent such practices are, this is not essential to the matter at hand.

Third, a Gosbank inspector claimed that his income depended materially upon uncovering false reportings of plan fulfillment in the enterprises he monitored. The respondent was well informed on other matters; it is logical for the Soviet system to encourage bank inspectors to uncover false profit reporting. Yet no other Gosbank employee reported being motivated by strong material incentives to uncover this kind of wrongdoing. In this case, it is crucial to know whether this type of incentive is common among individuals occupying this position (no other respondents had exactly that position), for it suggests a real incentive to uncover false reports of plan fulfillment. If commonly applied, this would suggest an independent auditing system of plan fulfillment that had previously not been given attention in the Western literature. There is no way to draw firm conclusions; one can only report that a single former Gosbank employee reported being financially motivated to uncover false enterprise reporting of profits.

The firmest results are repetitions, those confirmed by published Soviet sources, and those that represent logical behavior by a self-interested bureaucrat. Such evidence would most likely pass the test of duplication by other researchers. The patterns among these results are so strong that they could scarcely be overlooked by other researchers working with the same data. The evidence that is least likely to pass the duplication test is unique testimony provided by a single respondent.

Problems of small numbers

The universe of former members of the Soviet economic bureaucracy, living outside the Soviet Union and available for interviews, is limited. In only rare cases could respondents be interviewed who occupied similar positions in different organizations or locations. The more highly placed the respondent, the rarer it was to have an equivalent respondent with whom to compare experiences.

With a large number of respondents, people who had occupied different positions in the bureaucracy could have been interviewed, and conclusions could have been drawn concerning differences among bureaucratic units. For example, it might have been determined that ministries of type A (or regions of type X) behave in a significantly different manner than ministries of type B (or regions of type Z).

With a small number of respondents, it is not possible to control for such differences. It would be interesting to know, for example, whether different bureaucratic units respond in systematically different ways to reforms that increase the authority of a region. One could get at this issue by comparing differences in evaluations to the regionalization reform of the late 1950s (Khrushchev's *sovnarkhoz* reform). One would assume that regional authorities welcomed this reform, while national organizations (such as state committees and national ministries) resisted it. Only a few older respondents were able to offer informed opinions. Those who worked in regional bodies agreed that the reform improved the supply system, whereas those who worked in national bodies felt the reform worsened the system. Although the interviews support the hypothesis (the regionalization reform improved the supply situation of regional authorities and worsened it for national authorities), the number of responses is much too small for hypothesis testing.

The variation in assessments of the *sovnarkhoz* reform presents the problem of small numbers in its most agreeable light. In this case, respondents in the different response groups (regional vs. national authorities) agreed among themselves, and the response pattern is consistent with conventional wisdom. More typically, two respondents disagree on a matter that cannot be checked with other respondents and for which no conventional wisdom exists.

Given the limited number of respondents, this study must aim at unearthing common bureaucratic patterns. Relatively little can be done in terms of detecting systematic differences within the bureaucracy. Any differences must be stated as hypotheses rather than as conclusions.

Index

accepting commissions, 106, 119–20
"administrative-command economy," 6
*apparatchik*s: under *perestroika*, 148, 150–1, 157, 159, 165; role of, 54, 71–4, 76, 149–50
assortment plans, 84, 90, 94

Bahry, Donna, 171n6
banking, 3, 67–8, 131, 140, 157, 158; *see also* Construction Bank; State Bank
Barone, Enrico, 14–15
Bergson, Abram, 14
Berliner, Joseph, 141, 173n8
Brezhnev, Leonid, 4
bureaucratic behavior: admitting guilt, 58n8, 69–70; appearing progressive, 49, 74, 128; being a "yes man," 173; creating a paper record, 68–9, 71, 76, 135, 139; efficiency costs of, 70–1, 72, 76, 156; "not spoiling relations," 12, 35, 64n20, 68, 91, 93, 95, 96, 98, 119, 122, 173; seeking advance approval, 69, 73; using collective guarantees, 67–8, 69–70, 76, 173; and utility maximization, 15

capitalist societies, 78, 151, 155–6, 159
cash balances, 101–2, 103, 140, 157–8
Central Committee, 54; and economic decisions, 35, 81, 85, 123, 138, 139, 140; members of, 2, 29–30, 124; relations of, with the Council of Ministers, 25n2, 29–30, 123, 138, 139; relations of, with local party organizations, 124, 138, 139, 140, 144; and staffing decisions, 55, 123, 135, 136
Central Statistical Administration, 93
Communist Party, 25, 123, 124, 125, 126, 127, 149; *see also* Central Committee; local party organizations
Construction Bank (Stroibank), 71n33, 113, 119
construction projects: approval for, 19n16, 31–2, 107, 108n6, 109–10, 122, 138; contract negotiations for,

110–13, 122; costs of, 107, 109, 110, 111, 118, 122; defects (*nedodelki*) in, 120; designs for, 109, 111, 118, 121, 138; interministerial coordination for, 33, 38, 57, 119; monitoring of, 106, 108, 116, 118–20, 122; overauthorization of, 106–8, 113; political pressure and, 105, 107, 116–17, 124, 138–9, 142; and principal–agent problems, 117–20, 121, 122; priorities for, 108, 115–18, 122; and self-supply, 121, 122; site selection for, 43, 105, 116; and supply problems, 107, 116, 117, 118, 132
Council of Ministers, 2, 103, 131; edicts (*postanovlenie*) of, 25, 26n5; functions of, 20, 23, 25–8, 29, 47, 52, 54, 55, 56, 60, 81, 103, 123; and planning decisions, 26–7, 28, 35, 36, 40, 44, 49, 58, 81, 84, 85, 87, 89, 90, 139, 153; and principal–agent problems, 29–30, 34–6, 52; role of, in construction, 19n16, 32, 105, 107, 108, 109, 115, 116, 138; staff of, 28–9, 40
credit funds, 39, 100–1, 102, 113
curators (*kuratory*), 28–9

decision making, 8, 10; authority for, 19–20, 30, 36, 45, 57–8, 129; process of, 42, 45, 47, 59, 60–1, 74–5

economic bureaucrats: balance mentality of, 156–8; categories of, 54, 149, 164–5 (see also *apparatchik*s; *khoziaistvennik*s; technocrats); levels of, 2–4, 10, 15–18, 26–8; in organization theories, 13–15; and *perestroika*, 148, 149, 150–1, 156, 161–2, 165–6
*edinonachalnik*s, 57–8, 59, 60, 61, 63, 75, 129
émigrés, as informants, 9–10, 11, 126–7, 168–71, 172, 173, 174, 175–6
enterprise managers, 94, 105, 106, 110; behavior of, 5–6, 17–18, 139; relations of, with local party officials, 97,